OXFORD LEGAL PHILOSOPHY

Series Editors: Timothy Endicott, John Gardner, and Leslie Green

Reason and Restitution

OXFORD LEGAL PHILOSOPHY

Series Editors: Timothy Endicott, John Gardner, and Leslie Green

Oxford Legal Philosophy publishes the best new work in philosophically oriented legal theory. It commissions and solicits monographs in all branches of the subject, including works on philosophical issues in all areas of public and private law, and in the national, transnational, and international realms; studies of the nature of law, legal institutions, and legal reasoning; treatments of problems in political morality as they bear on law; and explorations in the nature and development of legal philosophy itself. The series represents diverse traditions of thought but always with an emphasis on rigour and originality. It sets the standard in contemporary jurisprudence.

Allowing for Exceptions
Luís Duarte d'Almeida

The Ends of Harm
Victor Tadros

Corrective Justice
Ernest J. Weinrib

Conscience and Conviction
Kimberley Brownlee

The Nature of Legislative Intent
Richard Ekins

Why Law Matters
Alon Harel

Imposing Risk
John Oberdiek

Reason and Restitution

A Theory of Unjust Enrichment

Charlie Webb

OXFORD
UNIVERSITY PRESS

OXFORD
UNIVERSITY PRESS

Great Clarendon Street, Oxford, OX2 6DP,
United Kingdom

Oxford University Press is a department of the University of Oxford.
It furthers the University's objective of excellence in research, scholarship, and education by publishing worldwide. Oxford is a registered trade mark of Oxford University Press in the UK and in certain other countries

First edition published in 2016

Published in the United States of America by Oxford University Press
198 Madison Avenue, New York, NY 10016, United States of America

British Library Cataloguing in Publication Data
Data available

Library of Congress Control Number: 2016930706

ISBN 978-0-19-965320-1

Series Editors' Preface

As compared with the rest of the common law of obligations, the law of unjust enrichment is still in its infancy. At any rate it is in its infancy as a distinct area of law. Cases that could be held to exemplify its main themes go back a long way. Yet only fifty years separate us from the seminal first edition of *The Law of Restitution* by Robert Goff and Gareth Jones. Lately that book has been renamed *The Law of Unjust Enrichment* to reflect changes in the way the subject is understood that are largely owing to changes in the analysis offered over the years by the subject's greatest guru, the late Peter Birks. It is thanks to Birks more than anyone else that the subject now benefits from such a developed literature and such lively debate. But Birks was openly resistant to the idea that philosophers could enhance or augment the debate. His influence, while accelerating the development of the law of unjust enrichment, slowed down the development of the *philosophy* of the law of unjust enrichment.

With that in mind we are delighted to include in *Oxford Legal Philosophy* this provocative book by Charlie Webb. Webb is a leading light in the new wave of unjust enrichment scholars who bring a more philosophical eye to the subject. The book is already provocative for that reason alone, but it is also provocative for another reason. Webb argues for the minority view, given short shrift by Birks, that the law of unjust enrichment is best understood as an incident or offshoot of the law of property. His defence of that view does not involve a Birksian attempt to show how the cases line up in support of it. He is interested in themes and undercurrents in the law of unjust enrichment. Ultimately he is interested in how that body of law could be justified morally. This book makes more than a start with that justificatory project. It makes a powerful case that the justification of unjust enrichment law will only be found by focusing first on the question of ownership.

TAOE
JG
LG
September 2015

Acknowledgements

In one respect at least, this book is long overdue. When, in the autumn of 2010, Oxford University Press agreed to publish the book, I had envisaged having it ready within a year. By this point I had a more or less complete draft and planned to make only a few minor additions. That it's taken so much longer is due more to my own fussiness than to any significant changes in my thinking or in the arguments the book presents. My thanks to all at OUP for this indulgence.

I didn't come to study, or to think about, the law of unjust enrichment until I moved to London, first as a master's student, in 2001. The move was a good one and I doubt this book would have been written had I not made it. But the broad direction the book would end up taking was, in some important respects, set earlier. For this, and much else, I am indebted to my first law tutors, Adrian Zuckerman, Martin Matthews, and John Finnis, who encouraged a certain attitude or approach to law, one that, years later, led me here. (My footnotes may suggest a more direct link. In fact I left Oxford with little understanding of Finnis' work. My own fault: I picked a tutorial on the enforcement of morals over one on natural law. The reading list was shorter.)

Many others have helped along the way. My thanks, in particular, to all those who read and commented on draft chapters and on earlier work upon which this book builds: notably Charles Mitchell, Simon Gardner, Robert Stevens, Neil Duxbury, Grégoire Webber, and, most of all, Sarah Worthington.

Contents

Table of Cases

1

Law and Evaluation

I Object and Existence

Some still question whether the law of unjust enrichment exists. On the face of it the answer is simple: it does. When lawyers talk of unjust enrichment they express a particular concept or idea. It is not always the same idea and the various ideas expressed through the language of 'unjust enrichment' can be, and sometimes are, expressed in other terms too. But all of these ideas or concepts exist (*as* ideas, concepts) and they can all be applied to our own and others' legal practices, irrespective of whether these concepts, expressed in these or other terms, are grasped and employed by participants in those practices. So any legal system which has rules providing for, say, the recovery of some mistaken payments or for the return of money paid under a judgment later reversed has a body of law we can describe as its law of unjust enrichment, notwithstanding that the association of these various rules is one those operating within that system do not themselves make. Indeed, it was against such a backdrop that the first textbooks on unjust enrichment and restitution were written.

But the aim of unjust enrichment lawyers was not to establish that such claims existed. This had never been in doubt. Nor was it simply to show that these various cases and claims could be brought together under a single heading. As a general rule, we can divide up the law however we like. Though the identification of a 'law of unjust enrichment' (or 'of tax', 'trusts', 'negligence', 'banking',...) involves a claim as to the unity and distinctiveness of the body of law so described, there are any number of alternative sorts of common denominator we can identify and around which a body of law can be defined. We see this in the categories conventionally employed by lawyers and law teachers (such as those just listed) which reflect the diverse practical concerns of those wanting to understand the law and what it requires of them. Wherever we can ask 'What does the law have to say on *x*?' we can define a body of law by reference to it. So a category such as banking law or media law *has* a unity and a distinctiveness in that it collects together all those rules which apply to its subject matter and omits all those which don't, but it need possess no unity beyond this. Nor need the identification of a given rule as a rule of, say, banking law involve any claim that the rule expresses any distinctive concern for *this* subject matter, such that it may not also be applicable to other subject matters and so be classified in other ways too.

It would have been possible to claim for the law of unjust enrichment no greater unity than that provided by a common subject matter. What subject matter? Early accounts of unjust enrichment took it to be addressed to liability for gains. More recently, the focus of many accounts has narrowed to gains resulting from non-consensual or defective transfers. On either view, there could be no sensible challenge to unjust enrichment's existence. For while there may be skirmishes over the place of particular rules and doctrines—Does this or that case really concern liability for a *gain*? Can the provision of a service really be said to involve a *transfer*?—there can be no doubt that these subject matters are addressed, systematically or not, by our legal practices and that the relevant collection of rules can be assembled under a common heading.

But the unity claimed for the law of unjust enrichment wasn't simply the unity of a body of rules which all have something to say on a given subject matter. Rather unjust enrichment was, and is, held up as a category of the same order and importance as contract and tort. While the category of contract is often framed by reference to some object—promises, agreements—to which its rules are addressed, its distinctiveness is typically taken to rest on more than the identification of some such subject matter to which these rules collectively apply. For contract is presented and understood as a category identifying a distinct *ground* of rights and duties, its unity not simply the unity provided by a common subject matter but a unity of principle or rationale. So viewed, the classification of a rule as a rule of contract law tells us not simply where the rule applies but also something about what idea it expresses, what considerations underpin it. It is such an understanding of contract that is presupposed when claims that contract law expresses no distinctive principle or idea are presented as signifying the 'death of contract'.[1]

Denials of unjust enrichment's existence are best read in the same way: as denials of unjust enrichment's existence as a category of claims united by a common rationale or principle. The existence of unjust enrichment *in this sense* is not established by demonstrating the existence of the various cases and claims collected together in unjust enrichment texts. That unjust enrichment identifies a distinct ground of legal claims and liabilities is sometimes taken to be settled by the fact that the courts have now said it does. There was noticeably less enthusiasm for treating prevailing judicial attitudes as determinative when the courts were in the habit of insisting it didn't. The question unjust enrichment lawyers first raised was whether what had long been seen as a series of discrete claims, lying at the edges of the law of contract, torts, and trusts and in the gaps between them, might better be seen as resting on a common ground or principle. How lawyers and judges presently understand these claims no more settles this now than it did then. Then and now, the existence of unjust enrichment as a distinct ground of rights and liabilities is neither determined by nor dependent on others accepting or endorsing its existence. If the law of unjust enrichment possesses the sort of unity and distinctiveness unjust enrichment lawyers have claimed for it, it does so not by judicial consensus or ruling but by virtue of the distinctiveness of the reasons that body of law identifies and on which these claims are founded.

II Aims and Strategies

Yet accounts of the law of unjust enrichment made little effort to identify what these reasons were. This was in part a matter of strategy. There had long been suspicion that ideas of unjust enrichment left judges free, in effect if not in intention, to reallocate gains on the basis of whatever sense or idea of justice happened to strike them as sound on a given day.[2] The correct response to these concerns was to specify

[1] See Grant Gilmore, *The Death of Contract* (Ohio State University Press 1974).

[2] See eg W S Holdsworth, 'Unjustifiable Enrichment' (1939) 55 *Law Quarterly Review* 37; cf *Baylis v Bishop of Durham* [1913] 1 Ch 127 (CA) 140 (Hamilton LJ); *Holt v Markham* [1923] 1 KB 504 (CA) 513–14 (Scrutton LJ); *Pettkus v Becker* [1980] 2 SCR 834, 859 (Martland J).

what reasons really are *good* reasons for requiring gains to be given up, showing that there are grounds of imposing liability for gains which no legal system could reasonably deny and which indeed already find expression in our legal rules and practices. But unjust enrichment lawyers sought instead to suggest that acceptance of the law of unjust enrichment did not depend on a commitment to—and so required no consideration and assessment of—any particular reason or set of reasons for imposing liability. Unjust enrichments were those enrichments the law held to be unjust and so could be identified and detailed from the facts of legal practice alone.[3] Whatever justified treating these enrichments as unjust enrichments was not unimportant; it just wasn't necessary to answer this question before unjust enrichment could be defined and its existence established.

One hurdle was that the language of unjust enrichment was, in the main, absent from the cases that were claimed to make up the subject. As such, identifying what cases were cases of unjust enrichment could not be a matter of simply looking for references to 'unjust enrichment' in the case law. In the absence of any such judicial pre-packaging, some account of the *idea* or *concept* of unjust enrichment was needed to know what it was that we were looking for. But while the idea of unjust enrichment could not simply be lifted from the cases, it could be applied to them. So if unjust enrichment is defined—as early accounts defined it—as any legally recoverable gain, an account of the law of unjust enrichment of any given community could proceed by gathering together all those cases in which claims for the recovery of gains have been allowed. The same can be done, with the relevant adjustments, whatever alternative idea of unjust enrichment one might put forward. In this way, an account of the law of unjust enrichment (however defined) could remain wholly 'downward-looking',[4] following what the cases themselves reveal to be unjust enrichments, even where those cases themselves make no reference to unjust enrichment and even in communities which make no use of this concept.

If these accounts had been content to do no more than track legal practice, identifying and detailing the circumstances in which courts have ordered gains to be given up, they could successfully have held

[3] Peter Birks, *An Introduction to the Law of Restitution* (rev edn, Clarendon Press 1989) 16–19, 22–24; Andrew Burrows, *The Law of Restitution* (3rd edn, Oxford University Press 2011) 4.

[4] Birks, ibid 19.

off the question of what reasons support these claims, what goods and values they express and advance. But the accounts unjust enrichment lawyers in fact put forward did not stop there. Their aim, as we have seen, was to show not simply that there existed a body of law that provided for the recovery of gains but that these claims shared a common rationale and expressed a common principle. Unjust enrichment was a ground of rights and liabilities 'as important and as central as, say, contract and tort'.[5] Its recognition allowed us 'to see which are the like cases that should be treated alike'.[6]

These claims couldn't be made out on the cases alone. For one thing, the cases these accounts brought together were cases the courts had traditionally regarded as *dis*similar, scattered across a range of other categories. Nor could it be said that behind these diverse concepts and formulas lay a common pattern of reasoning that accounts of unjust enrichment simply brought into the open. The dispersal of these claims to a variety of other categories meant not only that they received no uniformity of treatment or approach, but also that they became associated with other claims and ideas instead. We see this in the then orthodox placement of many of these claims into a category of quasi-contract. Whatever its historical origins, this idea of quasi-contract led some courts to treat these claims as analogous to true contracts: liability rested on 'implying' a promise to give up the relevant gain, and this implied promise could generate an obligation to give up that gain only if a genuine promise to this effect would itself have been contractually binding.[7] Unjust enrichment was put forward as an alternative to and improvement on this idea of implied contract, not as an articulation of it.[8]

[5] Andrew Burrows, *The Law of Restitution* (Butterworths 1993) vii. See too Andrew Burrows, *Understanding the Law of Obligations: Essays on Contract, Tort and Restitution* (Hart Publishing 1998) 100: 'the law of restitution is as fundamental as, for example, the law of contract or the law of tort, which are similarly...categories of law based on underpinning principle'. The relevant principle is, for Burrows, the principle of unjust enrichment.

[6] Burrows (n 3) 4. See too Birks (n 3) 20–22; Peter Birks, *Unjust Enrichment* (2nd edn, Clarendon Press 2005) 10.

[7] *Sinclair v Brougham* [1914] AC 398 (HL).

[8] Burrows complains that judicial reliance on the idea of implied or quasi-contract was 'contrary to the rule of law' on the basis that it failed to explain the courts' true reasons for imposing liability: (n 3) 28. Yet the courts employing this idea really did consider that liability turned on the possibility of implying a contract: this was the very reason the claim was denied in cases like *Sinclair*. It may be that the courts failed to explain what reason there was for making liability depend on the implication of a contract, or why it was that these contracts were then implied. No doubt, for most courts in most cases, this simply wasn't in issue. The law as established at the time required the implication of a contract; there was

So the like cases identified by accounts of unjust enrichment were not cases the courts took to be alike, the like treatment advocated for them not the treatment they were in fact accorded. If the claim that these cases were alike was true, it was true despite, and not by virtue of, the case law. Rather its truth could be established, if at all, only by inquiry into the reasons which support these claims, reasons which, by their unity and distinctiveness, mark out unjust enrichment's position alongside contract and tort as an independent source of rights and duties. Only by reference to these reasons can we say that these cases, long treated as diverse, are truly alike and merit like treatment.[9] And this task necessarily requires some assessment of what possible reasons really are *good* reasons for imposing liability for gains in cases such as these. If the only rational distinctiveness or likeness that can be claimed for the law of unjust enrichment is one provided by reasons we should reject as unsound, as *un*reasonable, our conclusion should be that in truth these cases are not rationally alike or distinct at all.

In these ways, the failure of unjust enrichment lawyers to identify what these good reasons were compromised the accounts of the law of unjust enrichment they put forward. Without an inquiry into these reasons, the claim that unjust enrichment identified an independent ground of rights and liabilities could not be adequately defended. And this meant in turn that they could not support the further claim that the cases they gathered together were truly *like* cases such as require their like treatment; the like treatment which these accounts then set out to provide.[10]

These were claims that these accounts could have avoided, claims they should have avoided if they were serious about remaining wholly 'downward-looking'. Establishing the existence of a body of law addressing the question of liability for gains required no inquiry into what reasons exist for imposing such liability. It was enough simply to

little for a law-abiding judge to do other than apply that law (see too Dan Priel, 'In Defence of Quasi-Contract' (2012) 75 *Modern Law Review* 54, 55). In the teeth of cases like *Sinclair*, Burrows reckons that courts were in truth applying the 'unjust enrichment principle' all along. But if (as Burrows claims) unjust enrichment only looks down to the cases, it no more identifies a reason for restitution than a fictional implied promise. If Burrows wants judges to give us their (full) reasons, they must address the very questions of justice and reasonableness that his own account eschews.

[9] See further 2.V.

[10] See too Peter Jaffey, 'Two Theories of Unjust Enrichment' in Jason W Neyers, Mitchell McInnes, and Stephen G A Pitel (eds), *Understanding Unjust Enrichment* (Hart Publishing 2004) 139–42.

set out the cases that did this. Nor was any such inquiry needed when it came to arranging this material, drawing out broader themes and structures from the case law, so long as the overriding aim remained to be true to those cases. But it was a different matter once these accounts sought more than fidelity to the cases, even where the appeal was then only to such 'humdrum values' as consistency or rationality.[11] For a true, faithful account of the cases will on occasion reveal a body of law that is, in places, confused and inconsistent. However much the law aspires to consistency and rationality, it sometimes falls short, not least where the relevant case law has received little critical scrutiny. Where this is so, a purely descriptive, purely 'downward-looking' account of the law ought to manifest the very same inconsistency and irrationality one finds in those cases. And so, while inconsistency and irrationality are indeed failings of the law, it is no failing of such an *account* of that law that it reveals it to be, to this extent, irrational and inconsistent.

By contrast, if the aim is an account which provides a coherence and consistency to a body of law which may, in its practice, sometimes fall short of these ideals, we can no longer hold off the question of what reasons—what *good* reasons—can ground these laws and practices. For such an account there is no proper stopping point short of a full inquiry into the goods and values they protect and promote. Only by reference to these reasons, to these goods and values, can different approaches and different rulings be judged to be inconsistent or incoherent; only by reference to the same reasons, goods, and values can these inconsistencies rationally be resolved. So it was no error at all for unjust enrichment lawyers to think that an account of the law could be wholly 'downward-looking', omitting any inquiry into what good reasons exist for having this, or some such, body of laws and claims. But, unlike the accounts they in fact provided, it must then remain resolutely 'downward-looking', limiting itself to the faithful, uncritical reporting of the laws and practices to which it is directed.

III Description

We can take any community's laws and practices and ask how they in fact attend to a particular idea or respond to a given set of concerns.

[11] Peter Birks, *An Introduction to the Law of Restitution* (Clarendon Press 1985) vii.

An account of the law of unjust enrichment might, in this way, begin by identifying some such idea or concern and proceed to describe those laws and practices that address it. As we've seen, the existence of the law of unjust enrichment as a body of law that addresses such a concern isn't dependent on lawyers within that community grasping this idea, nor on their adopting this terminology. (Though whether the idea and the term find a place in that community's legal thought and discourse are among the facts such an account can usefully bring out.) Since there are different concepts of unjust enrichment, different ideas that have from time to time been expressed in these terms, there are different subject matters that an account of the law of unjust enrichment might take as its focus. Sometimes different accounts of the law of unjust enrichment will turn out to be accounts of different things.[12] Nonetheless, these diverse ideas or understandings of unjust enrichment are all, together and in isolation, capable of providing the object of an inquiry into the legal practices of any community.

Whatever idea of unjust enrichment we take, an account of the law of unjust enrichment (so understood) can set out to capture those aspects of legal practice that address or manifest this idea. So if we take the idea of unjust enrichment as an enrichment that the law would order to be given up, we can survey the case law for situations in which the courts have ordered defendants to give up gains and for situations in which claims for restitution have been refused. We can look too for what the courts have said about the circumstances in which such claims will be available, what tests they have applied, what rules they have formulated. From these cases, and from any relevant codes and enactments, we can then piece together an account of the conditions in which such claims do, under the rules and practices of this community at this time, lie.

But an inquiry into the facts of these practices needn't stop there, for these rulings and enactments are themselves the products of arguments in fact made and considered, of lines of reasoning in fact taken up, reflecting broader attitudes and understandings in fact held. So an examination of the cases, if sufficiently extensive, will reveal not just what rulings courts have issued, but also how they came to them: what arguments were canvassed, which were accepted, which rejected, what reasons the individual judges endorsed and acted on, which they did not, and so on. So too we can detail the way

[12] See further 2.I.

individual decisions have then been understood and employed in later cases, what arguments they have been taken to support, to what extent they were and are treated as settling similar questions faced by future judges. If we broaden our view yet further, we can see what generalities exist in the way officials respond to earlier rulings, how they go about identifying what standards these decisions set down, on whom they are taken to be binding, and so on.

None of this requires any evaluation of these practices or of the standards they express and endorse. And this is true notwithstanding the role of evaluation *within* those practices. A community's legal practices are in all cases matters of social fact, capable of identification and description without inquiry into the goods and values they serve. To acknowledge this is to assume nothing about the content of those practices, and to accept that the norms in fact set down and applied by officials can be identified from such facts alone is to make no claim about how officials *themselves* identify these norms. So it makes no difference that the practices of adjudication and legislation frequently take officials beyond the facts of their own practices and require them to make judgments of justice and reasonableness. For such evaluations—what some individual or group in fact adjudges or regards as just or reasonable—are social facts too. To identify what some person or group considers reasonable does not require one to decide for oneself what really is reasonable. A true account of an evaluative practice and of the various evaluations that make up this practice does not require that they too be evaluated. On the contrary: faithful description of the reasoning and judgments of legal officials and of the various other facts of legal practice permits no revision of those facts in the light of values other than the very value of their effective reporting.[13] 'Description may still be description, even when what is described is an evaluation.'[14]

This is not to deny that, in other ways, description is necessarily evaluative. For a start, we can always ask the question: 'Why describe *this*?' ('Why spend my time offering a description of the law of unjust enrichment?') Any answer to this question is likely to invoke some consideration of what is good or worthwhile, and sometimes the worth of the inquiry will be found in the worth of the subject matter of that

[13] See John Finnis, 'On Hart's Ways: Law as Reason and as Fact' (2007) 52 *American Journal of Jurisprudence* 25, 27–28.

[14] H L A Hart, *The Concept of Law* (3rd edn, Oxford University Press 2012) 244.

inquiry.[15] But it needn't. The practical inquiry that, in this way, precedes any description by defining its subject matter ('What am I to describe?') should be distinguished from the inquiry into that subject matter which its description then involves ('What is true about this subject matter?').[16] Once the subject matter is fixed, any true description must deal with the facts as they are. There is no question of their being rewritten or revised to accord with my own judgments of their merit. And, again, none of this is changed by the fact the subject matter I am seeking to describe is itself a practice of reasoning and evaluation. The evaluations that make up much of legal practice earn their place in an account of this practice not because these judgments are themselves sound—they may be, they may not—but because they are real features of the very practice being described. Of course, any description of any subject matter, and hence any description of law, requires a selection of what of the various facts about that subject matter to include in one's description and how to present them. But, here too, one's choices will ordinarily be directed not by assessing what is good or valuable in what one is describing but by the purposes for which the description is intended, the knowledge and interests of one's audience, how much time and space one has available, and so on.[17] That anyone seeking to offer a description of the law must identify what makes for *good description* of the law doesn't mean that he must identify what makes for *good law*.

In any event, a community's legal practices will typically provide their own criteria of relevance and their own orders and arrangements that a description of that practice can simply follow, without

[15] See Finnis (n 13) 27–28.

[16] Though, in this way, any act of description starts with some such practical concern or point which marks out the subject matter to be described, this marking out may be only provisional and so subject to later revision. We will often work back and forth between the practical concern which determines our subject matter and the subject matter itself: 'I have chosen to provide an account of this football match. But which of the countless possible descriptions of these countless facts do I offer?' To answer this I must (re)consider: 'Why am I providing this account? What are the interests of my audience?' Once identified, it will be clear that my description of 'this football match' will not be a description of each and every fact of this football match and so may omit various facts about that match (the parameters of the playing pitch, the length of each blade of grass, the star signs of the players ...). At least on occasion, we might conclude that these facts can be omitted because they are, in truth, not part of the subject matter that we are seeking to describe.

[17] I leave to one side the question of whether, once one moves from describing the law and legal practices of a given community at a given time to offering a general description of law as a particular kind of social practice existing across communities across times, the selection of ideas, practices, and attitudes to include or prioritize within such a description ought to be grounded in a judgment about what is (or might be) good or valuable in

evaluation or endorsement. Legal practice is systematic. Legal officials deciding cases and issuing directives act not as isolated agents making a series of one-off determinations, but instead take themselves to be engaged in a sort of joint venture. We see this in the law's institutional arrangements, in its (more or less) established hierarchies and processes. And we see it too in the reasoning of its officials, with each new decision or ruling an addition to an existing network of decisions and rulings, which in combination aim to provide a uniform and mutually supporting set of answers to a range of practical problems. Much legal reasoning is therefore concerned with showing how *this* decision relates to other decisions and determinations already made. This can be seen in the practice of following and distinguishing precedents and in the concepts and categories lawyers employ in reaching and explaining their decisions. Legal officials tell us all the time not just what they are doing but why they are doing it, and a large part of this lies in explaining how their actions and decisions fit into the broader set of practices of which they are part.[18] In this way, the law comes with its own running commentary, telling us its objectives and reasons, its principles and processes.

So it is an observable feature of legal practice that divisions are drawn between, say, criminal and civil law, between contract and tort, negligence and nuisance, and so on. And to these categories we may now add unjust enrichment, and its various sub-divisions and constituent parts. These concepts and categories play the role they do in accounts of the law and in legal reasoning precisely because they are seen to reflect, if only loosely and imperfectly, distinctions in the law's aims and reasons, in the sorts of practical problems to which it is addressed, and in the answers it gives. So too an examination of the decisions, statements, and reasoning of legal officials will reveal judgments about what within these practices is sound or core, and what is instead unsound, anomalous, or marginal. In these various ways, an account of a particular body of law which aims to provide a faithful account of legal practice can *and ought* to offer more than an unabbreviated, unsorted history of various statements,

those practices. For the argument that it should, see John Finnis, *Natural Law and Natural Rights* (2nd edn, Oxford University Press 2011) 3–18; cf Mark C Murphy, *Natural Law in Jurisprudence and Politics* (Cambridge University Press 2009) 26–28; Julie Dickson, *Evaluation and Legal Theory* (Hart Publishing 2001) 57–67.

[18] See N E Simmonds, *The Decline of Juridical Reason: Doctrine and Theory in the Legal Order* (Manchester University Press 1984) 1.

decisions, opinions, etc, instead prioritizing some features and some understandings of this practice over others. And it can do this precisely because some of the facts of this practice are facts about how these claims and standards are understood and ordered, about which of these statements, decisions, opinions are thought to be important, central, valid and which not, such that an account which reflects these judgments and structures *better* captures the practices it seeks to describe.

IV Implication and Prediction

An account of the law that aims in this way to be true to legal practice must take the facts of this practice as they are. There will be times when these practices reveal muddle and contradiction, times when the law runs out, when existing decisions and rulings provide no clear answer on a given point or problem. In such cases, an account of the practice as it is must acknowledge this. But it can also make some headway in filling some of these gaps by paying closer attention to the broader commitments and understandings of participants in those practices. For the judgments of point and principle, of soundness and significance, found throughout legal practice and evidenced most clearly of all in the reasoned decisions of courts, cast a light over the full range of disputes and interactions to which those legal practices are addressed. And so, while there may be countless questions to which these practices provide no conclusive answer, on few, if any, questions will they be wholly silent. So, in the same way as lawyers can provide legal advice on any number of points which have received no authoritative resolution by courts or statute, not by offering their own views of the merits of alternative solutions but by considering how courts are likely to resolve those questions given what they have said and done elsewhere, so too can an account of a community's legal practices spell out their implications and likely development.

Just as we can work down from the principles and reasons identified in the decisions of legal officials to see how they might play out in a range of other cases and contexts, so too we can work up from these decisions and the reasons they express to see what they might tell us about the law's broader normative commitments. Now, the laws of any community will be a product of decisions made by different individuals at different times, and it is inevitable that the decisions of these different individuals at these different times will, at least on occasion, express different reasons and priorities. We should not expect, therefore, that the law—understood still as a set of standards in fact set down and applied by legal officials—will express a single, coherent set and ranking of goods and values. Nonetheless, it may be that, as we step back from the detail of individual decrees and rulings and as the generalities of legal practice come into view, the basic structures and ideas that underpin these determinations reveal a clarity and uniformity that these determinations themselves lack. Whatever inconsistencies there may be in the spelling out of these ideas through the cases and legislation, bodies of law, such as the law of unjust enrichment (or tort or private law generally...), demonstrate a basic and established form that lawyers recognize. Similarly, there will typically be consensus on at least aspects of their content, on the sorts of disputes or problems to which they are addressed, and on the centrality of particular rules, doctrines, and decisions. Or, at least, we can examine the legal practices of any community to see if this is true. And, where it is true, we can then ask what explains these people's choice to do things this way, what these practices reveal about their normative commitments and ambitions.

At what point this crosses from mere description to (re-) construction—from uncovering and explicating ideas and understandings largely latent but nonetheless discernible in those practices to proposing principles and goals consonant with those practices and which might be said to make sense of them—will often be impossible to determine. This is only compounded by the fact that this sort of reconstruction of legal materials is, at least in common law systems, a feature of the legal practices these accounts seek to capture. Old decisions are marshalled in support of new rules, rules the judges who reached those decisions did not envision and which they may not have supported. A characteristic feature of judicial law-making is its reliance on prior decisions and practices in identifying norms those decisions and practices neither identify nor entail.

For these various reasons, attempts to flesh out the—or some conception of the—rational or normative foundations of a particular body of law will typically be inexact. The practical inevitability that a community's laws and practices will not express, from beginning to end, any one coherent set of goals and values means that any attempt to draw out such a set of goals and values from these practices can succeed only by prioritizing some aspects of legal practice and marginalizing others. So too some selection will be needed of which of the diverse goods and values that receive some such qualified expression within these practices are sufficient to account for these chosen features of legal practice. Guiding these selections will be some idea, however loose or unreflective, of what an account of that body of law's rational foundations is for. The goal might be simply to better understand these practices as they are, meaning how they in fact operate and are in fact understood within that community. If so, no principle, no consideration, no good or value should be taken to provide an adequate explanation of the relevant practices unless it is, or would be, endorsed by their participants. Alternatively the goal may be to provide support for these laws and practices, to show them in their 'best light'.[19] Now the question is not what participants within those practices take to be their point or their normative basis, but what genuine goods these practices in fact serve, whether or not they are identified or endorsed in the attitudes and reasoning of those participants. The best case for this way of doing things may be one which those engaged in those practices have not made or conceived. Here then we need to consider not just what possible goods and values square with the laws and practices we are seeking to explain, but which of these purported goods and values really are good and valuable. Accounts sharing this ambition will, in turn, differ one from another, depending on how good a fit with that body of law they wish to achieve and on what aspects of legal practice they are willing to leave undefended.

The upshot is that different theories of, say, contract or tort or unjust enrichment, though each offered as interpretations of the rational foundations of some such body of laws and practices, will rarely be in any true competition. Accounts aimed at bringing out how those practices are, for better or worse, understood and explained by those engaged in them address a different question to those which seek to defend those practices or to show what they have going for them. Those accounts which aim to identify goods and values which can be offered in support of a particular set of laws and practices will differ where the laws and practices they seek to account for differ.

[19] See eg Hanoch Dagan, *The Law and Ethics of Restitution* (Cambridge University Press 2004) 4; Jules Coleman, *The Practice of Principle: In Defence of a Pragmatist Approach to Legal Theory* (Oxford University Press 2003) 29. The phrase, in this context, is typically associated with Dworkin (see Ronald Dworkin, *Law's Empire* (Belknap Press 1986) 90), though his project is quite different.

A theory of, say, contract which explains certain features of contract law but leaves others unexplained and undefended is no real rival to a theory of contract which explains a different set of features. Each theory explains or accounts for only those features it reaches, and is no explanation or defence *at all* of those it doesn't. Where then these features differ, these alternative accounts of 'contract law' are simply accounts of different things.

V The Structure of Unjust Enrichment

It is something like this process of drawing out, or providing, a rational structure and basis for this body of law that was attempted by the first accounts of unjust enrichment. At that time, there existed no systematic approach to claims in unjust enrichment, no common or established formula for their resolution. Instead, the cases and claims these accounts collected together were viewed as disparate, conventionally strewn across a range of other categories and doctrines. Nonetheless, these claims had a common element: all involved the imposition of liability that could, in one way or another, be said to be gain-based. From this common factor, these accounts were then able to step back and ask what further commonalities (and what differences) there were in the way these claims were approached and dealt with.

So it could be seen that sometimes the claimant succeeded on the basis that the defendant's gain came about through a wrong committed against the claimant, whereas elsewhere the claimant's connection to the defendant lay in the fact that the gain came (in some sense) from him. This observation grounded the division these accounts drew between cases of unjust enrichment by wrongdoing and cases of unjust enrichment by subtraction. Within this second class of case, further divisions were evident: some were cases where the claimant's complaint was that he did not intend to benefit the defendant; others were said to be instances where the defendant had acted shabbily in his acquisition or retention of the gain; a few were left over fitting neither description. This then gave three 'families' of unjust factors: non-voluntary benefits, unconscientious receipt, and a residual class of 'policy-motivated' claims.[20] In this way, though these accounts

[20] Birks (n 3) 99; Peter Birks and Robert Chambers, *The Restitution Research Resource* (Mansfield Press 1997) 2–3.

presented these claims differently to the way they were presented in the cases, highlighting themes those cases didn't pick out, introducing terms they didn't employ, they could still maintain that they were doing no more than exposing the 'common sense' lying behind these claims, a common sense obscured by a fragmented and disordered case law, identifying a structure which 'adds nothing to the existing law and effects no change except what comes from a better understanding of what is there already'.[21]

This inquiry was taken only so far. These divisions and sub-divisions were generalizations from the specific fact patterns that generated individual instances of restitutionary liability, and pointed towards, yet never really identified, distinct reasons for imposing such liability. So cases of mistake, failure of consideration, ignorance, and duress—despite their various dissimilarities—were judged alike in that they all enabled the claimant to say that he didn't (fully, truly) consent to the defendant's receipt and retention of the benefit he conferred, and it was this element, or so it seemed, which grounded the conclusion that it was just to require this gain to be given back. But the question of *why* it was considered just to compel the return of such gains—what reasons led, or could have led, courts to the conclusion that these unintended gains should be reversed, and hence what goods these claims served—was not answered.

Perhaps it couldn't be answered. The old writ system tended to encourage the use of fictions in the presentation of legal argument and to obscure the true grounds of judicial decisions. Moreover, once these rules were in place, they could be, and no doubt typically were, applied without reflection on their rationale. In any event, one can come to the judgment that, say, mistaken payments ought to be reversed without first reflecting on the goods and values that support it. For while the soundness of this judgment can be established only by appeal to such goods, the order of justification need not be the order in which these conclusions are reached. Our convictions on various concrete practical questions will often be more secure than our commitment to whatever moral theory might be offered in their support. We see this clearly with unjust enrichment, where confidence that the law is right to allow recovery of mistaken payments is rarely matched by any such conviction as to why this is.

[21] Birks, ibid 1, 27.

One job for a theory of unjust enrichment—or, more precisely, *the* job for one sort of theory of unjust enrichment—is to fill this gap. We now know what sort of questions the law of unjust enrichment addresses and how, in the main, it answers them. What remains is to provide an account of the goods and values that ground this body of law, explaining why these questions get these answers. Where the cases give no lead, such an account can proceed only by proposing goods and values which, though they may receive no explicit endorsement within the case law, are at least consistent with this way of doing things. As we have seen, at this point different accounts will reasonably diverge, in part by their adoption of different tasks. We might aim to identify reasons that, for better or worse, those officials whose acts and decisions constitute these practices would, if they came to reflect on their decisions, endorse as *their* reasons. Or we might instead aim to provide a defence of this body of laws and doctrines, bringing out the goods and values they really do serve, whether or not the account is one those officials would themselves endorse.

It is possible that there is no theory of unjust enrichment, so understood, to be found; that there is no coherent, appealing scheme of goods and values that can account for this particular collection of doctrinal features. Again, the fact that a body of law such as the law of unjust enrichment is the product of the determinations of any number of individuals over any number of years makes it improbable that it possesses an unqualified coherence. But even when we look beyond the diverse determinations and dicta of these various officials to the basic structure of this body of law and the ideas on which it builds, we may still find incoherence and confusion. If this is thought implausible, consider how the first accounts of unjust enrichment made no effort to defend the idea of implied or quasi-contract, which was, at that time, central to how the courts both conceptualized and disposed of such claims; their fit with the law achieved only by disregarding this basic organizing idea.

If we loosen this requirement of fit, and so the more aspects of legal practice we are prepared to leave unexplained or to present as anomalous or foreign, the more likely we are to find goods and values we can square with these laws and doctrines and which can then be offered in their support. But so too the more likely it is that we'll be able to provide alternative explanations, different combinations of goods and values which can support different aspects of these laws and practices. On occasion, we may be able to rank these explanations on the basis of how well they fit the law and, alternatively, the substantive merits of the goods and values they identify.[22] But we shouldn't think that these two rankings can be brought into alignment, that a sounder, stronger defence of certain features of the law can intelligibly be offset against failures of fit elsewhere, or vice versa. And so, save where one account comes out on top on both measures, there will be no basis on which we can adjudge any one as, all things considered, best.[23]

VI Evaluation and Adjudication

An inquiry into the legal practices of a given community will, if sufficiently far-reaching, tell us all there is to know about how it in fact addresses any given question or subject matter. On some questions, perhaps many, the answers these practices give will be unclear or incomplete. But this lack of clarity and completeness is itself a fact of these practices and so one part of the reality that any account which seeks to be true to those practices must capture. In this way, any gaps in those laws and practices entail no such gaps in descriptions of those laws and practices. And so, even if filling those gaps within these practices requires an assessment of the merits of competing solutions, no such assessment is needed if our aim remains simply to capture these practices as they are. There is, therefore, no impossibility in providing an account of (say) the law of unjust enrichment, which seeks to do no more than describe how a given community in fact addresses claims of this kind, tracking the decisions and reasoning of its members, drawing out their premisses and implications, all while resisting

[22] But only on occasion. For one thing, assessing an account's measure of fit cannot be a matter of simply totting up the total number of decisions or data-points which it matches, since some aspects of legal practice are, from the point of view of (those participating in) that practice more central and more important than others. A theory that misses these features misses more than one that fails to accommodate aspects which those engaged in the practice view as peripheral, or indeed aberrant. As such, though there will still be clear cases where one theory fits the practice better than another, in many other cases the most we can do is say that they fit some aspects of the practice better than others and to detail the differences. Second, while at times we will be able say that one account provides a sounder (more just, more reasonable) grounding for this body of law than another, any true plurality and incommensurability of values will, on other occasions, render such a ranking impossible.

[23] See John Finnis, 'Natural Law and Legal Reasoning' in Robert P George (ed), *Natural Law Theory: Contemporary Essays* (Clarendon Press 1992) 143–45.

any inquiry into what good reasons exist for such claims and what goods and values they truly serve.

An account of this kind has its practical purposes. Often it is enough to know what the law is: what it directs, what options it gives us, how our cases will be handled. This is true for those who wish to live their lives, so far as possible, free from the law's intrusion, sidestepping its sanctions and penalties. But it is no less true for those who want the law's assistance or to understand and take advantage of the range of options it provides. So the law gives me the power to determine where my assets go on my death. If I am to take that option, however, I need to know what counts as an effective exercise of that power, which means in turn what are the conditions in which, as a matter of fact, a court will uphold my choices.

We see the same with the law of unjust enrichment. While the safety net that unjust enrichment claims provide may occasionally influence the choices we make when disposing of our assets, the principal function of the law of unjust enrichment is remedial or corrective. So there is no duty not to make or to receive mistaken payments and, at least in the main, the job of the law of unjust enrichment is to say what happens once these mistakes have been made and the money paid. Moreover, there is good reason to think that the effect of such a payment is not to put the recipient under an immediate duty to make restitution but simply to empower the claimant to obtain a court order requiring the recipient to give up his gain.[24]

So, to this extent, we may see the law of unjust enrichment not as duty-imposing but rather as a set of power-conferring rules, providing claimants with the option of calling on the state's coercive machinery to assist their recovery of the enrichment.[25] As with other power-conferring rules (such as that conferring the power of testamentary disposition), what we, as holders or potential holders of the power, need to know is what this power amounts to and whether we have it. Is this an enrichment for which the law will order restitution? If restitution is ordered, what will I recover? (And beyond this: How do I go about making such a claim? What evidence will be admissible?...) All these are questions that can be answered, indeed can only be answered, by inquiry into the facts of positive law and practice.

[24] See too Stephen A Smith, 'A Duty to Make Restitution' (2013) 26 *Canadian Journal of Law and Jurisprudence* 157.

[25] Hart (n 14) 27–33.

However, there are other questions this sort of account cannot answer. Often the law seeks not just to expand or otherwise shape our options, but to tell us what option we should take. So, while the law of unjust enrichment may not, in the first instance at least, seek to direct the choices of unjust enrichers and enrichees, it does seek to direct those of judges charged with resolving their disputes. Indeed the very rules which tell citizens when they have claims in unjust enrichment also tell judges hearing such claims how they are to dispose of them. Where the law identifies an enrichment as an unjust enrichment, it both empowers the claimant to demand that the defendant be ordered to make restitution of that enrichment and obligates the court to make that order. But while an inquiry into a community's positive laws and practices will be enough for a claimant to know what his options are and will likewise tell judges faced with deciding unjust enrichment claims how others have decided those claims in the past and have directed that they be decided now, still it won't be enough for the judge who wants to know what decision he truly ought to reach in the case before him.

We can see this most clearly on those occasions where a community's laws and practices fail to answer the question the judge faces. Laws are often indeterminate. A jurisdiction might adopt a rule that a certain class of mistaken dispositions can be undone only where the mistake is sufficiently serious that it would be 'unconscionable' for the court not to order relief.[26] This formulation tells us little about the circumstances in which relief is to be ordered and so what this rule actually requires is unclear. Sometimes indeterminacies can be resolved by attending to other facts of legal practice: the intentions of the law-maker, how that rule has in fact been understood and applied by other officials, that community's broader rules and practices of construction and interpretation, and so on. But at other times indeterminacy remains even once all the facts are in. In such cases a judge looking to apply this rule must make a determination of his own. How? Not by 'an intense focus...on the facts of the particular case'.[27] Or at least not just by this. For the problem is not that we don't know enough about the facts but that we don't know enough about the rule we are to apply to those facts. Here the judge must make a choice; a choice which, though set against and responsive to the facts of the case and of wider legal practice, is not determined by or derivable from those

[26] Cf *Pitt v Holt* [2013] UKSC 26, [2013] 2 AC 108.
[27] Ibid para 126 (Lord Walker JSC).

facts alone, but which requires a judgment on the merits of alternative interpretations of that rule and their application to the case at hand ('the justice of the case'[28]).

Where the law is indeterminate, whatever ruling the judge makes will supplement the existing law. If this ruling is taken not just to settle the case at hand but also to govern later cases raising the same question, the ruling makes new law. But common law judges' law-making powers aren't limited to situations where the law runs out. Courts may have powers to overrule earlier decisions and otherwise to reject rules previously set down, making new law not where no law existed previously but where the law was hitherto different. These law-changing powers are generally, perhaps invariably, law-given and the law will likewise police their exercise. Nonetheless, the question of how these powers are to be exercised is one that, typically, the law neither settles nor seeks to settle. So, for some time English law barred recovery of mistaken payments where the mistake was of law rather than fact. In *Kleinwort Benson v Lincoln City Council*, the House of Lords abolished this rule.[29] It was clear that English law gave the court this option. But whether it should take that option was a question the law did not answer. Instead, it could be answered only by an assessment of the arguments for and against making the change, arguments often rehearsed in the cases and elsewhere but which take their force—such force as they have—not from the fact of their having been made before but from the goods and values to which they appeal. Of course, an inquiry into a community's legal practices will reveal not only how far such law-making powers are taken to extend but also how they are in fact exercised. But the same inquiry will also reveal that the proper exercise of the discretion thereby accorded to courts to make or change law is not taken to be fixed by how that same discretion has been exercised in the past. And so, any decision to exercise such a power to make new law, and so too any decision *not* to exercise that power but instead to keep the law as it is, will require an assessment of the merits of such a change.[30]

Even where they aren't free to overturn prior decisions and rulings, courts will typically be empowered to effect more limited changes to the law by distinguishing the decisions of other courts and the

[28] Ibid para 128 (Lord Walker JSC).
[29] [1999] 2 AC 349 (HL).
[30] See further Joseph Raz, *The Authority of Law: Essays on Law and Morality* (2nd edn, Oxford University Press 2009) 183–206.

rules they stand for. Before the rule barring recovery for payments made under a mistake of law was removed, the courts had developed a series of exceptions to that rule. For instance, in *Kiriri Cotton Co Ltd v Dewani*, the Privy Council held that money paid by mistake of law *was* recoverable if the parties were not *in pari delicto* (ie if the payee bore a greater responsibility for the mistake than the payer).[31] Lord Denning stated: 'The true proposition is that money paid under a mistake of law, by itself and without more, cannot be recovered back....If there is something more in addition to a mistake of law—if there is something in the defendant's conduct which shows that, of the two of them, he is the one primarily responsible for the mistake—then it may be recovered back.'[32] Often, as here, there is no express acknowledgment that the court is redrawing, and hence to this extent changing, the relevant rule. We are simply told that this is what the rule really is. But so framed, the question of what the rule truly is or requires is no longer settled exclusively by past practice but turns on an assessment of the merits of different versions or interpretations of that rule. And, again, this is true not only where prior authority is distinguished and the rule modified, but also wherever a court with that power decides not to exercise it and keeps the rule as it was.

It is sometimes suggested that the positive law is radically indeterminate or that its indeterminacy extends at the least to every case that reaches appellate level. But we don't need to go this far to see that some measure of indeterminacy is unexceptional, arising (for instance) wherever the law adopts standards of 'reasonableness', '(un)fairness', 'proportionality', and the like. Even where the law is determinate and where courts have no or only severely restricted powers to overrule that law, powers to change judge-made law through distinguishing precedents are a general feature of common law adjudication.[33] Here then there are questions that judges face, and face not simply on occasion but as a matter of course, which the law leaves unsettled and for which no inquiry into the facts of legal practice, however extensive, can provide an answer. In these cases, judicial decision-making requires an assessment of the reasonableness of the various options the law leaves open, an assessment which, in the end, must appeal to or

[31] [1960] AC 192 (PC).

[32] Ibid 204.

[33] Raz (n 30) 186, 195; cf Grant Lamond, 'Do Precedents Create Rules?' (2005) 11 *Legal Theory* 1.

presuppose some conception of the goods and values these decisions may serve and advance.

Often, as in the examples just given, it is the law itself that directs judges to look beyond the positive law. But the question of when the law permits us to look beyond law arises only if we have reason to look *to* law in the first place.[34] The law claims authority over us, telling us what we can and cannot do. But the mere fact that it claims this authority doesn't mean it has it, and the mere fact it identifies certain conduct as obligatory doesn't mean that we really are obligated—and so truly *ought*—so to act. When the law identifies certain conduct as obligatory, it is not simply saying: 'This is what the law says you must do [and/or: this is what will happen if you don't], so you may want to factor this in when making your choices', nor even: 'This is what the law says you must do, so, if you want to act in accordance with the law, this is what you should be doing.' It is saying: 'Do this.' Accordingly, when issuing such directives, the question it sets out to answer is not, or not simply: 'What does the law, as a matter of fact, say I ought to do?' or 'What will in fact happen to me if I don't?', but rather: 'What ought I do?' This question is not a question of social or institutional fact, but is instead practical: a question of choice and action, of what there is good reason to do. To answer questions of this kind it is never enough simply to inquire into the facts of our legal practices, or indeed of other practices, however extensive that inquiry. For while such an inquiry can tell us how others have in fact chosen and would have one choose, what they in fact identify and have identified as good reasons for action, determining what one ought to choose and do requires in all cases an assessment of what truly are, rather than are simply thought to be, *good* reasons for action. No ought from a mere is.[35] So the question of whether there is an obligation to obey the law or to conform to its demands is one the law itself cannot resolve. Even where the law is clear, the conclusion that what the law, as a matter of fact, *says* one ought do is

[34] See John Gardner, 'Ethics and Law' in John Skorupski (ed), *The Routledge Companion to Ethics* (Routledge 2010) 425: '[J]udges are human beings like the rest of us. By virtue of that fact, morality has an inescapable hold over them. Whereas their relationship to law, like yours or mine, is escapable. They need a moral reason to hold themselves answerable to law, but they need no legal reason to hold themselves answerable to morality.' See too Joseph Raz, 'Incorporation by Law' (2004) 10 *Legal Theory* 1; John Finnis, 'Law and What I Truly Should Decide' (2003) 48 *American Journal of Jurisprudence* 107, 128–29; cf Ronald Dworkin, *Justice in Robes* (Belknap Press 2006) 13–21, 251–54.

[35] See Finnis (n 17) 33–42, 441; Finnis (n 13) 44–45.

what one truly ought to do is one which can be justified only by virtue of the good that comes of complying with its directives.

No doubt there often is such a good. The standards posited by legal officials and institutions are frequently sound standards, standards by which our choices and actions ought in any case to be guided. But, more importantly, whatever their independent merits, the very fact that these norms have been posited as binding by these institutions may earn them a place in our deliberations. Any community faces choices as to how it shall arrange itself: what are to be its decision-making processes, the terms of its members interactions, its mechanisms for dispute resolution, and so on. Yet, after discounting those arrangements which are unjust and unreasonable, it will often be left with a range of reasonable options, none more reasonable than the others still in play, yet each more reasonable than leaving these matters unsettled. In such instances, there is a value in a choice being made and so in such matters being settled, notwithstanding that none of these ways of settling the issue has anything more going for it than the others. So, while reason cannot determine which option we should choose, it does tell us that we need to pick one and move on. And, once a choice has been made, it means we have good reason to stick with it. This then tells us why we need institutions and processes—such as those constituted in our legal practices—which will make such determinations and why we will generally have good reason to do as they direct, even where no sufficient reason so to act existed prior to and independently of the directive being issued.[36]

Moreover, once a legal system is in place and it demonstrates some measure of regularity and consistency in its practices, it creates expectations, encouraging those who live under it to plan their affairs in its light. Much of law's effectiveness is down to the expectation each of us has that our legal institutions will apply the rules they say they will apply and that we won't be the only ones willing (for the most part) to subordinate our preferences to conform to its directives. These expectations, and the contribution they make to the effectiveness of our legal system and so to values it serves and promotes, provide further reasons for complying with its posited norms.[37]

[36] See generally Finnis (n 17) 231–54; John Finnis, 'Law as Co-ordination' (1989) 2 *Ratio Juris* 97.

[37] There may be other reasons too. For instance, legal officials swear oaths of office, committing them to uphold or 'do justice according to' the law. It may then be that these undertakings, like other undertakings, provide reasons to do as one has undertaken to do and so, here, to accord law such a place in one's official actions: see Gardner (n 34) 425.

So there are good reasons for judges to comply with the rules posited by other officials and often it is the fact that, whatever their intrinsic merits, *these* are the rules other officials have posited which makes it reasonable for this judge, here and now, to endorse and act on them. And so often, far more often than not, good judicial decision-making will be decision-making in accordance with the laws of that community; the answers the law *in fact* gives, the answers a judge *ought* to give. Nonetheless, the question of what place to give the law's directives in one's deliberations is ever-present and confronts all those to whom these directives are addressed, including those officials charged with applying and upholding the law. If a claimant comes to court arguing that the defendant has been unjustly enriched at his expense and seeking an order for restitution, the bottom-line question for the judge is whether he should grant that order, which is to say, whether, all things considered, he has good reason to order restitution.[38] If the fact that other officials have ordered restitution in analogous circumstances or have endorsed a rule which identifies this as a case where such an order should be granted means that this judge has good reason to order restitution here and now, then it does so only by virtue of the values served by having some such set of common and public standards for the resolution of these claims and by the judge's own commitment to this project.

Accordingly, while it may be that legal standards are picked out by their sources—by their origins in the decrees and rulings of other officials—rather than their merits, the priority accorded to legal standards in judicial reasoning is one which can be established, if at all, on its merits. And while there will very often be good reasons for judges to accord these posited norms some such priority in their decision-making, these reasons don't exist in isolation and in all cases must be considered alongside other reasons, expressing other goods and values, which will, on occasion, be served by departure from these settled norms and practices. Judicial decision-making cannot get by without some inquiry into the facts of legal practice, but it doesn't end,

[38] And so the question for the judge is at root *neither* 'What is the law?'—if by that is meant 'What are the norms in fact posited by other officials for the resolution of this case?'—*nor* 'What ought the law to be?'—if by that is meant 'What would be ideal law here?' The question the judge does face is, however, categorically normative. The idea, seemingly common amongst private lawyers, that normative (or prescriptive) accounts are *ipso facto* unconcerned with and removed from the facts of legal practice, is badly mistaken.

in a sense cannot begin, with such an inquiry. Adjudication is, in this way, never immunized from questions of value and involves in all cases an assessment of what are truly good reasons for decision and action.

All this leaves open all questions of what these good reasons are and so what decisions judges ought reach. To say that adjudication is inescapably evaluative, requiring judges to engage in an inquiry that requires them to go beyond the facts of legal practice is not to advocate judicial 'activism' over 'restraint'. Judicial restraint is itself an answer to the question of how judges should decide cases, what reasons courts should prioritize in their decision-making, and it can be defended only by an appeal to the goods and values this style of adjudication promotes. Judicial reasoning is practical reasoning and is answerable to the full range of goods and values which bear on human choice and action generally. But what these goods and values require—what they give us good reason to do—will depend on the factual setting in and against which these decisions are made, including the circumstances of the decision-maker. So, as we have seen, there are good reasons for judges to comply with existing laws and practices, including those which mark out zones of competence, identifying some questions as properly belonging to one decision-making body rather than another. There will in any case often be good reason for judges to defer to the decisions of those with greater expertise and to respect the enactments of democratically elected representatives. Adjudication is not legislation. But the various good reasons for deferring to legislation and precedent are never simply the product of legislation and precedent. No judicial approach or technique can escape the question of its own reasonableness.

This does not mean that judicial reasoning, or for that matter practical reasoning generally, must start from first principles or requires in all cases explicit reflection on the basic goods to which it may be directed. As noted earlier, one's grasp of the reasonableness of a given decision—'I should keep this promise' or 'I should, when deciding this case, follow the directive of this statute'—will often precede and be firmer than one's grasp of the considerations which make these decisions reasonable. So judges typically won't have and won't need anything like a conscious, worked-through theory of law, or of contract, tort, unjust enrichment, etc, to decide reasonably. Their commitment to law and the direction of much of their reasoning is as likely to come from what one may call a feel for or sense of what is, in these instances, fair, just, workable, and so on, fortified by an experience of and expertise in dealing with cases of this kind and how other officials have dealt with them in the past. Only in cases of uncertainty or disagreement does it become necessary to widen one's perspective and give fuller consideration to the goods and values at stake in these decisions. So it may well be that judges rarely need to reflect on why it is reasonable to have and to follow laws, and more broadly on the goods and values which give law its point and judicial reasoning its direction. Nonetheless, judicial reasoning is always practical reasoning and there is no judicial decision which does not rest on or presuppose some conception of what is good and valuable.

VII Two Objects of Inquiry

It was no mistake to think that an account of the law of unjust enrichment could get by without inquiry into or account of the reasons that justify the recognition of unjust enrichment claims. Where the accounts unjust enrichment lawyers in fact offered went wrong was in thinking that such an account would also be good for the job of telling officials how they should decide these cases. The existence of the law of unjust enrichment as a body of claims which respond to the question of liability for gains (or some such subject matter) could, as we have seen, be established simply by appeal to the cases, without inquiring into the reasons which support these claims. But the same wasn't true of unjust enrichment's existence as an independent and unified ground of such claims. Yet, for these accounts, it was unjust enrichment's existence as such a ground of rights and liabilities which really mattered, since this provided the basis for the further claim that cases of unjust enrichment were like cases deserving like treatment; a like treatment which these accounts then sought to prescribe. In these ways, the refusal to address the question of what reasons—what truly *good* reasons—support these claims did not simply undermine the contention that unjust enrichment identified a distinctive ground of rights and liabilities; it undermined the accounts of the law unjust enrichment lawyers then put forward: from the basic frameworks they adopted—premised as they were on the idea that these were a collection of like claims—to the specific directions they then gave as to how individual cases and questions were best resolved. This is not to say that these directions were always unsound. They weren't. But they were, in all cases, inadequately grounded, assuming the correctness of arguments never made.

The basic failing of these accounts—and, indeed, of the broader approach to law and legal theory they exemplify—is in seeing just one object of inquiry where there are really two.[39] So one can take as one's focus the positive laws and practices of a given community or set of communities, and the ideas and standards expressed in those laws and practices. These practices are in large part practices of reasoning and evaluation: each legislative enactment and each judicial decision the output of a process of reasoning, aimed in turn at providing reasons for action to those officials and citizens to whom they are directed. Nonetheless, observing and reporting others' reasoning is not to engage in such reasoning, and describing others' evaluations doesn't require their evaluation in turn. Alternatively, one's inquiry may be directed not to the laws and practices a community has in fact adopted in response to a range of practical problems but to the answers those problems truly merit. Here the focus is on the reasons which bear on the choices and actions of those engaged in these practices and hence on the goods which mark out certain choices as reasonable or unreasonable. As we have seen, these goods will identify the value of having a system of positive law and so of adhering to the rules and rulings in fact issued by legal officials within that community; the answers the law gives to these questions will often be the answers these questions then merit. But while an inquiry into how these questions ought to be answered will in this way require an inquiry into how they are in fact answered and hence into the positive laws and practices of the relevant community, it is never reducible to the latter inquiry and, in all cases, involves some assessment of what is truly good and valuable.

Every unjust enrichment claim invites the court to order that a particular gain of the defendant's be given up to the claimant. The question for the court is, at root, whether it ought—ie has good reason—to make this order. Just as every claim in unjust enrichment asks this question, every verdict, every judgment gives an answer. An account of the law of unjust enrichment as it exists in any particular community is, therefore, an account of the answers officials within that community have given to this question. But such an account is

[39] See too John Finnis, 'Natural Law: The Classical Tradition' in Jules Coleman and Scott Shapiro (eds), *The Oxford Handbook of Jurisprudence and Philosophy of Law* (Oxford University Press 2002) 11–12, 16.

not itself an answer to that question and is not itself an examination of what these good reasons are. The laws and practices of any community may be more or less just, more or less reasonable, reflecting the more or less sound answers officials within that community have in fact given to the question of what good reasons exist for ordering the restitution of such gains. But their lack of soundness doesn't make them any less the answers these officials have in fact given and the lack of reasonableness of these laws and practices doesn't make them any less the laws and practices that community has in fact adopted. Conversely, while the requirements of good reason are shaped by the factual setting in which choices fall to be made—and hence while the circumstances in which there is good reason to order restitution will often be dependent on, indeed fixed by, a community's existing legal practices—identifying what reasons really are good reasons is not a question an inquiry into legal practice can answer.

VIII Practical Reasoning and Practical Scholarship

Some have suggested that time spent inquiring into unjust enrichment's 'ground theory' is time better spent on 'practical scholarship', scholarship which speaks directly to judges, legislators, and lawyers.[40] But while legal scholarship can, if it chooses, serve the same practical needs that law serves, these needs vary. At times—for the lawyer advising his client, for the potential litigant wanting to know his chances of success—it is enough to know what the law is: how it in fact responds to a particular concern, how officials will in fact deal with such disputes. An account that sticks to tracking and reporting judicial and legislative practice, therefore, has its uses.

But the law of unjust enrichment doesn't exist simply to advertise its own existence but to resolve certain social problems. I pay you money by mistake. I want it back. Should the state assist me by ordering you to repay? Once we have a rule providing restitution to

[40] See Burrows, *Understanding the Law of Obligations* (n 5) 112–14, 118–19, referencing and approving Harry T Edwards, 'The Growing Disjunction between Legal Education and the Legal Profession' (1992) 91 *Michigan Law Review* 14. For one judge's view of the practical limitations of Burrows' own 'practical scholarship', see P J Millett, 'Review of Andrew Burrows, *The Law of Restitution*' (1995) 111 *Law Quarterly Review* 517.

mistaken payers, those payers and the lawyers they consult need to know about it. But we don't get to that rule other than by a judgment that it would be unreasonable to treat those payments as final, unjust to deny the payer recovery and to leave the payee enriched. This rule, like the rest of the law of unjust enrichment, is itself an answer to a prior inquiry: one which asks why the state ought, on occasion, to provide claimants with the means to obtain restitution from those who have been enriched at their expense. It is this question that is at the heart of the law of unjust enrichment, and it is this question that is likewise at the heart of every judicial decision and every legislative enactment on unjust enrichment.

Again: for judges deciding unjust enrichment claims and, even more clearly, for legislators framing unjust enrichment statutes, the bottom-line question they face is not how others have decided and legislated previously, nor how others would have them decide and legislate now, but how they *ought* to decide and legislate. The questions judges and legislators face are, therefore, rightly described as practical. As practical questions, their resolution requires on all occasions an assessment of what are truly good reasons for action, an assessment which is necessarily evaluative. These practical questions are in turn questions unjust enrichment scholarship can set out to answer. But if they are to be answered well, unjust enrichment scholars must address the same questions of reason and value too.[41]

The principal good to come from such an inquiry is not then the resolution of academic squabbles over unjust enrichment's existence and status but the practical guidance it offers, its principal beneficiaries not legal scholars but officials charged with resolving these claims. A study of the reasons which apply to the resolution of this or any other set of cases and claims won't always yield a set of concrete proposals which a judge can simply take up. This sort of inquiry can be conducted at different levels of abstraction and generality. A general account of the goods and values that the law of unjust enrichment

[41] Much private law scholarship displays a failure to appreciate that (1) practical questions are always, in this way, normative; (2) an account that seeks to answer these questions must be normative too; and (3) normative inquiry is not limited to the questions 'How ought the law be reformed?' and 'What would be ideal law?' For a neat example of these confusions in action (and a misreading of the intentions—the practical point—of the sort of account proposed here), see Ben McFarlane, 'Reply: Property Law and its Structure' (2011) 2 *Jurisprudence* 217, 217.

serves and the basic principles they support may leave the work of spelling out their implications to other lawyers on other occasions. Often the ground-level application of these reasons can be fixed only by the kind of specific determinations that a community's positive laws provide. Nor, as we have seen, does practical reasoning require on all occasions an appeal to first practical principles. There are easy cases in law and in morality, and reasonable decisions don't always require that we work first through the reasons for them. Nonetheless there is here a continuum, a single movement from general theory to its various factual applications, or, reversing the order, from such answers to specific practical problems all the way back to the basic goods and first practical principles they instantiate. It is in this sense and for this reason that we can regard every judicial decision as 'itself a piece of legal philosophy, even when the philosophy is hidden and the visible argument is dominated by citation and lists of facts'.[42]

There is no single task for unjust enrichment scholarship. An account of the law of unjust enrichment can look to do no more than provide a faithful description of unjust enrichment law as it exists in practice, a task that requires no inquiry at all into the goods and values to which these laws and practices are properly directed. But if there is a task, a form of scholarship, which can claim to be truly practical, it is to address the same practical questions unjust enrichment law addresses through the decisions and enactments of judges and legislators. Here, however, there is no option to hold off an inquiry into these goods and values and the reasons they give. So there's a choice to be made. Unjust enrichment lawyers can indeed choose to deal only in the hard facts of legal practice, dismissing any inquiry into the goods and values it serves as appealing to 'an unknowable justice in the sky'.[43] But then they had better give up claiming that unjust enrichment *is*—and is not simply seen to be—a distinct ground of rights and liabilities, that cases of unjust enrichment *are*—and are not simply regarded as—like cases deserving like treatment. So too had they better give up seeking to guide judicial decision-making beyond detailing the decisions that other officials have in fact taken, and avoid assessments of these decisions beyond pointing out, without appraisal, their similarities with and differences from other such decisions.

[42] Dworkin (n 19) 90.
[43] Birks (n 3) 19.

Alternatively, they can choose to go on maintaining that unjust enrichment really is an independent source of rights and liabilities, that these cases really are like cases that really do merit like treatment, and to continue to direct and assess judicial decisions on this basis. But, whether they like it or not, they are then in the business of making arguments of justice and reasonableness, of goods and values, and these are arguments which cannot be fought and won on the facts of legal practice alone.

2

Concepts of Unjust Enrichment

I What is Unjust Enrichment?

Within legal discourse we see 'unjust enrichment' used to identify two different sorts of idea. One is as a description of a set of factual conditions in which a court will order gains to be given up. It is this idea we see when unjust enrichment is described as the 'generic conception of all events which give rise to restitution';[1] so too when it is defined (more narrowly) as 'all events materially identical to the receipt of a mistaken payment of a non-existent debt'.[2] More commonly, however, we see in references to 'unjust enrichment' a second idea, identifying not the factual conditions in which a defendant will be ordered to give up a gain, but the reason for such an order. '"Unjust enrichment" is, simply, the name which is commonly given to the principle of justice which the law recognises and gives effect to in a wide variety of claims of this kind.'[3] Sometimes—as here—'unjust enrichment' is employed as a principle or reason which grounds all claims to restitution of gains. At other times we see it used more restrictively,

[1] Peter Birks, *An Introduction to the Law of Restitution* (rev edn, Clarendon Press 1989) 17.

[2] Peter Birks, *Unjust Enrichment* (2nd edn, Clarendon Press 2005) 21. See too James Edelman and Elise Bant, *Unjust Enrichment in Australia* (Oxford University Press 2006) 3–5; Charles Mitchell, Paul Mitchell, and Stephen Watterson (eds), *Goff and Jones: The Law of Unjust Enrichment* (8th edn, Sweet and Maxwell 2011) [1-02]–[1-03].

[3] Robert Goff and Gareth Jones, *The Law of Restitution* (Sweet and Maxwell 1966) 11. See too Warren A Seavey and Austin W Scott, 'Restitution' (1938) 54 *Law Quarterly Review* 29, 32; Andrew Burrows, *The Law of Restitution* (3rd edn, Oxford University Press 2011) 9–12.

identifying just one of a range of reasons why a court might require a gain to be given up.[4]

Perhaps the term 'unjust enrichment' is better reserved for one or other of these ideas. Even so, any such choice we make as to terminology is not a choice between what concepts we go forward with. If, say, we were to stipulate that the term 'unjust enrichment' be used only as a description of a set of factual circumstances in which a court will order a gain to be given up, we still face the question of what reasons we may have for making such an order. So whatever competition there may be between these alternative uses of the term 'unjust enrichment', there is no competition between the ideas they express. There are circumstances in which the law imposes liability for gains and there are reasons why liability is imposed in such circumstances, and any complete account of how this or any other jurisdiction deals with liability for gains cannot but be concerned with both.

II Gain-based Liability

Nonetheless, if unjust enrichment is to merit a place alongside contract and tort as a basic organizing category of the law, it will be by virtue of the second of these ideas. We saw this in the previous chapter, and we can see it too in the difficulties encountered by those unjust enrichment lawyers who have sought to downplay or do without this idea, defining unjust enrichment not by reference to any such reason or principle, but rather as a set of factual conditions from which such claims arise.

The starting point for accounts of the law of unjust enrichment was the observation that there existed a collection of cases and doctrines, traditionally scattered over a range of categories and falling under a variety of headings, which imposed liability which was, in one way or another, gain-based. Given their common subject matter it was possible, and no doubt for some purposes useful, to group these cases together under a single heading: the law of restitution, restitution meaning here gain-based liability. Unjust enrichment was introduced in turn as an idea or theme that underpinned these claims,

[4] See Graham Virgo, *The Principles of the Law of Restitution* (2nd edn, Oxford University Press 2006) 8–9, 51–52; Ross B Grantham and Charles E F Rickett, *Enrichment and Restitution in New Zealand* (Hart Publishing 2000) 3–4.

doing the job of explaining why it is that the law requires these gains to be given up. One obstacle to unjust enrichment being accepted as a discrete category or ground of rights and liabilities was that it was thought too vague and, worse, gave licence to courts to reallocate gains on whatever notion of justice happened to strike that judge as sound on a given day. The challenge faced by lawyers seeking to provide accounts of the law of unjust enrichment was to provide a framework for the presentation and analysis of claims for the recovery of gains that would head off these criticisms.

One common strategy was to say that this idea of unjust enrichment, which was held out as grounding recovery in these cases, was simply responsive *to* those cases. On this view, unjust enrichment, though capturing some principle of justice which grounded these many instances of liability, was to be identified not by any moral inquiry but rather by reference to the case law: unjust enrichments were simply those enrichments the courts had determined to be unjust.[5] But this was self-defeating. If unjust enrichment was to provide any explanation of the defendant's liability, it needed to do more than just repeat the fact of that liability.[6] 'Why must I give up this gain?' 'Because it is an unjust enrichment?' 'Why is this an unjust enrichment?' 'Because you must give it up.' One way out would have been to articulate a concept of unjust enrichment which stood apart from those cases and claims, indicating a principle or ground of recovery whose content was not fixed solely by those cases but which was instead identifiable independently of them. An alternative, however, was to deny that unjust enrichment was in truth such a principle at all.

This alternative line received its most sophisticated and most effective treatment by Birks, starting with his *An Introduction to the Law of Restitution*.[7] Here too the point of departure was the identification of a

[5] Seavey and Scott (n 3) 36; Burrows (n 3) 4.

[6] In the *Restatement (Third) of Restitution and Unjust Enrichment* (American Law Institute 2014), § 1, comment b, it is suggested that the term 'unjustified enrichment' might be preferable to unjust enrichment on the basis that, by being more obviously tied to the cases, it has greater 'explanatory power' (the idea being that there are plenty of enrichments that might be thought 'unjust' yet which generate no liability). But if all unjust(ified) enrichment does is tell us that these are cases in which the law requires the relevant gain to be given up, it tells us nothing that is not already plain from those cases. To say that the explanation of the defendant's liability to give up his gain is that this is a gain that the law requires him to give up is no explanation at all. The same goes for Grantham and Rickett's preferred terminology of 'restorable enrichment': (n 4) 18–20.

[7] Birks (n 1).

body of law—the law of restitution—directed to the recovery of gains and the observation that these claims were, at least in many cases, independent of contract and tort. Restitution could not, however, simply be added on to these existing categories. While restitution described the objective or measure of these claims—the giving up of a gain—contract and tort identified, in Birks' view, sets of facts (or 'events') from which rights and duties arise. Contracts (when thought of as promises or agreements) and torts were things that happened, factual circumstances that gave rise to claims. Restitution wasn't. If this body of claims was to line up next to contract and tort, it needed a term that similarly captured the circumstances in which these claims arose.

This is where unjust enrichment came in. If restitution was the giving up of a gain, it followed that any liability to make restitution was dependent on the defendant having received some such gain or enrichment. Wherever an enrichment had to be given up, it could be described as 'unjust'. Wherever it was the claimant to whom the enrichment had to be given up, we could say that the enrichment was 'at the claimant's expense'. As such, unjust enrichment at the claimant's expense—unjust enrichment for short—became, by a simple unpacking of the idea of restitution, the 'generic conception' of those circumstances in which rights to restitution arise.[8] None of this revealed or presumed anything about why it was that the law required gains to be given up in these circumstances. The 'unjust' in this concept of unjust enrichment was in this account, as it was in others, 'downward-looking', simply descriptive of those fact-combinations in which the law provided for recovery. But, more than that, this concept of unjust enrichment didn't even purport to identify any principle of justice, any reason for ordering restitution, so shutting the door even more firmly—Birks hoped—on any suggestion that unjust enrichment licensed judges to decide on the basis of 'abstract conceptions of justice' rather than authority.[9]

III Restitution Without Unjust Enrichment

There is nothing incoherent in aiming simply to describe the factual conditions in which gains are recoverable, and so in employing

[8] Ibid 16–18.

[9] Ibid 19.

a concept of unjust enrichment that does no more than this. But this refusal to engage with the question of why recovery is allowed in these circumstances and not in others came at a cost. For the unity of the law of restitution as a body of law directed towards the recovery of gains is not matched by any unity in the reasons courts have in providing for their recovery. This disunity in turn compromises the identity of the law of restitution—or the law of unjust enrichment when so understood—as a body of law which can sensibly be aligned and contrasted with contract and tort.

Birks first saw the problem in relation to restitution for wrongs: cases where the claimant sought a defendant's gains on the basis that they were the product of some wrong the defendant had done the claimant.[10] These were cases of liability for gains and, as such, cases of restitution. Applying the logic of the *Introduction*, they had to be instances of unjust enrichment too. However, the facts of these cases also reveal a wrong committed by the defendant, and it is this wrong on which the claimant relies when claiming that the resulting gain should be given up to him. Because of this, these cases fell within both the category of unjust enrichment and the category of wrongs (which extended from torts to other breaches of duty). This in turn seemed to give the lie to any suggestion that unjust enrichment described either a class of 'events' or a body of claims that was genuinely distinct from contract and tort/wrongs.

Is this a problem? Lawyers, in their everyday reasoning and discourse, employ a range of categories that cut across each other in various ways.[11] As long as these overlaps are understood, none of these categories needs to be revised or rejected, no confusion needs to result. And so if the law of restitution—and, so defined, the law of unjust enrichment—overlaps with the law of torts, so be it. Nonetheless, this particular overlap did at least suggest that something was missing from the account of the law of restitution presented in the *Introduction*. For not every instance of restitutionary liability can also be classified as a wrong or, for that matter, as arising from a contract. For those cases that don't, the account of what it is that triggers the claim to restitution remained incomplete. What we lack is that part of the account

[10] See Peter Birks, 'Misnomer' in W R Cornish, Richard Nolan, J O'Sullivan, and G Virgo (eds), *Restitution—Past, Present and Future: Essays in Honour of Gareth Jones* (Hart Publishing 1998); Peter Birks, 'Unjust Enrichment and Wrongful Enrichment' (2001) 79 *Texas Law Review* 1767.

[11] See 1.I.

which, in the restitution for wrongs cases, is provided by the wrong or, in cases of contractual restitution, by the contract. But this something extra is something that the concept of unjust enrichment employed in the *Introduction*, devised as it was to capture all recoverable gains without discrimination, could not give us.

Birks' response was to retain the idea that unjust enrichment was descriptive of a set of factual conditions in which gains could be recovered, but to refine it so that the cases that also fell under wrongs or contract/consent were excluded.[12] Unjust enrichment was no longer the generic conception of all events from which rights to restitution arise, but the generic conception of such events which were neither contracts (acts of consent) nor wrongs, nor for that matter examples of some other class of 'right-creating' event. This was no solution at all, indeed a step backwards. For one thing, while this removed the overlaps with contract and wrongs, it did nothing to fill the gap in the account of those claims falling within this narrower category of unjust enrichment. The new account admitted that there were cases of restitution which were to be explained through the ideas of contract (consent) and tort (wrongs), but then provided no equivalent explanation of those which remained. In the *Introduction*, to say a case was one of unjust enrichment was to say the facts supported a claim to restitution; under the new approach, it was to say that the facts supported a claim to restitution that fell outside contract (consent) and wrongs. Unjust enrichment had shifted from a concept defined by some positive feature—the recoverability of gains—to one marked out by what it is not.

In fact the problems posed by this new concept of unjust enrichment ran deeper. Many rights and liabilities arise independently of any act of consent, wrong, or anything that could be described as an unjust enrichment. This is true, for example, of our rights not to be assaulted or defamed, so too title to assets acquired by possession or prescription. Any list of right-creating events must therefore extend beyond contract/consent, wrongs, and unjust enrichment. Birks gathered up these cases into a residual fourth class, designed to catch everything left over from the three nominate categories. Included within this miscellany, so Birks thought, were some cases of restitutionary liability.[13] So far

[12] See eg Peter Birks, 'The Law of Unjust Enrichment: A Millennial Resolution' [1999] *Singapore Journal of Legal Studies* 318, 328.

[13] See Birks (n 2) 2–8, giving the examples of income tax liability and restitutionary rights and duties emerging from court orders. Cf Edelman and Bant (n 2) 294, 317, who

as restitutionary claims were concerned, however, unjust enrichment was itself a residual class, defined to capture all instances of gain-based liability not falling into one of the other three categories. This meant that we were left with two categories whose content was determined by what wasn't in the others. The class of 'miscellaneous others' was fixed by what wasn't a contract/consent, wrong, or unjust enrichment, but the content of unjust enrichment was itself fixed by what wasn't a contract/consent, wrong, or other right-creating event. The result was that—so far as restitutionary claims were concerned—we couldn't say what was in either. Unjust enrichment was a category consisting of some, but only some, of the restitutionary claims not grounded in consent or wrongs. Which ones? Well, those covered in Birks' account of the law of unjust enrichment and in the accounts of those who followed him. But why *these* were cases of unjust enrichment but others were not could not be established by the concept of unjust enrichment they proposed.[14]

It would be easy enough to come up with some criterion that could draw a line between unjust enrichment and this miscellaneous class of other restitution-triggering events. So perhaps unjust enrichment might be refined to cover only those leftover cases of restitution where the defendant's gain comes *from* the claimant. We'd still need to do some work on the contours of 'from', but this too could be managed and, at the end of it, we'd be left with a concept of unjust enrichment distinct from the other categories of causative event. But the challenge would be to show why any such refinement isn't simply ad hoc, why *this* provides a better concept or definition of unjust enrichment than one that draws just as clear a line, but in a different place. Indeed, the central problem in Birks' revised account of unjust enrichment is that it appears ad hoc throughout, the distinctions it draws—even where clear—arbitrary or, if not arbitrary, then resting on premisses nowhere stated or defended.

So the initial move of excluding the restitution for wrongs cases from the category of unjust enrichment was presented as necessary to

propose a broader and, on the whole, better-defined class of restitutionary claims arising from 'other events'.

[14] For more on this, see Charlie Webb, 'What is Unjust Enrichment?' (2009) 29 *Oxford Journal of Legal Studies* 215. Birks acknowledged that whether a given restitutionary claim was better classified as an unjust enrichment or as an 'other' was at times difficult: Birks (n 2) 27. But, given the concepts and divisions he presented, this question wasn't simply difficult but impossible, unanswerable.

avoid overlap between the wrongs and unjust enrichment categories. But even if avoiding this overlap were necessary, this wasn't the only way to do it. Rather than taking 'unjust enrichment by wrongdoing' out of unjust enrichment, we could just as well take it out of wrongs. Just as Birks qualified unjust enrichment so that it covered only those gain-based claims which didn't arise from consent or wrongdoing, we could qualify wrongs so that it covers only those claims following breaches of duty which don't fall within unjust enrichment (as defined in the *Introduction*). Or we could split the restitution for wrongs cases off from both categories, leaving three classes where there were previously two: (non-enriching) wrongs, wrongful enrichments, and (non-wrongful) unjust enrichments.

Either of these alternatives would provide just as clean divisions as the approach Birks took. Indeed, if the only concern is to provide a scheme of 'causative events' which avoids overlaps, there are countless ways this could be done, providing countless alternative event-based classificatory schemes. Any factual difference between two cases could be used as a basis for putting them in distinct categories, any factual likeness could be adopted as a basis for grouping them together (e.g. gains [not otherwise falling within some other nominate category] received from LSE graduates, gains received by Librans...). But while Birks countenanced that there may sometimes be difficulties placing individual cases and claims within the scheme he proposed, there was no recognition that the categories themselves and the lines between them could be drawn differently, and so no defence of why they should be drawn this way.

IV Classification

A proper defence of Birks' scheme and so of the concept of unjust enrichment employed within it would need, therefore, to go beyond its success in avoiding overlaps and duplications. We might start by getting clearer on why overlaps were thought to be a problem in the first place. At times Birks gestured towards the claim that overlapping categories were simply irrational.[15] But there is nothing irrational or

[15] See eg Peter Birks, 'Equity in the Modern Law: An Exercise in Taxonomy' (1996) 26 *University of Western Australia Law Review* 1.

incoherent in lawyers using the categories of (say) contract, trusts, commercial law, and property, notwithstanding that each identifies a different sort of subject matter and mark outs no territory fully distinct from the others. This is no less true for categories that, unlike these, are of the same order, directed to the same sort of subject matter. No error is committed in talking both of the law of contract and of the law of misrepresentation, which, though both (on Birks' view) categories of 'causative event', overlap. And so too, there was nothing irrational or confused in the concepts of unjust enrichment and wrongs put forward in the *Introduction*, only in the suggestion—which Birks himself was careful not to make—that there was no crossover between them.

So why think that we need to avoid overlaps rather than simply to be alert to them? The truer proposal is that overlaps in the categories lawyers employ threaten rational law-making and legal decision-making where and to the extent that these categories are taken to be determinative of how the cases assigned to those categories are to be dealt with.[16] On this basis, the categorization of a given case as a wrong or as an unjust enrichment matters where and because it makes a difference to how we then respond to that case: if we treat it as a wrong, it is then to be treated as we treat other wrongs; if we treat is as an unjust enrichment, we should treat it instead like other unjust enrichments. It doesn't follow that all cases within a single category then fall to be dealt with identically. There may—as in the law of torts or wrongs—be further sub-divisions marking differences between cases and claims which are otherwise alike. But by grouping a set of cases or claims within a single category we mark them out as, to this extent, like cases and claims that, again to this extent, call for like treatment.[17] And so by putting the restitution for wrongs cases into the category of wrongs, these cases are channelled in one direction rather than another; their affinities with one body of law prioritized over whatever affinities they may also have with another. In this way, we can understand both why a choice is needed and why it matters which choice we make.

As this brings out, these classificatory concerns arise only if the questions we are addressing are indeed practical: if, that is, we are

[16] Cf Frederick Pollock, 'Divisions of Law' (1894) 8 *Harvard Law Review* 187, 187–88.

[17] See Birks (n 15) 5; Peter Birks, 'Definition and Division: A Meditation on *Institutes* 3.13' in Peter Birks (ed), *The Classification of Obligations* (Clarendon Press 1997) 34.

looking not just to capture how particular cases are or have been decided, but to make or to direct such decisions. Where, by contrast, the object is only to describe decisions courts have reached, the only classificatory concern is how this information may best be conveyed. The information remains the same however it is classified. Indeed, as long as our aim is mere description, there's no objection to putting the same information in multiple places. If all we want is to know how courts have in fact addressed restitution for wrongs cases, there's no debate to be had over whether this material should be collected in texts covering other aspects of the law of wrongs or in books on restitution: we can do both. Birks' concern, common to unjust enrichment lawyers, with orderly classification and the avoidance of overlapping or misaligned categories is intelligible only if, or to the extent that, their accounts are not simply 'downward-looking' but instead offer themselves as guides to legal reasoning and decision-making.

We classify for different reasons, and not all categories lawyers employ are used for the purposes of reaching or explaining their decisions. All these categories have some common denominator, and so some basic likeness that distinguishes what falls within the class and what outside. Often, perhaps more often than not, this common feature will have some bearing on how the cases belonging to that class are to be dealt with. So the category of commercial law identifies a common contextual setting which this group of cases share and it's possible that this setting raises common questions and concerns which merit common consideration and, perhaps, some commonality of approach. In this light, we might, for example, find it helpful sometimes to employ a category of commercial contracts, which we oppose, for some purposes, with categories such as consumer or employment contracts. But no competent lawyer would think that there is any opposition between commercial law and contract law (or between commercial law and property law or, indeed, the law of unjust enrichment), and hence that we need to determine to which one of these categories a case or claim properly belongs.[18]

What then marks out those categories that *can* sensibly be opposed in this way? For Birks, contract/consent, wrongs, and unjust enrichment were categories of 'causative event', with each category marked out by the distinct factual circumstances it describes, and from which its respective rights and duties arise. But as the *Introduction* itself showed,

[18] See too Birks (n 1) 73–74.

there's no necessary opposition between different categories of causative event. It just depends on how we choose to define them. And even if we choose to define them in such a way as avoids overlaps, there are, as we have seen, countless ways this can be done, picking up on any of the countless similarities and differences that exist between the cases we're looking to categorize. So, while the restitution for wrongs cases did have factual differences from those cases Birks left in the category of unjust enrichment, they had their likenesses too. This made it possible to frame categories that kept them apart and categories that kept them together, as Birks himself did at different times.

The conclusion that these cases were better placed in the wrongs category, therefore, could only rest on a judgment that these cases shared a closer affinity with other wrongs cases than they did with cases of 'autonomous' unjust enrichment, that their likenesses with cases of wrongs mattered more (and their differences less) than the likenesses they shared with those cases left within unjust enrichment. But what was missing from Birks' account, and from the accounts of those unjust enrichment lawyers who followed him, was any analysis of why some likenesses and differences matter more than others: why some cases, despite their differences, are alike in such ways that they ought to be grouped together; why others, notwithstanding their various commonalities, are not truly *like* cases and so should be grouped apart. Only on the back of such an inquiry is it possible to say why we should endorse or adopt these categories defined in these ways.

V Treating Like Cases Alike

The maxim that like cases must be treated alike is sometimes described as a principle of formal justice, the idea being that the like treatment of like cases is a condition of justice whatever substantive principles of justice one endorses. Sometimes too the principle is taken to bear only on the application of a pre-determined rule or body of rules. So understood, it directs that those rules not be applied partially or capriciously, requiring instead their full, or at least their consistent, application to all those who fall within them.[19] Here then, like cases are those which

[19] See eg H L A Hart, 'Positivism and the Separation of Law and Morals' (1958) 71 *Harvard Law Review* 593, 623–24. Cf H L A Hart, *The Concept of Law* (3rd edn, Oxford University

the relevant rules provide are to be treated alike, and to say that those like cases must be treated alike is to say simply that those rules should indeed be applied. As such, this formulation of the principle is otiose, adding nothing to the rules whose application it governs.

More commonly, however, the principle is used and understood differently. Here the principle calls for more than the application of whatever rules happen to be in place, and is addressed instead to the way we determine what rules we should have and what decisions we should make. So we can ask whether a rule or set of rules in its substance—and hence if applied in full—treats like cases alike, and a legal system whose rules are clear and consistently applied may nonetheless fail to meet this standard. Necessarily, therefore, the likeness of cases is not simply a product of the rules a legal system adopts, and cases can be (in this sense) alike even where the law views and treats them differently. Indeed, the principle that like cases be treated alike is often invoked when and for the purpose of challenging some distinction presently found in the law. It is clear too that like cases need not, and indeed will not, be in all respects alike. That cases can be alike, in this sense, despite their differences is sometimes accommodated by saying that the likeness we are concerned with is material likeness. The difficulty is that cases can resemble and differ from one another in countless ways. Until we know which of these likenesses and differences are material, the principle remains 'an empty form'.[20]

How then do we determine what is material? The principle requires that like cases be treated alike, so the likenesses (and differences) we are concerned with are those that are relevant to how those cases ought to be treated. Cases which differ in various respects are nonetheless alike if their shared features, however few, are sufficient to require their like treatment. They are different where their differences, whatever likenesses they also exhibit, give us cause to treat them differently. So we can determine whether cases really are alike only by inquiring into what reasons bear on their proper treatment.[21] Their likeness is then a function of the

Press 2012) 159–63, where Hart acknowledges that this is just one possible application of the principle.

[20] Hart, *The Concept of Law*, ibid 159.

[21] See too Joseph Raz, *The Authority of Law: Essays on Law and Morality* (2nd edn, Oxford University Press 2009) 203. Cf Andrei Marmor, 'Should Like Cases be Treated Alike?' (2005) 11 *Legal Theory* 27, who limits the principle to cases which are left underdetermined by the reasons which bear on them on the basis that, for all other cases, their proper treatment is determined by those reasons, so making the like cases principle superfluous.

reasons that apply alike to them and can be established only by determining whether the reasons that bear on their resolution bear on them in the same way. If the same reasons apply to them in the same way, it follows that they call for the same treatment.

VI Reasons for Restitution

If we want a concept of unjust enrichment which is not simply distinct from contract and tort (or consent and wrongs) but which reflects the material differences, such as there are, between these cases and categories, we cannot, therefore, avoid an inquiry into the reasons which ground these claims. It is sometimes thought that all restitutionary claims share a common rationale, resting on a common principle: the unjust enrichment principle.[22] This suggestion is undermined when combined, as it often is, with the further suggestion that the idea of unjust enrichment simply looks down to the cases, involving no appeal to any particular principle of justice. As Birks saw, this downward-looking, fact-focused understanding of 'unjust' made the principle redundant. If an unjust enrichment is simply an enrichment that the law requires to be given up, then to say that there is a principle against unjust enrichment is simply to restate that the enrichments that the law requires to be given up must, in law, be given up.[23]

When we do look up from those cases, we find a diversity of reasons or principles supporting the recognition of such claims. So Birks' decision to separate the restitution for wrongs cases from those restitutionary claims that arise independently of wrongdoing was a sound one. But this wasn't because of their factual differences alone, but because of the different reasons that exist for ordering restitution in each case. Requiring wrongdoers to give up their wrongful gains is often explained on the basis that this takes away one incentive for committing wrongs. If potential wrongdoers know there is a good chance that their wrongs won't pay, they are that much less likely to commit them. Down the line, more duties will be performed, fewer breached. Additionally, or alternatively, whatever the consequences of a rule requiring wrongdoers to give up their gains, and so however

[22] See eg Goff and Jones (n 3); Seavey and Scott (n 3); Burrows (n 3).

[23] Birks (n 1) 22–23. Cf Burrows (n 3) 4.

would-be wrongdoers respond to it, it might be thought *ipso facto* unjust that an individual wrongdoer should profit from his wrong. Neither of these reasons applies to, say, the standard mistaken payment, where liability must instead rest on some other ground, expressing some other principle of justice.

As we have seen, we can divide up the law in various ways and on various bases, and all such divisions will reflect some way in which claims are alike and unalike. But if we want groupings which capture claims which are alike such as to require their like treatment, then the only likenesses that matter are rational likenesses, the only divisions rational divisions. And this remains true even if we then present our scheme not as a scheme of such reasons or principles but as classification by 'causative event'. The conclusion, once more, is that if unjust enrichment is to identify a class of like cases and claims, marking out an independent ground of rights and liabilities, it does so by virtue of the distinct reasons it expresses. As such, even if then we choose to reserve the term 'unjust enrichment' to describe the sets of facts on which claims of this kind arise, unjust enrichment's distinctiveness from these other basic categories and claims is provided not by the various factual differences between these 'events' and others, but rather by the different reasons these claims express and effect.[24]

The line Birks took in the *Introduction* and followed by the mainstream of unjust enrichment lawyers, insisting on an account of unjust enrichment which only looked down to the cases, shunning any inquiry into the reasons which ground these claims, into the goods and values they serve, shut off the one line of inquiry by which unjust enrichment's existence as a body of like claims could be established. Without such an inquiry, the attempts in these accounts to identify a concept of unjust enrichment that could intelligibly and securely align with contract and tort ended up as increasingly sophisticated exercises in chasing their tails.

[24] Cf Birks (n 17) 17: 'It is enough to say here that whether or not you go in for subdivisions [by response or remedy]...you will in the end have to come to causative events. That is to say, no right can be understood without understanding the events which bring it into being. "You owe me five farthings!" The immediate response is, "Why?", meaning "Because of what facts?" This is the very heart of the law of obligations...what are their causative events?' But this line of inquiry stops too soon, for the follow-up to whatever fact-description one receives is 'Why *in light of these facts* do I owe you this?' or simply 'What *reason* do these facts give for me owing you this?' Indeed the more natural and more useful interpretation of 'Why?' here is not 'Because of what facts?' but 'For what reason?'

Only in Birks' last work do we see some recognition that unjust enrichment's existence and independence as a ground of claims is to be found not in the distinctiveness of the facts from which these claims arise but in the distinctive reasons that support them. So we still have unjust enrichment defined in terms similar to those of the *Introduction*, now adjusted to accommodate what Birks called restitution's 'multi-causality': 'unjust enrichment [is] the generic conception of one causative event from which restitutionary rights arise'.[25] Alongside this, however, we get a second definition: 'The law of unjust enrichment is the law of all events materially identical to the mistaken payment of a non-existent debt.'[26] Now there are, as we have seen, ways in which mistaken payments are like every other instance of restitutionary liability; so too are there countless ways in which they differ. So how do we know which of these cases are *materially* like Birks' core case of the mistaken payment?[27]

> Receipt of a payment supposes a receipt of money, and receipt of money generalizes to enrichment....Enrichment by transfer from another generalizes to enrichment at the expense of another. The mistake is or reflects the existence of the *reason*, not being a contract or a wrong, why the payment has to be given up. The generic *reason* why an enrichment at the expense of another has to be given up is that it is unjust....If we were to take the generalization of mistake to unjust as inviting us to search for any and every *reason* why an enrichment should be given up, we would gather in cases of contracts to give up gains and wrongs for which gain-based recovery is available. The most important feature of mistaken payments is the absence of contract and wrong....In recent years good maps of the response-based category of restitution have been made. But, precisely because restitution is a response, and multi-causal, those maps fall short of isolating unjust enrichment. They have gathered together each and every *reason* why a gain should be given up, but they have not drawn a careful line around the sub-set of those *reasons* which are not contracts and not wrongs.

Here restitution's multi-causality is revealed to be, more fundamentally, its multi-rationality, what distinguishes mistaken payments from cases of restitution for wrongs and contractual restitution a question not

[25] Birks (n 2) 21.
[26] Ibid 3.
[27] Ibid 10–11 (my emphasis throughout).

simply of fact but of rationale. But this insight is not followed through and, rather than inquiring into what positive reasons unjust enrichment identifies, we are told simply that these reasons are distinct from the reasons provided by contracts and wrongs. While this may suffice to show unjust enrichment's independence from those categories, it is not enough to establish its own material (that is, rational) unity. (We may doubt whether the category of tort or wrongs reveals any such unity either.) If we want to identify which restitutionary claims are indeed materially identical to mistaken payments we need to identify not just what reasons don't apply to such cases but, more importantly, what reasons do. Only then can we determine which of the claims left over when cases of restitution for wrongs and contractual restitution are removed are truly like claims, meriting the sort of like treatment which accounts of the law of unjust enrichment have called for.

VII Palm Tree Justice

In the main, the courts seem to have taken little interest in these definitional debates, making no conscious commitment to any one of the different concepts of unjust enrichment that unjust enrichment lawyers have from time to time put forward. Typically they treat unjust enrichment as identifying a principle rather than a set of conditions in which this, or some such, principle applies, though one can find formulations that fit each of these ideas. More clear and more significant is their rejection of the suggestion that unjust enrichment is purely 'downward-looking', its content fixed by the cases alone.[28] If unjust enrichment did no more than repeat what the cases already told us—that these enrichments were recoverable in these instances—then there was nothing for judges to gain by now addressing them as cases of unjust enrichment. The cases could speak for themselves. If the idea of unjust enrichment was to be a useful one, one worth judges taking up and employing, it needed to do some additional work, telling us something those cases, those rules and rulings, did not.

For the courts, the value of unjust enrichment was precisely that it appeared to point to some idea or principle that they could use

[28] Indeed, even the textbook writers who pushed the idea that 'unjust' looked only to the cases found themselves unable to tow this line: see Dan Priel, 'The Justice in Unjust Enrichment' (2014) 51 *Osgoode Hall Law Journal* 813, 817–21.

to resolve hard cases, cases that the existing authorities did not or could not settle. The last thing the courts needed was an idea of unjust enrichment that reflected what those authorities already said and no more. And so, while they ended up accepting the argument of unjust enrichment lawyers that unjust enrichment was indeed a ground of rights and duties, identifying a group of like cases and claims, they didn't adopt their position that it described only those circumstances where such claims had already been recognized. We see this, for instance, in *Woolwich v Inland Revenue Commissioners*, where the House of Lords held for the first time that a claimant who, without mistake or compulsion, had paid money to meet an unlawful tax demand was entitled to recovery of that sum plus interest.[29] This was, so said Lord Browne-Wilkinson, 'the paradigm of a case of unjust enrichment'.[30] Yet it wasn't such a paradigm by virtue of any line of authority clearly recognizing such a claim, for there was none. Rather it was a case that, the court considered, clearly called for such a claim, where to leave the defendant with its gain really would have been unjust.[31] No purely 'downward-looking' understanding of unjust enrichment here.

Now, unjust enrichment lawyers, while insisting on a concept of unjust enrichment fixed by the cases, accepted that the courts could recognize new 'unjust factors', recognizing unjust enrichment claims in situations not previously covered by the cases and statutes.[32] But, having ducked any inquiry into the reasons on which unjust enrichment claims were grounded, the question of when and why a new class of unjust enrichment claim should be recognized was one they were in no position to answer. Instead a framework for addressing these claims was proposed, listing a set of questions by which 'every problem in unjust enrichment can be unlocked' and so, presumably, any novel claim resolved.[33] One of these questions is 'Was the enrichment unjust?' But if 'unjust' remains tied to the existing cases, this framework is incapable of providing an answer (or at least an answer which

[29] *Woolwich Equitable Building Society v Inland Revenue Commissioners* [1993] AC 70 (HL). See too *CTN Cash and Carry Ltd v Gallaher Ltd* [1994] 4 All ER 733 (CA) 737 (Nicholls VC).

[30] Ibid 197.

[31] See too ibid 197: 'the concept of unjust enrichment suggest the plaintiffs should have a remedy'.

[32] See eg Birks (n 1) 294; Burrows (n 3) 87; *Goff and Jones* (n 2) [1-23]–[1-24].

[33] Birks (n 2) 39. See too Peter Birks, *Restitution: The Future* (The Federation Press 1992) x; Burrows (n 3) 27; Edelman and Bant (n 2) 6. The framework was endorsed by the House of Lords in *Banque Financière de la Cité v Parc (Battersea) Ltd* [1999] 1 AC 221 (HL).

isn't an automatic no) in those cases where it is most needed: where the authorities are unclear or as yet recognize no claim. The courts have been able to employ this formula when addressing novel claims only by rejecting (if only by implication) the idea that 'unjust' is merely descriptive of existing authority. And, though they have been keen to stress that unjust enrichment is no invitation to 'palm tree' justice, and that the determination of when novel claims should be recognized is one which requires 'clear reasoning' and the closest attention to the judgments (of value and reasonableness) reflected in the case law, in such cases the courts must, in the end, make such a judgment, such an evaluation of their own.[34]

The courts were right to reject these purely 'downward-looking' understandings of unjust enrichment. There is no difficulty making sense of the notion of a legally recoverable gain, and there is no obstacle to using the term 'unjust enrichment' simply to describe those (or some such set of) situations in which courts have held defendants liable to give up their gains. But this concept of unjust enrichment isn't adequate to answer the questions courts face when judging restitutionary claims, lending no assistance in determining the circumstances in which such claims should lie or the considerations by virtue of which such liability may reasonably be imposed. Unjust enrichment, so understood, can be identified only once we know that the gain is one the defendant must give up. But it plays no role in getting us to that conclusion, adding nothing but a label to decisions reached on other grounds, expressible, and often in fact expressed, in other terms. Through their well-intentioned efforts to counter the challenge

[34] See eg *Gibb v Maidstone and Tunbridge Wells Trust* [2010] EWCA Civ 678, [2010] IRLR 786, paras 26–27 (Laws LJ). Laws LJ goes on to suggest that recognition of new claims should be by 'extension' from existing cases, looking for 'analogues' within that case law. Perhaps it should. But this process of incremental, analogical development is no substitute for consideration of the reasons that ground those claims. As we have seen, the question of whether a given case really is analogous to—ie like—some other case or line of cases isn't simply a matter of their factual similarities but of the common reasons that apply to them. As such, the statement of Mann J in *Uren v First International Finance Ltd* [2005] EWHC Ch 2529, para 16, that the law as yet provides no 'freestanding claim of unjust enrichment in the sense that a claimant can get away with pleading which he says leads to an enrichment which he says is unjust' and that he must instead 'establish that his facts bring him within one of the hitherto established categories of unjust enrichment, or some justifiable extension thereof' sets up a false opposition. The only way that we can determine whether some such extension is justifiable is by consideration of the very same questions of justice that a 'freestanding claim' would require we consider.

that unjust enrichment left judges free to reallocate gains on a whim, guided simply by their own diverse, intuitive notions of justice, they ended up proposing an understanding of unjust enrichment which, by its refusal to go beyond the case law and so to offer any guidance on how novel claims were to be approached, left just this eventuality open.[35]

VIII Unjust Enrichment as One Reason for Restitution

There is no single idea, no one body of law, which has exclusive claim to the name 'unjust enrichment'. We can identify a concept of unjust enrichment, like that set out in the *Introduction*, which encompasses all instances of restitutionary liability, all possible reasons why a court might make such an order. There is nothing incoherent or mistaken in this idea or in using the term 'unjust enrichment' in this way, and such a concept may have its uses. But, so understood, unjust enrichment doesn't mark out any distinct ground of rights and liabilities and, while the cases it comprises have their likenesses, reflecting a common subject matter of liability for gains, these likenesses do not extend to a common rationale or the expression of some common principle. There is no one principle which accounts for all claims for restitution, no one reason which uniquely justifies ordering defendants to give up their gains. All attempts to formulate such a principle fail, reducing to the proposition that enrichments that ought in justice to be given up ought indeed to be given up. This identifies no reason for restitution at all.

The diversity in the grounds for restitution is most apparent when we compare the unjust enrichment lawyer's core case of the mistaken payment with those cases where the defendant's gain comes about through the commission of a wrong, or where recovery is expressly provided for by a contract between the parties. If we move these cases to one side, we are left with a body of law which is now independent of contract and tort and, should we choose, a concept of unjust enrichment which is likewise distinct from these other concepts and

[35] See too Hanoch Dagan, *The Law and Ethics of Restitution* (Cambridge University Press 2004) 23–25.

categories. Once more, there is nothing confused or unsound in this understanding of unjust enrichment, nothing mistaken in collecting up the miscellany of restitutionary claims left over once the contracts and wrongs cases are removed. But if we are looking for unjust enrichment to identify a body of law which is not simply distinct from contract and tort but which has a material unity of its own, we must go on. For within the claims left over we find further differences of rationale, identifying further sub-classes of restitutionary claim which are, one to another, no more alike than they are like the restitution for wrongs and contractual restitution cases already excluded.[36]

There is within the law of restitution a body of like claims, arising independently of contract and tort, which are typified by cases of the payment of a non-existent debt. Determining the extent of this class of claims is not a matter of simply abstracting from the facts of this core case, but of identifying what reasons there are for ordering restitution of these payments and seeing to what other cases these reasons extend.[37] Any account which seeks to identify unjust enrichment with such a body of like claims, even one which then aims to do no more than detail the situations in which these claims have been recognized and how courts have in fact responded to them, must then address the question of what distinctive reasons for restitution unjust enrichment describes. Once we know what these reasons are, we are in a position to say not only which of these cases are alike, but also (to this extent) what like treatment they merit.

Any account that seeks to isolate some such body of like claims will omit much that unjust enrichment has, at times, been taken to cover. The term 'unjust enrichment' has a natural reach set by the everyday

[36] Cf *Goff and Jones* (n 2) [1-02]–[1-08], where unjust enrichment is said to be 'a distinct source of rights and obligations', excluding from the category cases of restitution arising from contracts and wrongs, while also noting that '[t]he reasons why the courts have held a defendant's enrichment to be unjust vary from one set of cases to another'. The reality is that unjust enrichment, so understood, identifies not a single 'source' of rights and obligations but a collection of such sources, which have no more in common with one another than they do with those restitutionary claims which are classed instead under the headings of contract/consent and wrongs. Likewise, the authors contend that unjust enrichment 'is an organising concept that groups decided authorities on the basis that they share a set of common features, namely that in all of them the defendant has been enriched by the receipt of a benefit that is gained at the claimant's expense in circumstances that the law deems to be unjust'. But these common features are shared by all instances of restitutionary liability, with the wrongs and contract cases excluded simply (though not necessarily unreasonably) by fiat.

[37] Cf Birks (n 2) 10–11.

meanings of these words. This reach no doubt extends comfortably to wrongful gains; indeed ordinary language would put these gains at unjust enrichment's core. Those not versed in the definitional debates of unjust enrichment lawyers would likely be unimpressed by the suggestion that the liability of a dishonest fiduciary to give up his unauthorized profits is not a case of unjust enrichment (while admitting that it is a case of an enrichment which it was unjust for the recipient to make and which it would be unjust for him to retain). So the term 'unjust enrichment' may well be ill-equipped to capture what is characteristic or distinctive of the body of law unjust enrichment lawyers now take as their subject. But the measure of an account of 'unjust enrichment', understood as a set of like claims which takes mistaken payments as its paradigm, is not how well it accords with linguistic convention, nor indeed with the conceptual and classificatory conventions of other unjust enrichment lawyers, but rather its success in capturing what is truly distinctive of these claims: (namely) the distinct reasons for restitution these claims identify, and to which they respond. This is the idea of unjust enrichment to which this book is addressed.

3

Reasons

I A Paradigm

Mistaken payments, in particular those where the claimant's mistake goes to his liability to make the payment, are usually taken to be the core or central cases of unjust enrichment. Whether they merit the status of central case may be doubted. If what we are after is a case which best—most clearly, most fully—exemplifies the category, and if the category is one framed by reference to a common reason or principle, then the core case is one which provides the clearest, cleanest example of the nature and operation of that reason or principle. So even if we're clear that mistaken payments are examples of unjust enrichment, what elements of this case make it a case of unjust enrichment and hence how well it isolates and captures what is distinctive of unjust enrichment can be established only once we have a better sense of what this reason is. Nonetheless, mistaken payments do at least give us undisputed examples of unjust enrichment, even for those who dispute the usefulness of this classification. The defendant comes under a liability to give up his gain and this liability can, and often will, attach without any wrongdoing on the part of the defendant and in the absence of any contract providing for recovery. And so, central case or not, they provide a convenient entry point to an inquiry into the distinctive reasons for restitution that unjust enrichment identifies.

Sometimes the claimant's mistake is itself identified as the reason for restitution. No doubt the mistake goes to explaining why it is that the claimant should be entitled to demand that he be repaid. But the bare fact of the claimant's mistake cannot alone get us to the normative conclusion that the payment is one that ought to be given up. No 'ought' from a mere 'is'. To get from the 'is' of the defendant's receipt of the mistaken payment to the practical conclusion that the court ought to order the defendant to make restitution, we need to identify some good which ordering restitution serves.[1] Only if (1) there is a good that comes from the law providing for the restitution of mistaken payments; and (2) this payment was made by mistake; can we conclude that (3) the court ought—has good reason to—order restitution of this payment. So when we are asking what reason exists for ordering restitution of mistaken payments, we are asking: 'Why *on these facts* is a claimant entitled to restitution?' The answer to this question is not, in the end, to be found in further facts about the parties' interactions or their broader setting, but in the identification of some good or value these claims serve.

II Corrective Justice

The rule that a defendant must make restitution of mistaken payments can be identified as a rule of corrective justice. Indeed, on one view, we know this is a rule of corrective justice even before we consider what grounds this rule, and so whether or not it turns out that the rule is itself just. Here, to say a rule is a rule of justice is to say that it is a rule of allocation (of some resource, role, opportunity, burden, etc). To say a rule is one of corrective justice is to say that it is a rule that allocates in such a way as to correct (put right, undo) some

[1] John Finnis illustrates the general point in this way (John Finnis, 'On Hart's Ways: Law as Reason and as Fact' (2007) 52 *American Journal of Jurisprudence* 25, 44–45): 'The fact that it is raining is in itself no reason to carry an umbrella, no reason at all, even in conjunction with the fact that without an umbrella I'll get wet. But facts like these can play their part in the reason, the warranted conclusion (that I should [had better] carry an umbrella) which gets its directive or normative element from some practical, evaluative premise such as: it's bad for one's health to get wet or: it's bad for one's ability to think and function to get uncomfortably wet and cold. *By virtue only of that* or some similar truth (as one supposes) about good and bad, the plain fact that an umbrella can prevent these evils by keeping me dry can contribute to the normative conclusion that I have reason to, ought to, carry an umbrella.' See too John Gardner and Timothy Macklem, 'Reasons' in Jules Coleman and Scott Shapiro (eds), *The Oxford Handbook of Jurisprudence and Philosophy of Law* (Oxford University Press 2002) 447–55.

prior injustice or other misallocation.[2] This is, on any view, what a rule imposing liability for mistaken payments does. So understood, not every rule of corrective justice is itself correctively just. To know whether it is, we have to inquire into its merits, into what reasons can be offered in its support. For others, however, the idea of unjust rules of justice is an oxymoron and so to identify a rule as a rule of justice is to identify—or at least to claim—it as a *just* rule of allocation.[3]

But there's no real disagreement here and no need to adjudicate between these formulations. Regardless of whether we take the term 'rules of justice' to mark out a class of rules of a particular form or a class of rules identified not only by their form but also by their merits, it's clear that the only rules of justice which do any justificatory work are the just ones. To determine whether a particular rule is just we then need to consider what good reasons there are for such a rule, and to know what good reasons there may be, we need to consider the goods and values that rule may promote or serve. So, contrary to what some have thought,[4] there is no opposition between 'corrective justice-based' accounts of the law of unjust enrichment and accounts which seek to justify these claims by the goods or values they serve. Any defence of the law of unjust enrichment must take these rules to be correctively just *because* of the good they do or values they serve or instantiate. And because the corrective justness of these rules is a consequence of the goods and values they serve, the real focus of any justification of this body of rules and claims is not the concept of corrective justice but the goods and values which give just rules of corrective justice their content.

For a rule of corrective justice to be a just one the allocation it directs must be justified, and this means justifying both why the

[2] See John Gardner, 'What is Tort Law for? Part 1. The Place of Corrective Justice' (2011) 30 *Law and Philosophy* 1, 6–10, 14–16; Prince Saprai, 'Restitution without Corrective Justice' [2006] *Restitution Law Review* 41, 52–54.

[3] Does justice only concern questions of allocation? The term 'justice' can be and sometimes is used to identify a broader range of practical concerns: see, eg John Finnis, *Natural Law and Natural Rights* (2nd edn, Oxford University Press 2011) 161–93; John Finnis, 'Reflections and Responses' in John Keown and Robert P George (eds), *Reason, Morality, and Law: The Philosophy of John Finnis* (Oxford University Press 2013) 502–06. Since the questions raised by the law of unjust enrichment are plainly allocative, they are, on all views, questions of justice.

[4] See eg Dennis Klimchuk, 'The Normative Foundations of Unjust Enrichment' in Robert Chambers, Charles Mitchell, and James Penner (eds), *Philosophical Foundations of the Law of Unjust Enrichment* (Oxford University Press 2009).

relevant item be removed from the defendant and why it be given to the claimant. This point is occasionally put in terms of the need to account for the bipolarity and correlativity of private law claims and relations. So long as this means simply that any successful justification of a given rule or practice must indeed justify that rule or practice in its entirety, then it is unobjectionable. But those who have emphasized private law's bipolarity have sometimes meant more than this, taking it to address not just what any such account must justify but also *how* private law rules and relations can be justified, what sorts of considerations might be invoked in their support. The bipolar form of the claimant–defendant relationship must be matched, so it is said, by justificatory considerations of the same structure; the only reasons capable of supporting such claims being reasons which are themselves bipolar or relational in character.[5] This then precludes any recourse to public or collective goods, whose reach extends beyond the relationship between these two parties, and to individual interests and responsibilities, which don't reach far enough and so are incapable of explaining what brings these parties together.

The suggestion here is not merely that these other sorts of considerations do not in fact justify a particular set of private law rules and claims, nor that they cannot do so without supplement from other sorts of considerations: those which *are* bipolar in structure, which can both isolate and link these two parties. Rather, it is that they can play no role whatsoever in justifying or determining the proper content of any private law claim or relationship. On this understanding, it never counts in favour of some action of mine, in determining how I should act towards you, that I am (also) advancing some collective good or interest; it never counts against it that in so acting I am harming such an interest. Indeed public goods and goals are never rationally implicated in the interactions of any members of the public one to another, these collective goods and goals having nothing to say to any dealings between members of that collective. This suggestion is rightly rejected or simply never considered in the practical deliberations of each of us daily and by all real-world systems of private law.

The bipolarity of private law is in any case overstated, and indeed in an important sense simply untrue. One way to see this is that when it comes to private *law* there is always a third party involved. The

[5] See Ernest J Weinrib, *The Idea of Private Law* (Harvard University Press 1995) 32–36; Ernest J Weinrib, *Corrective Justice* (Oxford University Press 2012) 2–4.

question is no longer simply how should these individuals deal with each other, but also how should the state deal with them: What direction, if any, should it give them? When should it take action against one at the behest of the other? Law, including private law, is directed not only to citizens but also to officials. Indeed, though the law of unjust enrichment is at the service of unjust enrichment claimants, it speaks perhaps most directly to judges, instructing them as to how they ought to resolve disputes over gains.[6] Of course, in determining how a given dispute ought be resolved and, more broadly, how the law ought to regulate the dealings of private individuals, among the considerations which will be central will be those that bear on the reasonableness of the parties' actions one to another. But the question of what the state ought to demand I do in my dealings with you is not reducible to the question of what I ought to do in those dealings.

As this starts to bring out, emphasis on the bipolar structure of private law, and particularly private law litigation, blurs what is in truth a series of distinct, though connected, practical questions faced by the relevant parties. Say I agree to sing exclusively in your opera house for the next three months. I then receive an offer of more money to sing elsewhere. What ought I to do? Should I stick to my agreement with you or would it be reasonable of me to take up the more lucrative offer, so long as I see that you receive adequate reparation? If I take up the better offer, how should you respond? Should you sue me, or my new employer, or would your interests be better served by keeping this out of court? If you sue, should the judge order me to keep to my agreement with you? If not, should he at least prevent me from singing for your rival? If damages are instead to be awarded, how should they be measured? Beyond our dispute, what general directions should officials give to contracting parties? What direction should they give to judges charged with resolving their disputes?[7] These are all questions that the law—private law, the law of contract—addresses. And when it addresses these decisions, the law speaks to us as individuals,

[6] See 1.VI.

[7] The failure to distinguish these different questions, and in particular to distinguish the question of what the law says to the parties from what it says to the judge called on to resolve their dispute, goes some way to accounting for the popularity of the view that the law gives contracting parties the option of performing or paying damages (see eg O W Holmes Jr, *The Common Law* (Little, Brown, and Company 1881) 301); so too the idea that the imposition of a duty of care means 'only' that the defendant is liable for negligently caused harm (see eg Peter Cane, *Atiyah's Accidents, Compensation and the Law* (8th edn, Cambridge University Press 2013) 67).

to the choices each of one of us must make and must, in the last resort, make alone. No doubt some of my choices bear directly on you, and no doubt too there are times when your interests alone are enough to make some action obligatory. When the law seeks to direct our choices it too will often have good reason to prioritize the interests of those our choices affect. Nonetheless, the reasonableness of individual choices can be determined only by considering the full range of goods and values that human action can serve, and the same goes for the choices of legal officials when seeking to direct these choices.

The bipolar form of private law litigation matters because it shapes some of the questions that private law seeks to answer. Should this claimant be accorded standing to police or complain against the conduct of this defendant? Should the defendant be ordered to pay compensation *to this claimant*? But this justifies no categorical restriction on the considerations that go to how these questions should be answered. To ask what good reasons exist for restitution of mistaken payments is to ask what goods and values are served by the law providing such redress to mistaken payers. Only if we can identify genuine goods and values which are well served by these claims and orders is the rule that mistaken payees are liable to make restitution of their gains a sound rule of corrective justice.

III The Elements of Unjust Enrichment Claims

Unjust enrichment lawyers have, in the main, made little headway in identifying what these goods or values might be. Most accounts got so far as to identify mistakes as just one of a broader class of 'unjust factors' which centre on the claimant's lack of full or effective consent to the defendant's enrichment. But they didn't go on from there to ask why the claimant's consent should make the difference to the defendant's entitlement to that enrichment. (After all, the defendant would, presumably, rather keep the enrichment for himself, its receipt and retention something to which *he* did and does consent.) As we have seen, the question of what justified treating these enrichments as unjust enrichments was not one these accounts sought to answer; their express aim was limited to detailing the circumstances in which such claims would lie. Yet here too the failure to inquire into the reasons that grounded these claims compromised the accounts they put forward.

So one function of identifying the mistaken payment as unjust enrichment's core case was to provide a template from which, by extrapolation from its basic facts, the essential elements of unjust enrichment claims generally could be worked out.[8] Accordingly, the receipt of money was broadened to the receipt of any enrichment; that the money was paid to the defendant by the claimant could be generalized to the defendant being enriched by subtraction from the claimant or, broader still, at the claimant's expense; paying by mistake was just one instance of an enrichment to which the claimant did not fully or properly consent, which in turn described just one class of 'unjust factor'. Once one added in the possibility that, even where these elements are present, a claim may be defeated on the basis that the defendant may raise an effective defence, we have a basic formula through which (it was suggested) all unjust enrichment claims could be analysed and resolved.[9]

The formula suggested that every enrichment that was mistakenly conferred was a presumptively unjust enrichment. Any benefit I confer on you is an enrichment at my expense. If I can identify an unjust factor, and mistake is as clear an unjust factor as they come, I have all the elements of a cause of action in unjust enrichment. My claim might yet fail: you may be able to raise a defence, or there may be some 'justifying ground' for your enrichment. Nonetheless, on this view, I make out a case for restitution simply by showing that I enriched you by mistake. And so the implication is that in every case of mistaken enrichment there is a reason to order restitution of that enrichment and, if my claim is to be denied, this will be by virtue of some additional factor (eg the defendant's change of position, a contract obligating the claimant to confer that enrichment or barring its recovery) which provides a reason *against* ordering restitution sufficient to outweigh or exclude whatever reason *for* restitution the mistake gives.

[8] The clearest example of this is Peter Birks, *Unjust Enrichment* (2nd edn, Clarendon Press 2005) 9–11.

[9] See eg Peter Birks, *Restitution: The Future* (The Federation Press 1992) x; Andrew Burrows, *The Law of Restitution* (3rd edn, Oxford University Press 2011) 27; Charles Mitchell, Paul Mitchell, and Stephen Watterson (eds), *Goff and Jones: The Law of Unjust Enrichment* (8th edn, Sweet and Maxwell 2011) [1-09]; endorsed by the House of Lords in *Banque Financière de la Cité v Parc (Battersea) Ltd* [1999] 1 AC 221 (HL); cf Birks (n 8) 39.

The cases, however, tell a different story. I forget to turn off the heating in my flat when I go away over Christmas. This heats your flat above, saving you money on your own heating bill. I have no claim to restitution.[10] Yet your gain comes from me—from my actions and from the application of my resources—and there's no doubt I made a mistake.[11] In *TFL Management Services Ltd v Lloyds Bank Plc*, Floyd LJ thought the result could be explained on the basis that '[t]he heating of the flat above was the entirely foreseeable consequence of heating the flat below. The owner of the lower flat must be taken to have accepted this as an inevitable consequence of turning on her own heating.'[12] But it is likewise an 'entirely foreseeable consequence' of my paying you that you will receive and be enriched by the money I pay. The fact I pay you in this knowledge doesn't support the conclusion that I have 'accepted this inevitable consequence'—at least so as to justify then denying me restitution—even if it turns out that my payment is mistaken.

Perhaps the 'at the claimant's expense' requirement could be massaged to have my claim excluded. Where you benefit from my heating my flat in the ordinary course of things, your benefit is merely incidental to mine, or to my pursuit of my own ends, and it's been suggested that such incidental benefits aren't enrichments at my expense.[13] But this is hardly the case here. Your benefit is not a side effect of some self-interested course of action on my part. Or, to the extent that it is, it is no more so than where I pay you in the mistaken belief that I am thereby discharging my debt to you. In any event,

[10] *Edinburgh and District Tramways Company Ltd v Courtenay* 1908 SC 99; *TFL Management Services Ltd v Lloyds Bank Plc* [2013] EWCA Civ 1415, [2014] 1 WLR 2006, paras 35–36.

[11] This hypothetical modifies the facts of an example deployed in the *Edinburgh and District Tramways* case (ibid) to reject the contention that a defendant is liable (at least presumptively) to make restitution of all gains provided without donative intent. The example used there involved no mistake: the neighbour simply benefits from the claimant's heating of his house. Some then argued that no claim would lie because the enrichment was in fact intended, since it was an inevitable side-effect of the claimant's intentional heating of his own house: see eg Birks (n 8) 158–59. The example given in the text shuts off this argument, as it does too the suggestion that no claim lies because the claimant has intentionally 'abandoned' that benefit: see Eli Ball, 'Abandonment and the Problem of Incidental Gains in the Law of Restitution of Unjust Enrichment' [2011] *Restitution Law Review* 49. More to the point: the question of whether the claimant has effectively given or given up the relevant benefit arises only if the benefit is the claimant's to give in the first place.

[12] *TFL Management Services Ltd v Lloyds Bank Plc* (n 10) para 36.

[13] See eg Andrew Burrows, *A Restatement of the English Law of Restitution* (Oxford University Press 2012) 54–55.

the reason for denying my claim is not any problem connecting me to the gain you made. The connection is clear. If it is suggested that this connection is insufficient to ground a claim, the question is why (to which the answer cannot be: 'Because no claim lies'). Certainly we cannot work out what connections count as sufficient simply by looking to the facts of the mistaken payment and trying to work out from them. The conclusion that certain gains you make from me are nonetheless insufficiently connected to me to satisfy the 'at the expense of' requirement is one which can be supported (if at all) only by reference to the reasons which ground and limit these claims. Yet the very value of the formula, as it was presented in these accounts, was its promise to provide a way for courts to resolve novel unjust enrichment claims without having to appeal to 'an unknowable justice in the sky'.[14]

Nor is this a case where the denial of my claim is best explained on the basis that you have a defence. None of the recognized defences fits and, more importantly, there is nothing in these facts that provides the sort of additional factor or additional argument that you might raise to counter my claim for recovery. The true position, I suggest, is that there is nothing for you to counter. You don't need to make the case against liability as there is no case for it in the first place. Whether I consent to a particular enrichment you take from me matters only where my consent is a condition of your entitlement to receive and retain that enrichment. But there are countless occasions in which it is not such a condition; where you are free to take the benefit of my actions whether I like it or not. Of course, I am ordinarily free not to act in these ways—it's me who gets to choose whether or not to turn on my heating—and so typically you don't get the chance to take any of these benefits unless I do in fact so act. In this way, and to this extent, the choice of who gets the chance to benefit from my actions is indeed mine to make. But if I do so act—or indeed if the same

[14] Peter Birks, *An Introduction to the Law of Restitution* (rev edn, Clarendon Press 1989) 19. In truth, most accounts, including Birks' own, equivocated on this point. On the one hand, they were often prefaced by explicit denials of any normative commitment or agenda, claiming only to look down to the cases and proposing that novel questions could be answered simply by identifying and following through the logic already implicit in those cases (see eg ibid 1, 27). Yet in the main body of these accounts we find no shortage of arguments, arguments that, though often incomplete and rarely expressed in these terms, appealed time and again to the justice of particular approaches and solutions. So, when one looks beyond what these accounts say and to what they do, it is plain that there is no suggestion that the framework obviates all need to consider these questions on their merits.

effect is brought about without my participation (say someone else switches my heating on)—I have no veto on who derives a benefit from this, and you are entitled to take and keep that benefit irrespective of whether this is something to which I consented. And so, while the law recognizes and protects my freedom to perform the action of flicking the switch, it doesn't recognize any distinct freedom to control who gains from the taking of that action, however it was taken.

Cases such as these are best seen as the restitutionary analogues of those tort cases where compensation is denied on the basis that the claimant's loss is *damnum absque injuria*: loss without injury, without infringement of any legal interest of the claimant's. For instance, in *Bradford v Pickles*, the defendant made excavations on his land to extract water from an underground stream passing through his property.[15] The stream, when uninterrupted, continued on to the town below and so the effect of Pickles' actions was to reduce the flow to the town, limiting its water supply. Town officials sought to stop this. Their claim failed: though Pickles was depriving them of water which would otherwise have come their way and though this therefore left them worse off than they would otherwise have been, they had no entitlement to the flow of that water into the town and so no right that he refrain from interfering with it.

Perhaps it is always unreasonable to act with the intention of causing harm.[16] Perhaps too, the fact that an act will cause someone loss always counts against it. Losses are setbacks, leaving those who suffer them in one way or another worse off than they would otherwise have been. But losses resulting from human conduct can be avoided only if people tailor their actions accordingly. Any right I have that you not set back my projects and interests means a duty on you, limiting your options and setting back your own projects and interests in turn. As such, the mere fact that your conduct interferes with my plans, depriving me of opportunities I wish to pursue or advantages I wish to enjoy, cannot be sufficient to demand that you compromise your pursuit of your plans, forgoing opportunities and advantages of your own instead. There is instead a judgment to be made as to what projects and interests ought to be protected from such interference,

[15] *The Mayor, Aldermen, and Burgesses of the Borough of Bradford v Pickles* [1895] AC 587 (HL). See too *Victoria Park Racing and Recreation Grounds Company v Taylor* (1937) 58 CLR 479.

[16] See John Finnis, 'Intention in Tort Law' in David G Owen (ed), *Philosophical Foundations of Tort Law* (Clarendon Press 1995). Cf *Bradford v Pickles* (n 15) 594 (Lord Halsbury LC), 598 (Lord Watson), 601 (Lord MacNaghten).

what losses are losses I shouldn't have to tolerate, but which I can instead reasonably demand that others avoid or bear.

There is, therefore, no presumptive wrong or injustice in the mere infliction of loss, even where that loss is a known consequence of our actions. And in the same way there is no presumptive injustice in others gaining from our actions, even where this gain is one to which we have not consented. Indeed with gains this may well be *a fortiori*. Though there is nothing unjust in the mere causing of loss, we should still prefer to see fewer losses, fewer people's interests set back, and to see those whose interests are set back have them set back less far. For gains the opposite is true. There are indeed situations where it is indeed reasonable to make a claimant's consent a condition of the benefit others may derive from his choices and actions. But the idea that we might have a general right to prevent others benefiting from our activities and to demand the surrender of whatever benefits others may derive from us without our consent has even less going for it than the suggestion that there is a general right not to be caused loss. So just as not every infliction of loss—even every knowing infliction of loss—is a *prima facie* tort, not every unauthorized enrichment is a *prima facie* unjust enrichment. And just as we need more than the fact that the defendant's actions caused the claimant loss before we have a reason to order the defendant to desist or pay compensation, so, as the earlier example and countless others like it show,[17] we need more than the fact the claimant didn't consent to the benefit the defendant took from him before we have a reason to require that that benefit be given up.

It is therefore only on occasion that a claimant's interest in determining what enrichment others may derive from him—from his choices and actions, from the resources at his disposal—grounds a claim for restitution against a defendant who so benefits without his consent; only on occasion that he is, as it were, entitled *to* those benefits. It is this idea we see expressed in the following terms by the reporter of the *Restatement (Third) of Restitution and Unjust Enrichment*: 'To be the subject of a claim in restitution, the benefit conferred must be something in which the claimant has a legally protected interest.'[18]

[17] For a few more, see Charlie Webb, 'Property, Unjust Enrichment, and Defective Transfers' in Robert Chambers, Charles Mitchell, and James Penner (eds), *Philosophical Foundations of the Law of Unjust Enrichment* (Oxford University Press 2009) 346–51.

[18] *Restatement (Third) of Restitution and Unjust Enrichment* (American Law Institute 2011) § 2, Comment *b*, and see too the illustrations there given. There appears to be greater recognition of this point among civil lawyers and comparativists: see Ernst von Caemmerer,

This formulation requires some refinement, and defence, but is at root sound. Where the claimant has no such protected interest in the benefit the defendant takes, his lack of consent to the defendant obtaining that benefit provides no ground for its reversal. Conversely, where he does, that interest, in conjunction with the fact of a lack of true or applicable consent to the defendant deriving such a benefit, gives us a reason to order that gain to be given up to the claimant.

IV Two Concepts of 'Interest'

The term 'interest' is used in different ways. Sometimes it is used to identify a set of concrete legal entitlements, as where my easement over a plot of land is said to constitute an interest in that land, the contours of that interest being settled by the legal rules applicable to it. Elsewhere, however, we see interests understood not as sets of bottom-line entitlements but as, or as indicating, a particular kind of ground of such entitlements. Here, to describe an individual as having a particular interest is to identify some aspect of his wellbeing, something which is good for him.[19] I have an interest, so understood, in my physical safety, in my good name, and in getting a good night's sleep. These goods—these things that make my life go better in various ways—may, if sufficiently important, ground duties on others not to interfere with, and occasionally to support, my enjoyment of, or participation in, that good. My interest in physical safety is a reason why you should drive carefully in my vicinity, my interest in a good night's sleep means that you should turn your music down at night, and so on.

Not all interests of this kind merit legal recognition or protection. Those that do won't always receive the protection they deserve. Interests may be recognized and protected only in part. Not all interests are of equal value or weight. Some give stronger reasons than others: my interest in physical safety is a weightier consideration

'Grundprobleme des Bereicherungsrechts' in Hans G Leser (ed), *Gesammelte Schriften: Bd I, Rechtsvergleichung und Schuldsrecht* (J C B Mohr (Paul Siebeck) 1968) 374–75; Reinhard Zimmermann, *The Law of Obligations: Roman Foundations of the Civilian Tradition* (Juta & Co 1990) 889; James Gordley, *Foundations of Private Law: Property, Tort, Contract, Unjust Enrichment* (Oxford University Press 2006) 424–26.

[19] See eg Joseph Raz, *The Morality of Freedom* (Oxford University Press 1995) 166–70.

than my interest in sleeping well. Sometimes the value of a particular interest—that it does indeed identify a genuine aspect of my wellbeing—is self-evident. No argument is needed to get to the conclusion that my physical safety is worth preserving. At other times, however, more needs to be said to demonstrate that a purported interest really does identify something sufficiently good or valuable that it should act as a constraint on others' choices and actions. Some interests will derive their value, or part of their value, from other more basic interests or from broader social goods: my interest in a good night's sleep derives from my interest in my physical and mental health. That I have a particular interest counts in favour of requiring you, and others, to refrain from acting in ways that harm or interfere with the object of that interest. But the reason my interest provides is just one consideration to be factored in when assessing whether you ought to come under this or some such duty. Whether, all things considered, my interest justifies a particular duty depends on other considerations too, including the impact this would have on others' interests. Identifying an individual as having a particular interest is only one step towards working out what demands can reasonably be made of others in their dealings with him.

When Fuller and Perdue wrote about the different interests that contract damages might serve, they used the term in this second sense, identifying each interest as a different 'purpose' to which such an award may be directed, a different claim of justice such an award might express.[20] Hence we can say that a contracting party has an interest in performance of the contract and that this identifies a reason to see his counterpart as owing a duty to perform and for courts to take action against him if he doesn't. Determining whether this interest should be protected by a judicial order that the defendant perform, however, requires that we also consider the interests of the defendant, so too the cost and feasibility of administering such orders. Sometimes the defendant's interests and these considerations of practicality and efficiency will give the court good reason to refuse to compel performance and instead order the defendant merely to compensate the claimant for the losses caused by his failure to perform. But the refusal to compel performance doesn't establish that this claimant's interest in performance is going unrecognized or unprotected and, by the same

[20] L L Fuller and William R Perdue, Jr, 'The Reliance Interest in Contract Damages: 1' (1936) 42 *Yale Law Journal* 52.

token, the fact that damages do not provide the claimant with the performance he was promised doesn't mean that his interest in that performance is not the ground of the damages award. That this interest isn't given full protection does not mean it is being given none.

When understood as bottom-line legal entitlements, our legal interests are determined and delimited by our community's positive laws and by the claims and duties they describe. But, as this example shows, this is not true of the sorts of interests that ground those entitlements. My interests, so understood, will sometimes come into conflict with yours, and with other goods and values. Where they do, the law may accord my interests only limited recognition and protection. Interests of this kind are not, therefore, co-extensive with the legal rules that protect them. It follows that we can't infer from the fact that I am denied a particular claim that the law denies that I have any relevant interest worthy of legal protection. It may simply be that it is outweighed by some other consideration. Nor, where my claim succeeds, can we conclude that the interest which the law is recognizing goes only so far as the protection it is thereby accorded, for again this determination may represent a balancing of competing interests and considerations.

That the same term 'interests' can be used to identify both bottom-line practical conclusions and their grounds means we must be careful with statements to the effect that an individual has (or lacks) a particular interest. If a court rules that the claim against Pickles fails because the claimants had no interest in the water he extracted, this may just be another way of restating the conclusion that they had no right that Pickles refrain from extracting the water, that Pickles breached no duty when he did this. Or it may instead point towards the basis of this conclusion: no claim lies because, whatever good comes to the claimants, and to the townspeople for whom they act, from having access to the water, is not sufficient to deny Pickles the freedom to take that water for himself. As this shows, even when 'interest' is used in the second of these senses, it may tell us only so much. If we want the full reasons for denying the claim, we need to go on and ask what good there was in the town having access to the water, what good there was in Pickles' freedom to interrupt that flow, what weight those goods were given, and what other considerations were brought into the balance. In these ways, the idea that some losses are *damnum absque injuria* tells us neither what counts as *injuria* nor how that determination should be made.

Nonetheless, it remains useful for the reminder it gives that there is nothing presumptively wrongful or unjust in causing others loss. In *Donoghue v Stevenson*, Lord Atkin considered that there must be some 'element common' to all cases where a defendant was held to owe a duty of care.[21] When he looked to those cases, he saw that in each the defendant was engaged in some activity that made it reasonably foreseeable that, were care not taken, harm would result. He concluded that if the reasonable foreseeability of harm was sufficient to raise a duty of care in these cases, so it should in others and hence, wherever harm was reasonably foreseeable, we had the same reason to recognize a duty of care. But this didn't follow. That harm was foreseeable in all those instances where it was reasonable to require a defendant to take care did not mean it was, even presumptively, reasonable to require a defendant to take care in all cases in which harm was foreseeable. It is, at root, the same mistake that affected the accounts of the law unjust enrichment lawyers offered and the formulae for recovery they proposed. A range of cases exists in which the claimant's mistake or lack of true or effective consent to the defendant's enrichment provides a basis for a claim for restitution. But it doesn't follow from this that we have the same, or any, reason for restitution in all cases of mistaken or non-consensual enrichment.

The fact that a defendant's conduct poses a foreseeable risk of harm supports a requirement that the defendant take care to avoid that harm where the harm is to some interest of the claimant's sufficient to merit this protection. So too the fact that the claimant did not consent to the defendant's enrichment supports the imposition of liability to restitution of that enrichment where the claimant has some sufficient interest in that enrichment, (or more broadly) in determining what benefits others may derive from his actions and resources. Only where he has some such interest does his consent make a difference to whether the defendant is free to keep an enrichment made, in one way or another, at the claimant's expense. Sometimes, as in our earlier example, where I mistakenly heat your flat, there is no such interest. At other times, whether the claimant has, or ought to have, such an interest will be unclear. In these cases, there is no option but to ask what reasons support such interests, what good is served by according the claimant and others in his position this sort of control over enrichments of the kind the defendant has received. Here the law

21 *Donoghue v Stevenson* [1932] AC 562 (HL) 580.

of unjust enrichment—like the law of torts in cases like *Bradford v Pickles*—takes on the job of determining what interests merit legal protection and what protection they merit, delineating our legal entitlements by specifying what opportunities and advantages are ours to exploit and with which others must not interfere.[22]

But, very often, that the claimant has such an interest is not in doubt. And so we see in many unjust enrichment decisions no discussion of this question, indeed no reference at all to the interests these claims serve. Instead argument focuses on what is in dispute: whether the claimant was truly mistaken, whether this mistake caused the enrichment, whether the defendant changed his position, and so on. These are the standard cases of unjust enrichment, argued and decided without reference to the interest these claims serve, not because this interest is immaterial, but because it isn't in doubt.

V Title and Transfer

Yet these cases are commonly thought to resist any such explanation precisely because it seems the claimant has no interest in the enrichment the defendant receives, and so no interest that he can now invoke in support of its return. True, there are cases—for instance, where money is stolen from the claimant or paid under a mistake as to the recipient's identity—where the claimant is held to retain his title to that money. But these cases are the exception. In the unjust enrichment lawyer's core case of the mistaken liability payment, as in all the standard cases of unjust enrichment, this title passes to the recipient. Here, so it is thought, whatever interest the claimant once had in that enrichment is now gone, lost to the defendant through the very transfer which he now seeks to reverse. And so, for some, the question raised by these cases is: What reason do we have for granting a claimant restitution in respect of the payment *given that* he no longer has any interest in that money? What reason is there to require the defendant to give up this gain given that the money is now *his*?[23] The mystery at the heart of the law of unjust enrichment is then to

[22] See too Daniel Friedmann, 'The Protection of Entitlements via the Law of Restitution—Expectancies and Privacy' (2005) 121 *Law Quarterly Review* 400.

[23] See eg Klimchuk (n 4) 82–83, 88; Weinrib, *Corrective Justice* (n 5) 188–89.

explain the defendant's liability in respect of a transfer that, to this extent, the law regards as effective.

The real mystery is how so many unjust enrichment lawyers have made such heavy weather of this rule of positive law for so long. The rules of title mark out what we might call a set of provisional or default entitlements concerning the use and enjoyment of particular assets. So where I have legal title to an asset, I am identified as the holder of a collection of default claims, powers, and privileges related to its use and disposition. In what sense are these specific entitlements default? The rules of title aren't the only way the law regulates the use of assets, and so the claims, powers, and privileges I am accorded as title holder aren't the last word on what I and others are entitled do with that asset. While I have title to this land, you may at the same time have a distinct proprietary interest of your own—say a lease or an easement—in it. What use I may make of the land may be curtailed by various statutory and common law prohibitions and by permissions I have granted and undertakings I have made. In these instances, my all-things-considered claims, powers, and privileges in relation to the land are cut back. Yet these various qualifications to my bottom-line entitlements are not taken to qualify my status as holder of legal title. I do not become any less an owner each time I permit you or someone else use of my assets, and my position as legal title holder is compatible with my having, for the time being, minimal, or indeed no, access to that asset. My title instead provides a sort of baseline: a collection of use-privileges and control-powers which operate in default of and subject to any such licences and permissions and any relevant rules and rulings governing use of the asset, but which then cede (to this extent) wherever such licences and permissions, rules and rulings obtain.[24]

The rules on the location of title determine who holds this default set of privileges and powers. These rules are necessarily implicated every time those assets change hands, including in every mistaken or otherwise 'flawed' transfer. But they are implicated as one aspect of the law's *response* to such transfers. For the question for the law is what difference the fact of these transfers should make to the parties' respective entitlements: what (if any) use-privileges and powers of

[24] Cf Sir Frederick Pollock, *Jurisprudence and Legal Essays* (MacMillan & Co Ltd 1961) 97–98; A M Honoré, 'Ownership' in A G Guest (ed), *Oxford Essays in Jurisprudence: A Collaborative Work* (Oxford University Press 1961) 126–28.

disposition the transferee acquires, whether the transferor's powers and privileges are now curtailed or lost. As such, these rules—whatever they provide—are not part of the backdrop against which restitutionary claims following mistaken and otherwise flawed transfers fall to be addressed. Rather they are themselves central features of how the law then addresses these claims. If we're looking to explain the law's response to cases such as these, they are among the rules we need to account for.

So in those cases where title is held not to pass to the recipient, and hence where there is no doubt that the law takes the claimant to retain an interest in that asset, this subsisting title is not the explanation of the defendant's liability, but itself calls for explanation. It might be thought that, once we've determined that title has not passed, the defendant's liability to give up his gain follows, in a sense, automatically: the determination that title remains in the claimant entails or incorporates the conclusion that the defendant must give up his enrichment. But then the reason for restitution in such cases is the reason for holding title not to have passed. Such a line of reasoning might go as follows: (1) the fact the claimant held (we can, for now, assume) undisputed legal title to the relevant asset at the outset reflects a determination that he was, at least provisionally, the person authorized to determine how and by whom that asset is used, such that, to this extent, these decisions were his to make; (2) though the asset is now in the defendant's hands, meaning he is now, as a matter of physical reality, in a position to determine its use, this came about other than through some such decision of the claimant's, or at least only by virtue of a decision which was, in some way, impaired; (3) there is then good reason to treat the claimant as *still* the person authorized to determine the asset's use and disposition; (4) it is, therefore, reasonable to rule that legal title remains in the claimant and, hence, that the defendant must then surrender to the claimant that asset, or at least its monetary equivalent.

This leaves various questions unanswered. Even if all this follows from the determination that the claimant has legal title at the outset, what explains *this* determination? When, if ever, should a mistaken decision to transfer the asset be taken to be tantamount to no such decision at all? Why, given this line of reasoning, should the claimant have to make do—as in law he often must—with recovery of the monetary value of the asset, rather than the asset itself? (The essential fungibility of money is one reason for thinking mistaken payments may not provide the best focal point for a study of unjust enrichment.) Nonetheless, here we have a line of argument which takes us from the parties' pre-transfer positions and entitlements to this set of post-transfer entitlements, one which explains not simply why the fact of such a transfer has normative consequences but why *these* consequences.

To put the same point another way: when title does not pass following an asset's transfer, there are two senses in which the claimant can be said to retain an interest in that asset, reflecting the two senses of 'interest' described above. The claimant's title is an interest in the first of these two senses, identifying a (default) set of bottom-line legal entitlements.[25] But *this* (bottom-line) interest is retained by the claimant because the reasons for according him that title in the first place remain notwithstanding its physical transfer to the defendant, because, that is, he has an interest (in the second, justificatory sense of 'interest') in determining that asset's use and disposition which continues to merit that recognition and protection. For an explanation of the defendant's liability we need to look past the conclusion that the claimant retains title to the asset to reasons for that conclusion. It is not the claimant's title that justifies his claim for restitution but the (background, normative) interest in determining the disposition of that asset which that title represents and protects.

VI The Passing of Title

In the standard cases of unjust enrichment title passes. If we think that the reason for restitution in those cases where title doesn't pass is the claimant's title to the asset received by the defendant, it follows that, where title does pass, any liability to make restitution must have some other rationale. But, as we've now seen, the claimant's title does not explain the law's response to such cases, but is itself one aspect of that

[25] Or, as some prefer to put it, legal title and other such property interests are forms of legal response (ie conclusions, outputs of a chain of legal reasoning): see eg Peter Birks, 'Property and Unjust Enrichment: Categorical Truths' [1997] *New Zealand Law Review* 623. The fact that property (and the terms 'property interest' and 'property right') can describe both this sort of legal conclusion and a possible ground for such conclusions goes a long way to explaining, and unravelling, apparent disagreements about property's place in legal reasoning (cf R B Grantham and C E F Rickett, 'Property and Unjust Enrichment: Categorical Truths or Unnecessary Complexity?' [1997] *New Zealand Law Review* 668).

response; the reason for requiring the defendant to make restitution is not the title held by the claimant but the interest that title upholds and protects. The role of title is no different in the standard cases of unjust enrichment where the claimant's title passes. Here too the rules on the passing of title are not part of the explanation but part of what needs to be explained, and this explanation requires us to look beyond those rules to the reasons which support the combined effect of the law's rules of title and liability. So there is no doubt that the law's response differs between these two classes of case. But if we want to know whether or to what extent this difference in response reflects a difference in rationale, we won't get our answer by simply restating the very differences in response we are looking to explain.

In those cases where title does not pass, the rule that title remains in the claimant represents a judgment that his (background) interest in determining the disposition of that asset remains deserving of protection, notwithstanding that the asset is no longer in his possession. His legal title is an expression of that interest, a means by which it is accorded legal recognition and protection, and the conclusion that he retains that title even though the asset is now in the defendant's hands is a response designed to ensure that this interest and the authority it accords him over that asset's disposition are respected. So if the claimant's surviving title expresses the law's recognition that he has such an interest, doesn't it follow that, where title is held to pass, the law recognizes he has none? No. As we've seen, the interests which ground bottom-line legal entitlements are not defined or delineated by the entitlements they ground, for the protection accorded to individual interests will often be limited by the need to protect other interests and by other goods and values which also have a call on the law's attention. This is true of a contracting party's interest in contractual performance. One way the law can recognize and protect this interest is by compelling a recalcitrant defendant to perform. But this interest may also be recognized and protected in cases where the courts consider it unreasonable to compel performance and award the claimant only damages. For the preference for damages need involve no denial of that interest or of the value of its protection, and may instead signify only that compelled performance is not without cost—to the interests of the defendant, to the pursuit of other goods and goals—which justify giving the claimant's interest in performance something less than full protection. It is a mistake to think that interests must be protected in full or not at all.

The same is true of interests in the use and disposition of assets. These interests are likewise neither defined by nor co-extensive with the legal protection accorded to them. The idea that these interests begin and end with the acquisition and passing of title is a straightforward confusion of bottom-line entitlements and their grounds. And so it does not follow from the all-things-considered determination that, following a mistaken transfer, legal title passes to the defendant and that the claimant is entitled only to a claim to the money value of that asset that the claimant has no interest (in this sense) in that asset, nor that the defendant's liability is not in fact grounded in that interest.[26] Of course, the fact that title is indeed held to pass to the defendant and that the claimant recovers not the asset but only its monetary equivalent means that this interest isn't being given full effect or protection. But this may only go to show that there exist competing interests, competing goods and values, which, in these circumstances, justify giving it only partial protection.[27]

So one suggestion sometimes made is that the law's response to the standard cases of unjust enrichment—holding title to pass while enabling the claimant to demand that he be paid a sum assessed by reference to its value—is explicable along the following lines:[28] (1) the claimant, as legal title holder of the relevant asset prior to its transfer, was authorized to determine who may receive and use that asset; (2) though the asset is now in the defendant's possession, it came into his hands only by virtue of a decision of the claimant's which was qualified or, in some way, impaired; (3) there is then good reason to

[26] See too Peter Jaffey, *Private Law and Property Claims* (Hart Publishing 2007) 95–96.

[27] As a further illustration, note another way in which positive law often limits the recognition or protection given to interests of this kind. My interest in my assets is an interest in determining their use and disposition. Respect for this interest means respect for my choices. But the law sometimes denies me certain choices (think, for instance, of perpetuity rules) or recognizes them as effective only when manifested in a particular form. Sometimes these rules are explicable on the basis that they best support the interests of owners generally, for instance by cautioning them or by encouraging them to express their intentions more clearly, or by ensuring that future generations don't have their choices unduly limited by the choices of present owners. At other times, they serve broader interests and goals, such as publicity and the protection of others who later deal with the asset.

[28] See eg Kit Barker, 'The Nature of Responsibility for Gain: Gain, Harm and Keeping the Lid on Pandora's Box' in Robert Chambers, Charles Mitchell, and James Penner (eds), *Philosophical Foundations of the Law of Unjust Enrichment* (Oxford University Press 2009) 169, 177; Jaffey (n 26) 98, 156. Cf Ben McFarlane, 'Unjust Enrichment, Rights and Value' in Andrew Robertson and Tang Hang Wu (eds), *The Goals of Private Law* (Hart Publishing 2009) 604–07.

treat the claimant as *still* the person authorized to determine the asset's use and disposition; *but* (4a) if we were to allow the claimant to assert a continuing title to that asset, this may create problems for third parties who have dealt with the defendant on the reasonable assumption that the asset now in his hands is his to dispose of; *and* (4b) if we were to allow the claimant to reclaim that asset ahead of the defendant's other creditors in the event of the defendant's insolvency, this would unreasonably prejudice those other creditors; *so* (5) it is reasonable, all things considered, to limit the claimant to recovery of a sum of money of equal value, leaving the asset in the defendant's hands and his to dispose of.

Is this sort of qualified protection of a claimant's interest a truly reasonable response to the various considerations that bear on the law's resolution of these claims?[29] This can be determined only by a fuller examination of those considerations. But at the very least it offers a coherent, plausible account of the law's operation here, one that cannot simply be assumed to be unsound. Indeed it is quite possible that something like this line of argument accounts for how the law here developed and how, prior to the emergence of unjust enrichment as an organizing idea, these rules were in fact understood by the lawyers responsible for their application and development.[30] So the old cases and treatises contain numerous references to claimants recovering money which is 'theirs' or to which the defendant is 'not entitled', even where it is plain that title has passed.[31] On the view now taken

[29] Remember too that a claimant's interest in the disposition of his assets receives only partial protection, even in those cases where title is held not to pass, for here the claimant will often recover not the asset itself but its monetary equivalent (at which point title will be lost to the defendant).

[30] See generally S J Stoljar, *The Law of Quasi-Contract* (2nd edn, Law Book Company 1989) 6, 10–17; David Ibbetson, *A Historical Introduction to the Law of Obligations* (Oxford University Press 2001) 266–68, 273–76; Michael Lobban, 'Mapping the Common Law: Some Lessons from History' [2014] *New Zealand Law Review* 21, 48–54.

[31] Two notable examples: *Kelly v Solari* (1841) 9 M & W 54, 59 (Parke B), the case adopted by Birks as the exemplar of his core case of unjust enrichment, and *United Australia Ltd v Barclays Bank Ltd* [1941] AC 1 (HL) 27 (Lord Atkin). The trend continues to the case taken to have marked the official recognition of the law of unjust enrichment in England: *Lipkin Gorman v Karpnale Ltd* [1991] 2 AC 548 (HL). There, it was accepted that title to the money misappropriated from the firm's client account by the solicitor, Cass, was vested in him such that, when it was then paid over to the defendant, it took legal title in turn. Yet, in upholding the firm's claim for money had and received, the money was described as 'their [ie the claimant's] money', 'their property' (ibid 564, 572, 574). For extensive discussion of the case, which wrestles with these supposedly contradictory elements of the judgments before concluding that the claim may indeed best be analysed as resting on the firm's continuing interest in the money (though describing 'the nature of this interest' as 'something of a mystery'), see Lionel Smith, 'Restitution: The Heart of Corrective Justice' (2001) 79 *Texas Law Review* 2115, 2159–74.

by the mainstream of unjust enrichment lawyers, the conclusion must be that these judges were, to a man, hopelessly mistaken about the very rules they were applying, that their statements were flatly inconsistent with what they themselves must have known the law to be. The more charitable interpretation is also the more plausible: these judges knew full well that title to money (usually) passed on transfer, yet they also understood that these claims provided a form of protection for the interest which that title hitherto protected.

Here modern accounts of the law of unjust enrichment mark not progress but regress. Modern unjust enrichment lawyers exhibit a collective failure to grasp an idea, a manner of thought and of expression, which to their forebears was both simple and familiar. The rules on the passing of title do not provide the backdrop against which unjust enrichment claims are to be addressed, but are part of the larger body of law which addresses the question of the parties' respective rights and liabilities following such transfers. There is no reason to assume that the conclusion that title passes to the defendant is best understood independently of the conclusion that the defendant (at the same time) comes under a liability to give up a sum quantified by reference to the value of that very asset; no reason either to think that this liability is not itself an expression of the very same interest, the very same good or aspect of the claimant's well-being, which that title previously expressed. Perhaps there are other explanations of unjust enrichment's central cases, identifying reasons for restitution independent of any interest of the claimant's in the relevant asset. If so, all the better. But viable alternative explanations have proved hard to find and, in their absence, the rejection of this line of reasoning—a rejection in any case premature and ill-grounded—looks reckless.

VII Some Failed Explanations

The different legal responses to mistaken transfers, sometimes holding title to pass, sometimes not, need reflect no difference of rationale, any more than the distinctiveness of specific performance and damages need indicate distinct interests, distinct injustices. The idea that all these claims serve the same interest—the claimant's interest (with 'interest' here, as from now on, understood in the second of the two senses set out above) in the asset now held by the defendant—is not contradicted by the rule that, in the standard cases of unjust enrichment, title passes. Whether these cases really are materially, rationally distinct from those where title stays with the claimant is a question that cannot be answered simply by referring back to those very rules, but only by inquiry into the goods and values those rules serve and the reasons they give. The failure to conduct any such inquiry meant that those accounts which did address this division could do little more than restate that these differences in response do indeed exist.

For instance, it is sometimes said that it is only in those cases where title passes that the defendant's liability turns on the identification of an 'unjust factor'.[32] By contrast, where title doesn't pass, the claimant succeeds simply by establishing his title to the asset now in the defendant's hands. The ruling that title remains in the claimant may well presumptively entail liability of some sort on the part of the defendant. If so, then, no doubt, once we've determined that the claimant retains his title we don't need to go on to inquire into factors that make the defendant's retention of that asset unjust. But that ruling is itself a conclusion that we get to only by way of an inquiry into the circumstances of the transfer, the very sort of inquiry which elsewhere is framed in terms of unjust factors. The most we might say is that the law does indeed respond differently, asking different questions in different terms, where title passes than it does where title does not pass. None of this takes us any further in accounting for this difference.

The same goes for the suggestion that we can distinguish the standard cases of unjust enrichment from those where the claimant's title doesn't pass on the basis that it is only where title passes that the defendant can be said to have been enriched, or that it is only then that any enrichment comes at the claimant's expense.[33] Since there needs to be an enrichment before we can have an unjust enrichment, it follows that the cases where the claimant retains his title can't be cases of unjust enrichment, and so require some other explanation. The standard counter-argument here is that, though the defendant

[32] See eg Graham Virgo, *The Principles of the Law of Restitution* (2nd edn, Oxford University Press 2006) 11–14, 570–74; Lionel Smith, 'Unjust Enrichment, Property and the Structure of Trusts' (2000) 116 *Law Quarterly Review* 416, 420.

[33] See eg Andrew Tettenborn, 'Restitution of Property You Do Not Own Anyway' in Alastair Hudson (ed), *New Perspectives on Property Law, Obligations and Restitution* (Cavendish Publishing 2003); R B Grantham and C E F Rickett, 'Property Rights as a Legally Significant Event' [2003] *Cambridge Law Journal* 717, 742; William Swadling, 'Ignorance and Unjust Enrichment: The Problem of Title' (2008) 28 *Oxford Journal of Legal Studies* 627. Cf Birks (n 14) 13–16.

may not be 'technically' enriched without title passing, as a matter of 'factual reality' he is, for the asset is nonetheless at his disposal.[34] Those who take enrichment to be a factual issue have the better of this argument. If we are to say that the defendant isn't enriched where, though the asset is now at his disposal, title remains in the claimant, then we should likewise say he isn't enriched where, though title passes, he comes under an immediate liability to give up its value. Either way the law provides, from the word go, a mechanism to ensure that the defendant takes no benefit from his receipt.[35] The idea that there is a 'legal benefit' where, but only where, title passes is just another example of the failure to treat the rules on the passing of title as themselves part of the law's response to these cases and claims. So all this argument really does is to repeat that the rules of title do indeed apply differently as between these two classes of case.

If I pay you money I wrongly believe I owe you, title to the money passes; if I pay you the same money thinking you are someone else, it does not. Perhaps this difference in treatment reflects a genuine material difference between these two cases. But if it does, this won't be on the ground that only the first of these payments enriches you.[36] Money is no more enriching when the payer thinks he owes it to you than when he thinks you're someone else. Perhaps we might capture this difference in the way these cases are treated by saying that it is only where title passes that the law treats the payment as (presumptively) enriching. But this takes us no nearer to explaining this difference in treatment, no nearer to determining whether these two cases differ not only in response but in rationale. We won't find out whether cases are alike by asking whether they are in fact treated alike.[37] The only factual difference between these two cases lies in the nature of my mistake. If *this* difference is a material difference—a difference that supports the differing treatment of these two cases—it can only be because these different mistakes give us different reasons to order (or to deny) restitution.

[34] See eg Birks (n 25) 654–56; Burrows (n 9) 195. Cf Birks (n 8) 27, 64–68.

[35] See too Peter Watts, '"Property and 'Unjust Enrichment"': Cognate Conservators' [1998] *New Zealand Law Review* 151, 161.

[36] Nor because the recipient receives a different kind of enrichment: cf Robert Chambers, 'Two Kinds of Enrichment' in Robert Chambers, Charles Mitchell, and James Penner (eds), *Philosophical Foundations of the Law of Unjust Enrichment* (Oxford University Press 2009).

[37] 2.V.

VIII A Reason for, or a Reason Against, Restitution

English law does not respond to all mistaken or otherwise defective asset transfers in the same way. In the main, these differences in response do not track differences in what is transferred but differences in the circumstances of its transfer. So the law responds differently depending on whether I make a mistake or merely a 'misprediction', whether my mistake goes to my liability or to your identity, and so on. But alongside these differences these cases share some basic similarities. They have a common starting point: some asset in my possession and to which I have legal title. They have a common end point too: that asset no longer in my possession but in yours. The title I have at the outset expresses and recognizes my interest in determining that asset's use and disposition. When that asset changes hands, leaving my possession and coming into yours, that interest cannot but be a central consideration when working out what difference, if any, this makes to our respective entitlements. At the point of its transfer, I had the authority to determine how and by whom that asset was to be used. When that asset comes into your hands, it does so either with my authorization or without it. Either way, that authority and the interest it supports are implicated. Either way, it gives a reason which is presumptively determinative of how we are then to be treated.

So if you receive the asset without my authorization, there is reason to treat me as *still* authorized to determine its use and disposition, the transfer of possession marking no transfer of entitlement. Conversely, where I authorize the transfer, there is in that exercise of authority a reason to take that transfer as effective to alter our entitlements in the ways I intended. If my intention was to assign my full entitlement to this asset to you, and if this decision was indeed mine to make, then respect for my interest in the disposition of that asset supports treating that transfer as effective to pass that title to you. The authority you now have over that asset's disposition is then the realization of my exercise of such authority. Any entitlement you now claim on the back of such a transfer manifests and endorses *my own* entitlement to make this determination.

More needs to be said to explain whether and how mistakes and other factors influencing or deflecting my decision-making may be taken to have the effect of rendering an apparent exercise of my authority no true exercise of that authority.[38] For now, we can say that, if and when they can, my interest in determining that asset's disposition is sufficient, all else equal, to justify your liability to make restitution. Of course, if the proper conclusion is that my authority was truly exercised, however ill-judged or otherwise deficient my decision to exercise it in this way may have been, no claim for restitution can be justified on the basis of my interest in making these choices. But more than that: the conclusion that my decision to make the transfer was a true exercise of my authority means there is reason to *deny* me restitution. Recognizing and respecting an owner's authority to determine his asset's disposition means recognizing and respecting the decisions he has made. Where I authorize such a transfer, this means treating that transfer as effective to pass my entitlement to you, and so refusing any attempt to rescind that transfer or to undo its consequences.

As such, if I pay you money I mistakenly believe I owe you, my interest in determining the disposition of that money either provides a reason for granting me restitution or it provides a reason against it. Which of these reasons it provides depends, in the first instance, not on how the law in fact responds to my case, but on how my mistake may be said to affect my apparent exercise of my power to dispose of that money. The challenge for those who would deny that my interest in the money—the interest previously recognized and protected by my title to that money—can support my claim to repayment is, therefore, not just to identify some other reason for restitution, but to explain how this overrides the reason *against* restitution my legitimate exercise of my power to dispose of the money provides.

Few unjust enrichment lawyers have addressed this challenge, none successfully. It is sometimes suggested that we can make sense of the combined effect of the rules of title and liability in these cases—whereby title to the asset passes but the defendant becomes liable to pay over its monetary equivalent—on the basis that it in fact reflects the claimant's intentions: that it is merely his intention to benefit the defendant which is absent or compromised, not his intention to pass title.[39] No doubt these intentions can be distinguished. I can intend to give you some benefit from my asset without intending to

[38] I address this question in chapter 5.

[39] See eg Virgo (n 32) 583; William Swadling, 'A Claim in Restitution' [1996] *Lloyd's Maritime and Commercial Law Quarterly* 63, 64–65. Cf Ernest J Weinrib, 'Correctively Unjust Enrichment' in Robert Chambers, Charles Mitchell, and James Penner (eds), *Philosophical Foundations of the Law of Unjust Enrichment* (Oxford University Press 2009) 32–34, 38–41, 51.

pass title to you (as where I merely licence your use of it or where I deploy it in furtherance of your projects and interests). So too can I intend to pass title to you without intending you to benefit (as where I transfer the asset to you on trust). Given the separability of these intentions, it may not be impossible to imagine circumstances in which a claimant's apparent intention to benefit a defendant is affected by a mistake which does not likewise affect his intention to pass title.

But these are not the ordinary cases of unjust enrichment. Save where a title-holder intends a transfer on trust, the intention to pass title *is* an intention to benefit. If I mistakenly pay my debt to you twice over, my purpose, on each occasion, is to give you title to, and thereby the benefit of, that money. Without the mistake, I'd have intended neither. It is simply unreal, untrue to say that my mistake extends only to the intention to benefit, or that it bears any more or any differently on that intention than it does on my intention to pass title. My intent to pass title to you and my intent to benefit you go hand in hand. Of course, it may be said that the effect of the rules English law has adopted here is to deem my intention to pass title to remain intact and effective, my intention to benefit vitiated. But this conclusion gets no support from the reality of the choices I make and what I intend. Here, as in all these cases, there is no intention to benefit which is separate or separable from the intention to pass title, no sense in which the claimant consents to the defendant taking that title to the asset but not his being enriched by it.

Unjust enrichment lawyers are right to identify the central cases of unjust enrichment as cases where the claimant's mistake in making the transfer supports the conclusion that he did not truly consent to the benefit the defendant derived from it. But any lack of true consent to the defendant's enrichment is, at the same time, a lack of true consent to the passing of title. There is in these cases no decision to benefit distinct from the decision to transfer that title, no qualification of or flaw in the claimant's intention to benefit the defendant that doesn't likewise affect his intention that the defendant becomes entitled to that asset. The reason this lack of consent matters, and the reason it then supports imposing a liability on the defendant which is, in one way or another, restitutionary, is that the decision as to how that asset was to be applied, which encompasses decisions concerning the transfer of title to and beneficial use of that asset, were, by virtue of his own title and the interest it recognizes, the claimant's to make.

Why then is title held to pass in these cases? Why is it that, at least ordinarily, the claimant recovers not the asset itself but merely its monetary equivalent? It is, as we have seen, a mistake to think that the law must protect interests in full or not at all, and it may sometimes be reasonable to accord a claimant's interest in an asset's use and disposition something less than full protection. But whether this is truly reasonable can be determined only once we have a clearer grasp of what other interests, other goods and values, also vie for recognition and support in such cases. Once we do, it may or may not turn out that the very collection of rules (of title, of liability) that English law, at this point in its history, has adopted for the resolution of these cases marks out a fully reasonable response to the various concerns they raise. The aim of the account offered here is in any event different. For the question this study addresses is not how the rules and practices of a given community may best be explained, but what reasons bear on the resolution of these cases and claims generally, a question which faces and must be answered by all communities at all times. For such an account, the question of fit with any particular community's rules and practices—rules and practices that may or may not reveal a sound grasp and application of these reasons—does not arise.

4

Property

I Property and Unjust Enrichment

Where the law recognizes me as having an interest in determining the use and disposition of some item or advantage, it thereby recognizes a reason for restitution where that item or advantage is received by you without my consent. Unjust enrichment claims will, on occasion, test the boundaries of these interests, and of the legal protection they merit. Sometimes a court faced with such a claim must decide whether a claimant should be accorded this sort of authority in respect of a particular resource or how far this authority should extend. But in the vast majority of unjust enrichment claims no such questions arise and, in the main, we don't need the law of unjust enrichment to settle them. For there is a broader body of law which addresses, directly and systematically, questions of entitlement to assets and advantages, which takes as its task to determine how and by whom these items may be accessed and exploited: the law of property.

A community's laws of property provide its primary means of regulating access to resources. Proprietary interests, such as those recognized and assigned by rules of title, mark out clusters of powers and privileges over some such item, granting their holders a limited authority to determine their use and disposition. The law of unjust enrichment—or that part of the law of unjust enrichment as characterized by claims to recover mistaken payments—exists in the service of these rules and interests, by ensuring that those accorded such authority have that authority respected.

The suggestion that the law of unjust enrichment takes its lead from property law or from ideas of property is nothing new.[1] Indeed, once upon a time, before unjust enrichment emerged as the preferred candidate, this appears to have been the dominant understanding of these claims among lawyers and commentators alike.[2] But for the mainstream of unjust enrichment lawyers today this way of thinking is scarcely taken seriously. For while there's no doubting that property interests can support claims for restitution where the claimant's title survives the transfer, it's assumed that this explanation is straightforwardly ruled out in the standard cases of unjust enrichment by the rule that title passes.

They are wrong. That title passes means that the claimant's interest in that asset does not receive complete protection, not that it receives none. Again: it is simply a mistake to think that interests can be protected only in full or not at all, and hence it is a mistake to think that unjust enrichment claims may serve a claimant's interest in his assets only where his title remains. Indeed, those who think a claimant's interest in his asset cannot provide a reason for restitution where title has passed are soon in trouble. As we have seen, the claimant's interest in determining the disposition of the asset is implicated in every transfer of that asset, every time that asset changes hands. That interest provides a reason for restitution wherever the claimant's consent to that transfer was lacking. The conclusion that this interest provides no such reason is, therefore, one which can be supported only on the basis that his consent to the transfer was unaffected by whatever mistake or coercion accompanied his decision to make the transfer. But those

[1] See eg S J Stoljar, *The Law of Quasi-Contract* (2nd edn, Law Book Company 1989) 5–9; David Stevens, 'Restitution, Property, and the Cause of Action in Unjust Enrichment: Getting by with Fewer Things' (1989) 39 *University of Toronto Law Journal* 258, 325; Brian F Fitzgerald, 'Ownership as the Proximity or Privity Principle in Unjust Enrichment Law' (1995) 18 *University of Queensland Law Journal* 166; Peter Watts, 'Restitution—A Property Principle and a Services Principle' [1995] *Restitution Law Review* 49–70; Joachim Dietrich, *Restitution: A New Perspective* (The Federation Press 1998) 208–13; Andrew Kull, 'Restitution in Bankruptcy: Reclamation and Constructive Trust' (1998) 72 *American Bankruptcy Law Journal* 265; Peter Jaffey, *The Nature and Scope of Restitution* (Hart Publishing 2000) 275–360; Peter Jaffey, *Private Law and Property Claims* (Hart Publishing 2007) 93–103; James Gordley, *Foundations of Private Law: Property, Tort, Contract, Unjust Enrichment* (Oxford University Press 2007) 424–26; Andrew Botterell, 'Property, Corrective Justice, and the Nature of the Cause of Action in Unjust Enrichment' (2007) 20 *Canadian Journal of Law and Jurisprudence* 275; Simon Gardner, *An Introduction to the Law of Trusts* (3rd edn, Clarendon Press 2011) 296, 303–07; Dan Priel, 'The Justice in Unjust Enrichment' (2014) 51 *Osgoode Hall Law Journal* 813, 837–42.

[2] See Michael Lobban, 'Mapping the Common Law: Some Lessons from History' [2014] *New Zealand Law Review* 21, 48–54.

who take this line had better give up on the idea that these 'unjust factors' are significant for revealing 'defects' in the claimant's consent to the defendant's enrichment.[3] Either these factors call a claimant's consent into question or they don't. If they do, it is not simply his consent to the defendant's enrichment that is compromised, but his consent to the very transfer. And if they don't, we have reason not only to see the transfer as successful to pass title, but also to reject any attempt to deny the defendant of the benefit of that transfer.[4]

For others, explaining unjust enrichment by appealing to property is not so much wrong as empty, a pseudo-explanation. The invocation of property doesn't answer the question of what explains these claims, but only repackages it. Not only that: property is (so it is said) a contested concept. Legal discourse reveals different ideas and understandings of property, each of which requires elaboration and explanation if it is to play an effective role in the framing and resolution of practical problems. So, true enough, the word 'property' itself solves nothing. Nonetheless, there is a wider body of law directed to questions of access and entitlement to particular assets and advantages, and the name given to that body of law *is* the law of property. To draw a connection between unjust enrichment and the law of property is to position these claims within that wider body of law, to associate them with a broader, longer-established, and, on the whole, better-understood set of ideas. And so what matters here is not the terminology but these ideas, ideas expressed in the previous chapter without reference to 'property' but which, as we shall now see, can be illuminated by placing them in the setting of the practices and principles which that term still best captures.

II Private Property Interests and Their Protection

My legal title to my assets marks me out as the holder of a set of powers and privileges over their use and disposition. By recognizing me

[3] See too Peter Jaffey, 'Two Theories of Unjust Enrichment' in Jason W Neyers, Mitchell McInnes, and Stephen G A Pitel (eds), *Understanding Unjust Enrichment* (Hart Publishing 2004) 148, 150; Jennifer M Nadler, 'What Right Does Unjust Enrichment Law Protect?' (2008) 28 *Oxford Journal of Legal Studies* 245, 253.

[4] 3.VIII.

as holder of that title, the law takes me as having an interest in the use and disposition of those resources that is worth protecting in this way. Yet it will often be good for you—in your interests—to have access to those assets. Perhaps allowing you access to those items would do you more good than my access does me. The effect of my title is to make your access to that asset, and so to this good, conditional on my authorization, and I am free to deny you this. So why is title mine and not yours? Why is it my interest that is picked out for protection?

A system whereby private individuals and groups are given authority to determine the use and disposition of particular items, an authority which they are then free, within limits, to exercise in their own self-interest and towards their own ends, is a system of private property. The range of decisions reserved for private owners (ie title-holders) within such systems will vary from place to place and time to time, and from one class of asset to another. It need not, but often will, extend to the power to transmit that authority to another person or group. Where it does, the question of where this authority presently resides—and so why this title is mine and not yours—isn't answered by need or desert or by considering who might gain most from it, but rather is settled, at least presumptively, by the determinations of those who held that authority previously. As such, however the entitlements recognized within a system of private property are first allocated, from that point on their allocation is, in the first instance, left to those to whom they have been allocated. And so, more generally, whatever beneficial consequences are promoted through a system that recognizes and protects entitlements of this kind, their de facto promotion and realization is, to this extent, left in the hands of those who, from time to time, acquire and exercise this authority.

That private property necessarily grants individuals some such authority over some items of social wealth does not mean that it is unlimited or its grant unconditional. Any number of reasonable restrictions may, and in practice will, be placed on the uses to which those with title may put their assets. We miss much of property's role and operation if we attend only to the powers it accords to individual owners and not to the duties and disabilities that go with them.[5] Nonetheless, the distinctiveness of private property as a means

[5] See, in their different ways, John Finnis, *Natural Law and Natural Rights* (2nd edn, Oxford University Press 2011) 171–73; Hanoch Dagan, *Property: Values and Institutions* (Oxford University Press 2011) 41–44.

of regulating access to such resources is in the authority accorded to private individuals to determine their use and disposition. So, whatever limits are placed on the entitlements recognized within such a scheme, and hence on the authority individual owners are accorded, all such schemes—*as* schemes of private property—necessarily recognize a domain within which owners are accorded this sort of authority, where their say-so counts and counts conclusively, even should their determinations be in various ways unreasonable.

Adopting a system of private property is one way a community might respond to the practical need to regulate its members' access to scarce resources. It is possible that there are goods and values that can be advanced only by such a system. But more likely, the goods and values that private property serves may also be served by alternative forms of regulation. So it is sometimes argued that private property creates incentives for the careful management and profitable exploitation of resources, or that such entitlements reward those who have applied their skill and labour to natural resources.[6] But clearly private property rights aren't the only incentives or rewards that might be offered. Private property identifies what we may then see as a distinctive *means* to these ends. Different justifications of private property will identify different ends, different goods and values, that private property serves. On occasion, these different justifications will support different private property arrangements, differing in the range of resources to which they extend and/or in the conditions attached to the acquisition and exercise of the powers owners are accorded. But *as* justifications of private property—of this way of regulating access to such items—what they all aim to justify is the authority all such schemes grant, to a greater or lesser extent, to private individuals over the use and disposition of some such items. (Were this not the case, different theories of private property would simply talk past each other, offering theories of different things.)

So while an appeal to the goods and values private property serves is necessary to support the adoption and maintenance of such a scheme and to delineate the entitlements recognized within it, when it comes to uses and decisions which fall within the scope of the authority thereby accorded to an individual, what matters is that his authority is respected. This is done in part through rules

[6] See eg Aristotle, *Politics*, II: 1261b33–8, 1263a20–9; Aquinas, *Summa Theologiae*, II-II q 66, a 2c.

prohibiting others from unauthorized use of or interference with the asset.[7] But one cannot know what counts as an unauthorized use until one asks both how far the owner's authority extends and how that authority has in fact been exercised. So, more fundamentally, the authority title bestows on its holder necessitates a concern not only with the conditions attached to that authority, but also with the conditions of its exercise. This means measures aimed at ensuring than an owner's determinations take effect as intended: that the dispositions he wants are the dispositions he gets. The flipside of this is that, again so far as this authority extends, only those dispositions he really does intend are then treated as effective.

Just as a system of private property cannot exist without rules prohibiting trespass, so too every such system requires rules that respect and protect an owner's authority to determine that asset's use. Protection of that authority means providing him with redress where that asset comes into another's hands without his consent. Without this, an owner's claim to his assets would be no greater than my claim to the seat I happen to take on the bus: 'mine' to enjoy while I am in occupation, but free to all comers the moment I am not. Much of this job is done by rules now collected together under the heading of unjust enrichment and is typified by the liability that attaches in unjust enrichment's 'central case' of the receipt of a mistaken payment. These rules and claims are just as central and just as integral to the protection of the interests recognized and accorded within any system of private property as rules against trespass found in the criminal law and the law of torts.

III Justifying Private Property and Justifying Unjust Enrichment Claims

How we justify the practice of private property is then distinct from how we go about justifying the allocation of individual entitlements within such a practice.[8] The decision to adopt a system of private

[7] What Harris termed trespassory rules: J W Harris, *Property and Justice* (Oxford University Press 1996) 24–26.

[8] Cf John Rawls, 'Two Concepts of Rules' (1955) 64 *Philosophical Review* 3.

property is one that can reasonably be made only on consideration of the goods and values promoted by ordering access to certain resources in this way. Given private property's role as a distinctive means of regulating use of and control over resources within a community, this requires not only, indeed not principally, showing that there are goods and values such a system serves, but showing that it serves them better than alternative arrangements a community might otherwise adopt. Once such a system is up and running, however, an individual's entitlement to use and make decisions in respect of a given resource is settled, in the first instance, by the decisions made by those who held such an entitlement previously. Individual owners establish their proper ownership not by appeal to the values underpinning that property scheme—by showing how these goods and values support *their* having these powers ahead of others who would wish to have them—but by showing a chain of title, tracing their entitlements back through a series of authorized dispositions made by those previously accorded that authority.

Within a system of private property the proper allocation of entitlements is then rarely, if ever, a fully open question, to be resolved only by an unqualified assessment of the merits of alternative possible allocations. We do not, and do not need to, consider afresh the justice of making *you* owner of the relevant asset every time you receive a gift or make a purchase. The justice of your entitlement is, in the main, settled simply by the fact it was transferred to you by someone authorized to make that disposition (who in turn had it transferred to him by someone so authorized, and so on).

This matters when we come to claims in unjust enrichment, where your entitlement to some such asset or advantage is in dispute, for a range of arguments and considerations, which outside a system of private property would rightly bear on the merits of our respective claims, are now shut off. To choose a system of private property is to choose a particular way of ordering access to items of social wealth, and so to choose *against* other bases on which those resources might be managed and allocated. By adopting such a system, we shut off various arguments that could otherwise be made for or against particular allocations. I can't successfully challenge your title by alleging that, say, my need or desert is greater, or that the community would be better served by its reallocation. Perhaps I'm right, but if these arguments are open to me, they are open to everyone. Any property holding could be reopened by anybody at any time and our system of private property would be an illusion.

And so, within such a system, the dispositions of owners in legitimate exercise of their authority are not open to review on the basis that some other disposition might better serve a particular good or value, and this extends to those goods and values which support the devolution of these decisions to private individuals in the first place. As with other authorities, the authority to determine an asset's use can be exercised unreasonably and yet still count as a legitimate and effective exercise of that authority. Instead, the one capacity in which I can ordinarily challenge your entitlement without undermining the very scheme of private property by which such entitlements are recognized is as a prior owner; the one ground upon which I can base that challenge is that I did not authorize any disposition through which you may now claim to be entitled to that asset. And, if I can establish this, there is, again in the usual case, no need for me to go further, no need for me to adduce any further reason why I should be granted restitution.

The law of unjust enrichment takes its basic justification from the same goods and values as justify institutions of private property. But, as with the entitlements then recognized within such a regime, these goods and values justify individual instances of unjust enrichment liability only in so far as they support the devolution of decisions as to how given resources are to be used to private individuals, for it is this devolution which then requires that we give precedence to the choices these individuals in fact make. From here on in, the reasons for liability in specific cases of unjust enrichment are to be found not by direct appeal to these goods and values, but by attending to the choices made by those authorized to determine that asset's disposition. If we are uncertain where this authority lies then, again, the answer to this is to be found not by reference to the goods and values that support having a system of private property, but by tracking the choices made by those who held this authority previously.

In this way, the provision of a body of claims that responds to unauthorized transfers follows as a matter of rational necessity from the fact of according individuals such authority, whatever our reasons for according them that authority. So it makes no difference how we justify private property: by choosing such a system, we choose to recognize this sort of authority, and we cannot have this sort of authority without rules which protect and respect its exercise. Respect for its exercise means respect for an owner's choices, whether or not those choices, one by one, in fact promote the goods and values private property is designed to serve. And so, save where the scope of an owner's authority over the asset's use is itself in doubt, the resolution of claims in unjust enrichment not only does not require but does not permit consideration of the reasons for granting individuals such authority in the first place. So, as we've seen, one argument sometimes used in support of private property is that it promotes productive use and careful management of resources. Given a concern to ensure that resources are well managed, any community which adopts a private property scheme on these grounds will also have reason to take further measures that encourage those accorded such powers to exercise them well and penalize those who do not. But, so far as this concern leads us to adopt of a system of private property, we are committed to a system in which choices over how resources are to be deployed are left to private individuals, individuals who may or may not make those choices well. You cannot then challenge my claim to assets I have legitimately acquired on the grounds that you would do a better job of managing and exploiting them, and this is so even though our system of private property is directed towards promoting the careful management and beneficial exploitation of such items.

It is no different if an asset that I was authorized to deal with ends up in your hands and a dispute arises as to whether I can demand its return, or whether you should instead be free to keep it. The dispute is not to be settled by asking which of us would do this job better. Such arguments are neither needed by, nor available to, either of us. I have been accorded the authority to decide on the disposition of that asset. The question, in the first instance, is simply: What did I decide? If I chose—truly, effectively—that the power to use and decide on the disposition of that asset should become yours, alienating this authority to you, this is sufficient for you to resist my claim and be recognized as owner in my place. If I did not, there is here sufficient reason to reject your claim to that asset and to allow me to recover.

IV Choice

A system of private property, as a system in which decisions as to how some resources are to be used are reserved for specified private individuals, cannot get by without rules directed to ensuring that those accorded such decision-making powers have those powers respected. On the one hand, this means rules facilitating and recognizing true exercises of these powers. On the other, it involves rules directed at ensuring that, in the absence of such authorization, the owner's position as decision-maker isn't usurped, and one aspect of this is to provide a means of redress to those who have seen their assets pass into another's hands without their true or effective consent. This is a job taken on, in the main, by that body of claims which forms the better part of what we now call the law of unjust enrichment. For this reason, and to this extent, the law of unjust enrichment is a necessary element of any system of private property.

To say this is not to say that this body of law will, or ought to, be the same within all communities with such systems. Having chosen to adopt a private property regime, a community will face a series of further choices as to how it should be implemented: what resources will be governed by it, how the entitlements it accords will be delineated, what limits and conditions will be set for their transfer, and so on. Many of these options will be reasonable, others unreasonable yet sometimes chosen. Whatever options are taken, this will have knock-on consequences for the law of unjust enrichment, for when we demarcate the scope of an owner's authority, we also mark out the range of dispositions to which the law of unjust enrichment attends.

Nor should we think that the law of unjust enrichment, as it exists in a given community at a given time, is no more than a working out or working through of the positive laws of property then in place. Any such community will face yet further choices when it comes to fixing its practices for remedying unauthorized dispositions. Though any private property scheme requires some such body of claims, different communities may choose—and as a matter of observable fact have chosen—diverse rules and practices for their resolution. Owners' interests in the disposition of their assets can be protected in different ways and to different degrees. Furthermore, these claims are not without cost, to the parties and to the community as a whole. Sometimes we cannot protect an owner's interest in disposing of his assets without imposing burdens on others.[9] Moreover, litigation is expensive and time consuming, and it creates the risk of error and state-sanctioned injustice. Any community must decide to what extent the goods and values served by these claims outweighs these costs. For these and other

[9] See further Chapter 8.

reasons, the positive law of unjust enrichment will vary from place to place and time to time.

Not only, therefore, does the law of unjust enrichment follow inevitably from the adoption of a system of private property, but the contents of that body of law as it exists in any given community are, to a significant extent, determined by the contours of the private property scheme that community in fact adopts. But this does not mean that, when addressing unjust enrichment claims, all aspects of the laws of property of that community at that time must be taken as given. So it shouldn't be thought that, on this account, the rules of title come first and the job of the law of unjust enrichment is then to ensure that those accorded title under those rules have their authority respected. True, the law of unjust enrichment and the broader principle that those properly recognized as having authority over particular assets should have their determinations respected say nothing whatsoever about who should first be granted such authority. But once this first allocation has been made, this principle takes over. From that point on, as we have seen, entitlement is presumptively settled by the authorizations of those previously authorized to make such dispositions.

Within such a system it is, therefore, always a good argument that the owner did not truly authorize such a disposition. *This*—unlike a number of other arguments as to the proper distribution of resources—is an argument which private property admits and indeed invites. The argument won't always win. There are other considerations that will sometimes justify overriding an owner's authority over his assets, and so it will sometimes be reasonable to hold that this authority is lost even in the absence of some genuine authorization. This may justify the rule holding title to pass in many cases of unjust enrichment. But sometimes a community's positive laws of title will be unreasonable, holding title to pass in the absence of any true authorization of the prior owner and in the absence too of any consideration sufficient to make the usurpation of his title a just or proportionate response to some relevant practical concern. In such instances, the positive laws of property adopted by a given community are open to challenge on the basis of their inconsistency with this central principle of private property. Where these laws are open to challenge, so too are the entitlements they confer.

So one response to a claimant's allegation that he didn't properly authorize the defendant's receipt of the relevant asset is that *his* authorization was not needed, and this response may be available even where the claimant can show that he held title to that asset at the point of transfer. Nonetheless, we might expect such challenges to the claimant's authority to be rare. Unjust enrichment defendants have little to gain by challenging the claimant's authority to make the very transfer through which they now themselves seek to derive title. There will, in any case, be limits to the desirability and feasibility of reopening the long chain of transactions through which the claimant derived his title. The common law rule that holds that a claimant need only show that his title to the disputed asset is better than the defendant's, avoiding any broader inquiry into the quality or justness of his entitlement, makes much sense.[10]

V Scope

We can think of ownership of physical things as private property's central case. The central cases of unjust enrichment, in turn, involve the transfer or taking of physical things. Once we have such a set of rules in place—rules of title and property, and hence rules of unjust enrichment—the same ideas and reasoning can be applied outside cases of tangibles to other items and advantages. Accordingly, the property regimes of modern legal systems also encompass forms of intellectual and intangible property, while legal discourse sometimes goes further still, stretching 'property' to particular capabilities and to other entitlements.[11]

Not all of these extensions of 'property' support parallel extensions of the law of unjust enrichment. Ownership of physical things has various incidents, various features that might be said to combine to make this property's central case.[12] When property is extended beyond this, this will typically be on the basis that some subset of these features can be located in other cases too. Intellectual property, for example, shares some features of property in tangibles, and not others. Since these features can occur in different combinations at different times, concepts of property can branch out from this core in different directions. At

[10] Cf Torts (Interference with Goods) Act 1977, s 8(1).

[11] As seen, for instance, in Charles A Reich, 'The New Property' (1964) 73 *Yale Law Journal* 733.

[12] This is the basis of what is sometimes called the 'bundle of sticks' view of property. For one account of these features, see A M Honoré, 'Ownership' in A G Guest (ed), *Oxford Essays in Jurisprudence: A Collaborative Work* (Oxford University Press 1961).

what point the similarities with the core case become too few or the differences too many to merit the label 'property' is a question that cannot be answered in the abstract. We should, therefore, be neither surprised nor concerned that those who have sought to draw such a line have drawn it in different places.

In the central cases of unjust enrichment, my pre-transfer title to the asset now in your hands is significant because it marks me out as the person authorized to determine that asset's disposition. So my claim to restitution of the mistaken payment I made to you is grounded in the authority my title to that money gives me over its disposition, an authority which continues until I choose, in final exercise of that authority, to confer those powers on someone else or they are stripped from me by operation of law. Until this happens, respect for that authority means respect for my choices, which in turn means giving my dispositions such effect as I intend them and ensuring that my capacity to make, and go on making, such choices is supported. And so, in the absence of any such authorization, the fact that this money is now in your hands should no more empower you to use it than when it was safely in my possession. In calling for this money to be returned, I am seeking to be put back in the position to exercise those powers.

It is this feature of private property, this authority it grants to individuals over the use of particular physical things, which necessitates a law of unjust enrichment. Where the law accords individuals similar authority in relation to other items and advantages, there is an equivalent need for rules directed to ensuring that their authority is respected. Where, without the relevant individual's authorization, that item or advantage is put beyond his control, leaving someone else in a position to exploit it in his place, we have the same reason for providing a claim in unjust enrichment so as to ensure that he is put back in the position to exercise that authority (or at least to ensure that he is not prejudiced by its loss).

For instance, in *Cressman v Coys of Kensington*, Cressman owned a car with the personalized registration number TAC 1.[13] He wanted to sell the car, but keep the number. Ordinarily the registration number stays with the car to which is assigned, but it is possible for the owner to apply to retain the number when the car is sold and have it reassigned to some other vehicle. Cressman instructed Coys, the auctioneer

[13] *Cressman v Coys of Kensington (Sales) Ltd* [2004] EWCA Civ 47, [2004] 1 WLR 2775.

conducting the sale, that he wished to have the number retained, and Coys said they'd get this done. Coys didn't. As a result, though the car was presented without number plates and though it was made clear to the bidders that Cressman intended to retain the number, when the car was sold, the number went with it. Cressman succeeded in his claim in unjust enrichment against the purchaser, McDonald, and was awarded the monetary value of the number, minus a sum he had already received from Coys in settlement of his claim against them. The claim here was not in respect of some physical asset. The number assigned to the car was distinct both from the car itself and the plates that carried the number. But the option of retaining the number gave Cressman a similar (though more limited) authority over its disposition, an authority which was compromised when, by operation of law, the number was transferred to McDonald without Cressman's consent, and which justified his claim for restitution.

A more common, though in some ways less straightforward, example concerns bank transfers. If I direct my bank to transfer £1,000 to your account with your bank, mistakenly believing this is money I owe you, I have the same claim against you in unjust enrichment as I would have were I to have handed you the £1,000 in bank notes instead. Yet here no physical thing passes between us, and likely none between our banks. Indeed we might say there is no true transfer at all. There is nothing you receive which was previously held by me. My right to payment from my bank reduces by £1,000, yours increases by the same figure. But there is no right or asset of mine now in your name or at your disposal. Nonetheless, my claim against you is justified by an extension of the same reasoning as justifies my claim in the case where my mistaken payment takes the form of cash.

My bank account entitles me to call on my bank to put me in funds (at least) to the value of my credit balance. As an alternative, however, I can direct my bank to pay someone else, instructing it to debit the relevant sum from my account and credit my payee's account, or directing my payee's bank to credit his account, with the same amount. So, though the bank holds no cash earmarked for me, my account represents funds that are, in this way, truly at my disposal. When your account is credited as a result of my instructing my bank to pay you, this increase in the funds now at *your* disposal comes about by virtue of the application of those funds. This facility, this power to put myself and others in funds is, of course, mine and mine alone to exercise, and it is a facility *pro tanto* diminished each time that account is debited. This diminution is matched exactly and directly by an addition to the equivalent facility you have with your bank. So my bank account is not a repository of cash and the transfer of funds from my account to yours is not a handing over of cash from me to you. But it serves the same function, taking funds at my disposal and making them available to you. And so while this transfer of funds is in one sense notional, since there need be nothing which passes from me to you or from my bank to yours and there is instead simply a series of discrete steps taken by the parties in performance of their discrete contracts with one another—my instruction to my bank to debit my account and make payment into your account; my bank's instruction to yours to credit your account; your bank making these funds available to you at your demand—each of these steps is connected to the next as essential elements of a single transaction, with the single intended effect of my paying you.[14]

Saying that the money now available to you comes from me is, then, a shorthand for the composite legal effect of this series of instructions and accounting measures. But the shorthand involves no fiction. It is no mistake for the law to treat this sort of transfer as a payment, as (at least for most purposes) equivalent to the handing over of that same sum in cash. Or, to put it another way, though there are no specific funds which move from my bank to yours for your account and then on to you, this is how, given modern banking practices, I can exercise the facility my account provides to put you in funds. So when your account is credited as a result of such a transaction, you get access to funds that do indeed represent or manifest the funds which were, at the outset, mine to dispose of. And, therefore, if I did not truly authorize this transaction, respect for my authority as account holder—as the person entitled to decide how this facility be exercised—supports providing me with a claim for restitution of the funds credited to your account.

VI Unjust Enrichment as a Corrective Technique

In these cases just examined, the defendant is put in a position to exploit some advantage reserved for the claimant only with the law's

[14] See generally David Fox, *Property Rights in Money* (Oxford University Press 2008) 164–76.

assistance. Were it not for the legal rule which provides that, in the absence of a successful application for its retention, title to the registration number passes with the car, the defendant in *Cressman* would not have got access to the number. To this extent, the claim in unjust enrichment was a response to a problem of the law's own making, correcting an injustice only made possible by the legal rules on the transfer of title adopted for such items. The same may be true in some cases involving tangible assets. So we could imagine a system of land registration that takes the register as in all cases conclusive of title to land. If, through fraud or administrative error, your name replaces mine, you get title to land from me, notwithstanding that my occupation of that land remains (for now) undisturbed. Here too, even if it is thought that the sanctity of the register is such as to deny my claim that it be rectified and title returned to me, it may be reasonable to grant me a claim in unjust enrichment to ensure that I am not prejudiced by its loss.

This observation has led some to conclude that the law of unjust enrichment is addressed only to these sorts of problems.[15] So, as we have seen, in the ordinary mistaken payment title passes, notwithstanding my mistake. My claim in unjust enrichment then serves, so it might be said, to correct—or at least to mitigate the effects of—the rule that says title passes.[16] As I suggested in the previous chapter, the law of unjust enrichment is indeed better viewed as operating alongside the rules on title. Perhaps it is true that some or all of the body of rules and claims now conventionally classed as the law of unjust enrichment arose as a sort of corrective to the rules on the passing of title. But if that is so, that is all the more reason to take both sets of rules as directed to a common endeavour, with a common point or rationale.

Say I transfer an asset of mine to you by mistake, such as allows me to say that I had no intention that it be received and retained by you in these circumstances. We have in my interest in determining that asset's disposition—an interest recognized by my pre-transfer title—a reason to take my say-so as conclusive on your liberty to keep that asset for yourself and so a reason here, given my mistake and so

[15] See eg Ben McFarlane, 'Unjust Enrichment, Rights and Value' in Andrew Robertson and Tang Hang Wu (eds), *The Goals of Private Law* (Hart Publishing 2009).

[16] See McFarlane, ibid 607. Cf Lionel Smith, 'Property, Subsidiarity and Unjust Enrichment' in David Johnston and Reinhard Zimmermann (eds), *Unjustified Enrichment: Key Issues in Comparative Perspective* (Cambridge University Press 2002) 610–22.

given my lack of consent to its transfer, to grant me restitution. The law could respond to my claim in various ways: it could hold title to remain in me and enable me to demand the asset to be returned *in specie*; it could hold title to remain in me, but limit me to recovery of its monetary equivalent; it could hold title to pass, but create a distinct title in my favour, then allowing me to recover the asset *in specie*; it could reach the same conclusions on title, but entitle me to recover only its value; or it could hold that title passes to you and no new title arises in me, and yet allow me to recover its monetary equivalent. These differences of approach are sometimes significant, sometimes not. Where they are, the choice of one over another will be influenced by various other concerns and principles which are implicated in the law's resolution of these claims. It may be reasonable for a given community to adopt different approaches at different times.

It is, once again, a mistake simply to assume that different forms of response identify different injustices, a mistake to take the distinct ways in which an interest may be protected as the protection of distinct interests.[17] It is this same mistake made whenever it is said that enrichment must be legal—(such as by acquiring title to the asset) rather than factual (such as by merely taking possession and making use of it);[18] or where it is claimed that there is no enrichment which can be said to be at the claimant's expense if the claimant's title isn't lost;[19] or where it is said that (some of) these different responses reflect different kinds of enrichment;[20] or where it is suggested that justifying claims in unjust enrichment is a matter of better understanding the conceptual or structural features of the law's response to these claims.[21] The rational, material likeness of a body of cases and claims cannot be established simply by appeal to features of the law's response to these cases and claims, but only by examination of the reasons that properly

[17] As McFarlane sees: ibid 599. But what he, like others, fails to note is that the rules on the passing of title are themselves elements of the law's response to these cases.

[18] See eg William Swadling, 'Ignorance and Unjust Enrichment: The Problem of Title' (2008) 28 *Oxford Journal of Legal Studies* 627, 644.

[19] See eg Swadling, ibid 650–1; Robert Chambers, 'Trust and Theft' in Elise Bant and Matthew Harding (eds), *Exploring Private Law* (Cambridge University Press 2010) 232–35.

[20] See eg Robert Chambers, 'Two Kinds of Enrichment' in Robert Chambers, Charles Mitchell, and James Penner (eds), *Philosophical Foundations of the Law of Unjust Enrichment* (Oxford University Press 2009); A V M Lodder, *Enrichment in the Law of Unjust Enrichment and Restitution* (Hart Publishing 2012).

[21] See Ben McFarlane, 'Rights and Value; Means and Ends' in Charles Mitchell and William Swadling (eds), *The Restatement Third, Restitution and Unjust Enrichment: Critical and Comparative Essays* (Hart Publishing 2013) 1–2, 29–30.

bear on them. If we do this, it becomes plain that my mistaken transfer, *as* a mistaken transfer, is just the one injustice, an injustice we can identify before we know how the laws of a given community in fact go about remedying it. To put it another way: the reasons why we consider that the law should provide the claimant with some sort of restitutionary relief where title is held to pass, despite his mistake, are the same reasons why we consider, at other times, with other mistakes, that title does not pass. These are simply different means, different techniques for dealing with a common problem.

There are, as we have seen, different concepts of unjust enrichment. It is possible to define the law of unjust enrichment such that it embraces only those cases in which title is held to pass. So understood, unjust enrichment is a particular technique for addressing the problems of defective or unauthorized transfers. The concern of this book is not specifically with this or any such technique, but with the nature of these problems and the considerations that bear on their reasonable resolution.

VII Services and Value

The law of unjust enrichment rightly extends beyond the taking and transfer of physical things. But it ought not to extend so far as unjust enrichment lawyers have sought to take it, nor so far as some judges, following the textbooks' lead, have taken it. Determining the proper scope of the law of unjust enrichment has sometimes been thought to require no more than an extrapolation from the facts of its core case. If the mistaken payment is taken to be unjust enrichment's paradigm, the reach of the law of unjust enrichment could be established by generalizing from its basic features. This was typically presented as a matter of simple logical or linguistic inference: 'The receipt of money can be described as an enrichment. Other things can also be described as enrichments. *Therefore* the same rules as apply to money ought apply to these other enrichments too.' This was an error, the error again being to think that a set of like claims could be identified simply by their factual likenesses, and not by their reasons. No doubt money is enriching, no doubt other things are too. In this way, as in others, mistaken payments share common features with a broader range of cases. But whether this or any other commonality supports viewing these cases as truly *like* cases is a question we can answer only by inquiry into what reasons for restitution exist on these facts. Only then can we say how, if at all, this common element bears on how these cases fall to be treated.

Without this, there was little more to go on other than hunch and ordinary language. Take cases of services. Whether the law of unjust enrichment extended to the performance and receipt of services was treated in the first instance as a matter of language: are services 'enriching'? If so, or to the extent they are, then the 'logic' of the mistaken payment applies to them too. But, as some noted, unlike payments and other asset transfers, a service may leave the defendant with no 'marketable residuum', no increase in the stock of assets at his disposal.[22] Here then was a feature of unjust enrichment's core case missing from cases of such 'pure' services. Was this enough to make a difference to how these cases fell to be treated? Once again, the question was often treated as simply one of language: can we say that those who receive pure services are 'enriched'? Hence the standard textbook position: people are often willing to pay for pure services, *therefore* they are enriching, *therefore* they fall to be dealt with like other enrichments.[23]

But what matters is not whether linguistic convention permits pure services to be described as beneficial or enriching, nor whether we can pick out features of these cases shared by the central cases of unjust enrichment. The question is not one of language but of rationale. Accordingly, the scope of that body of claims typified by cases of mistaken payments is properly settled not by linguistic convention or circumstantial resemblance but by the reasons that ground liability in these cases. These reasons alone identify what features of mistaken payments, and of other cases too, are necessary elements of these claims. So it is simply a mistake to assume that because money is enriching, the same rules as apply to payments must also apply to other enrichments: *non sequitur*. Indeed, as we saw in the previous chapter, the cases themselves make plain that what is true for money is not true of

[22] See eg J Beatson, *The Use and Abuse of Unjust Enrichment: Essays on the Law of Restitution* (Clarendon Press 1991) 28–32.

[23] See eg Peter Birks, *An Introduction to the Law of Restitution* (rev edn, Clarendon Press 1989) 449–51; Andrew Burrows, *The Law of Restitution* (3rd edn, Oxford University Press 2011) 46–47; Graham Virgo, *The Principles of the Law of Restitution* (2nd edn, Oxford University Press 2006) 62–64.

all enrichments, that it is only on occasion that my consent is made a condition of your freedom to keep whatever benefits you may derive from me.

In the case of the mistaken payment, as in the other standard cases of unjust enrichment, what justifies the defendant's liability is not simply the fact that the claimant didn't consent to the enrichment, but that his title to the thing now in the defendant's hands gave him authority over its disposition. It is by virtue of this authority that the claimant's consent is (so far as this authority goes) a condition of the use others may make of that thing. The law of unjust enrichment takes up the job of protecting the claimant's interest in determining its disposition; the sort of interest that is recognized and protected within all systems of private property. We have seen too that this rationale can stretch beyond the receipt of physical things to cases where the defendant's enrichment is found in his acquisition of some intangible asset or advantage to which the claimant was similarly entitled. When it comes to services, the question is whether the law recognizes us as having a similar interest in and authority over the benefits that others may derive from our actions. If and to the extent that they do, we should be entitled to restitution of those benefits conferred without our consent.

Do we have such an interest? It is clear that the law protects our freedom of action and that, in allowing us to choose how we act, the law gives us some control over whom we benefit through our actions. It's my choice to sit on the couch all day and, if I do, nobody else is likely to benefit. If I choose to do some work, I typically get to choose what work and whom I'll work for. But it does not follow from the fact that the law protects our interest in choosing how to act and hence, to this extent, in choosing who benefits from our actions that it protects or ought to protect any interest in the benefits our actions confer. If I pay you by mistake, I can't go on exercising my authority over that money unless it is returned and, unless I recover *something*, my interest in determining its disposition comes to nothing. But where I mistakenly perform some beneficial service for you, my on-going freedom of action isn't compromised if I am denied a claim to the benefits you derived. I remain as free as I was before to choose my actions. So, though it is sometimes said that each of us has property in our labour, for we have a similar entitlement to decide on its application as we have in relation to our assets, the analogy breaks down if we seek to treat every application of our labour as a disposition or transfer of that property, for each such 'disposition' (at least ordinarily) leaves this property undiminished. The idea that as we own our labour we *therefore* own the fruits of our labour—an idea sometimes proposed to justify private property—is another simple *non sequitur*.

We cannot, therefore, justify restitution in services cases by appealing to the value of our being free to choose how we act, and so whom we benefit through our actions. Once the services are provided, our freedom of action isn't implicated either way. A bridge between the provision of services and the cases we have been examining until now, where some asset passes from claimant to defendant, is sometimes built on the basis that services involve a transfer of value from provider to recipient. It then appears just a small step to suggest that our consent is, and should be, a condition of transfers of value, just as it is a condition of transfers of our assets. Indeed it is sometimes thought that mistaken payments and other asset transfer cases are themselves merely examples of this broader category of transfers of value. Reducing the asset cases to transfers of value is a mistake. This computer, that house, your shareholding are things worth having, things that provide benefits in the same sense and of the same order that services can provide. (I expand on this below.) But they are more than this. They, unlike the services I receive, are items that can be exchanged for other valuable items and services and, beyond this, they have uses of their own, which the holder can apply to his own ends and interests. When I give you this computer or you give me your shares, we do more than abstractly enrich one another: we confer the power to deal with these specific assets in these ways. There is, in this way, no basic equivalence between, on the one hand, receiving a computer or some shares or money and, on the other, receiving a pure service. The thought that cases of asset transfers are significant for the law of unjust enrichment only as transfers of value is driven by the law's response to these claims: giving the claimant a claim to that asset's monetary value, but leaving the asset itself with the defendant. But this is the same old mistake of thinking that the remedy must be co-extensive with the interest it protects.

So the services cases are different. Can we nonetheless support the law of unjust enrichment's extension to these cases on the basis that they do involve transfers, not of assets but of value, and that we have an interest in determining who receives value from us in the same way as we have an interest in determining who receives our assets? On the understanding of benefit and value which unjust enrichment lawyers tend to advocate, one can benefit from an action or event irrespective of whether it adds to one's holdings, to the wealth at one's disposal. It is this that makes it possible to say that pure services—those that leave no marketable residuum, no increase in the recipient's patrimony—can be beneficial (or enriching). Giving you a tutorial or singing you a song may be of value to you even though they leave you with no addition to your disposable wealth or holdings.

As these examples show, you may receive a benefit not only where there has been no addition to your holdings, but also where there has been no change whatsoever in your physical circumstances. My song leaves no trace. Because of this, it is sometimes thought that pure services, though beneficial, can support no claim for restitution, since the benefit one derives from them cannot be given up. Birks contended that unless the service results in some addition to the beneficiary's holdings or saves him expense, preserving the stock of assets at his disposal, whatever benefit the recipient may take from the service is merely transitory: his enrichment is no sooner received than lost.[24] This position looks incoherent. If pure services are enriching, then enrichment requires no addition to the beneficiary's holdings. If no such addition is needed for a benefit to be received, then why think any is needed for that benefit to be retained? Conversely, if the absence of any surviving addition to your holdings means you retain no benefit, the fact that there never was such an addition or saving suggests that no benefit was ever received.

We see in Birks' account a confusion of two distinct understandings or concepts of benefit. So we might take benefit to be tied to the measure of one's holdings or transferable wealth. When used in this way, pure services don't provide even fleeting or transient benefits. But, alternatively, we might take a broader understanding of benefit, extending to all things that one values. So I can put a value on pure services, though they do nothing to increase my holdings. Since the benefit, so understood, of a service doesn't depend on the receipt or holding of any particular asset or on any increase to my total stock, there's no reason to conclude that the benefit I take from such a service evaporates in the absence of any such marketable residuum.

[24] Peter Birks, *Unjust Enrichment* (2nd edn, Clarendon Press 2005) 62–63. See too Ross B Grantham and Charles E F Rickett, *Enrichment and Restitution in New Zealand* (Hart Publishing 2000) 61.

Rather, to say that a service is beneficial (or enriching or valuable) is really to say that it serves my interests, that it advances my goals or satisfies some preference of mine. I benefit—it makes my life go in some small way better—when I listen to some songs. And, though the sensation of hearing the song passes, this doesn't mean that this benefit is then removed or lost. Otherwise, every time I pay to attend a concert, I should take myself to be immediately poorer the moment the music stops, the benefit of that performance now gone, and only the diminution in my funds remaining.

So, understood in this way, benefits are not increases in your holdings, in the wealth at your disposal, and are not co-extensive with such increases. Though the sources of these benefits are real-world actions and events, the benefits themselves, as shown by the examples given, have no physical identity or substance. We see this in the way that the very same item or service may be beneficial to one person but not to another. You would likely pay to avoid the concerts I pay to attend. As such, if services do effect transfers of value, they do so variably, with the very same services effecting transfers of differing value and sometimes none at all, depending on who is at the receiving end. Occasionally this is doubted and the value of a given service is thought not to be person specific, even accepting that what value a service has (and transfers) is not the same at all times and places. It is possible to put a value on all sorts of things without inquiring into who we're valuing them for, as we see whenever reference is made to the objective or market value of an asset or service. So can't we say that you, no less than me, would receive a valuable service if you were to attend the sorts of concerts I attend, notwithstanding your overwhelming desire not to receive that service? The implication of this way of thinking is that the market fixes what counts as a transfer of value, the measure of that transfer, and so the measure of the defendant's liability in a claim for restitution.[25]

Attendance at the concerts I attend has a market value. But that market value is one most people would not pay. Indeed most people, like you, would pay to avoid the experience. So to say that you receive something of value really means that you receive something for which there is a market, something which *some* people—though not you,

[25] See eg *Benedetti v Sawiris* [2013] UKSC 50, [2013] 3 WLR 351, paras 101–02, 122 (Lord Reed JSC).

and not many—value. There's no doubt, however, that you receive no benefit from the service. We might, if we wished, say without contradiction that you receive something of value that is of no value to you, which brings you no benefit. And this isn't because your value is idiosyncratic. You are no different to the vast majority of people who have no interest at all in attending these concerts. So when it comes to claims for restitution for the value of these services, what sense is there in measuring this by reference to the value those (few) like me put on it, rather than the value you put on it? Even if we can say—misleadingly, for the reasons given—that you receive something of value, there is no *transfer* of value to you. If unjust enrichment claims really are concerned with transfers of value, then unless the defendant receives something which can itself be sold on and so 'turned to value' in this way, what matters is *his*—not the market's, not anyone else's—value.

The way the unjust enrichment texts, and now it seems the courts, typically factor in this subjectivity of value is to say that, while market value provides the starting point for an inquiry into a defendant's enrichment, he is then able to argue that his valuation is different. This may often be a practical and convenient way in to establishing what benefit the defendant derived, so long as the objective or market measure is used only as a proxy for or means towards establishing that defendant's enrichment. It is sometimes said that permitting such 'subjective devaluation' of the objective value of the relevant service is necessary to protect the defendant's autonomy, his freedom of choice over how he deploys his resources.[26] If he was required to pay the market rate for a service he doesn't value, or doesn't value so highly, we would be compelling him to pay more than he would choose to pay for it. In most cases, however, the reference to freedom of choice is unnecessary. True, you would not pay to attend this concert. But this choice is simply a reflection of the value you attach to this service: you'd choose not to spend your money on it because you don't value it, because, for you, this service isn't beneficial. The value you place on it is in turn a product of your capabilities, tastes, goals, and circumstances, which, in the main, are not themselves chosen. No doubt it is typically unjust to make a defendant pay more for a service he didn't choose to receive than he would himself have chosen to

[26] See eg Birks (n 23) 109–10; Burrows (n 23) 44; *Benedetti* (n 25) paras 18 (Lord Clarke JSC), 113–17 (Lord Reed JSC).

pay for it. But we don't need to appeal to the value of choice to explain why an award aimed at removing a benefit the defendant derived from a service must attend to the value *he* attaches to that service. (The choice argument has a distinct role to play only where the value the defendant places on the item is greater than the price for which it could be acquired on the market. Then he can say that, though his valuation is higher than the market rate and so he would, if necessary, have paid more, the lower market price means he wouldn't have needed to pay this much to obtain this benefit. To make him pay the higher figure would be to compel him to pay more than he would have chosen to pay.)

Indeed the broader truth here is that benefits are subjective not merely in their measure but in their essence. What benefits me is a product of my circumstances, my tastes, interests, abilities, means, and goals. I benefit when I receive or experience or do something which accords with my tastes, or which satisfies these interests or advances these goals. It is sometimes said that the law of unjust enrichment is concerned only with benefits that have monetary or financial—rather than, say, emotional or intellectual—value.[27] But the opposition is false. Money provides a measure of value. Any benefit, whatever its form or source, can be measured in monetary terms. Of course, some beneficial items can be turned to value by being sold on. This is the idea of a marketable residuum. But once we leave to one side the idea of a benefit as some such increase to one's holdings, what makes a particular item or service or experience beneficial—and hence (financially) valuable—is, in all cases, its contribution to the recipient's goals and wants. So, though assets are distinct from services, and from knowledge and relationships, the benefit we may derive from each is of the same order or kind. Benefits are in this sense fungible. If they were not, restitution of the benefit of a pure service could not be achieved by a money payment.

There is nothing to my benefiting from a particular service or event (as against your not benefiting from the same service or event) other than the contribution it makes to the advancement of my goals and interests or, as we might put it, to my quality of life. The benefit I get from a particular service is the improvement it makes to the life I lead, through its accordance with my tastes and preferences, through its facilitation or furtherance of my objectives. And so despite the tendency of unjust enrichment lawyers to reify the idea of value,

[27] See eg Charles Mitchell, Paul Mitchell, and Stephen Watterson (eds), *Goff and Jones: The Law of Unjust Enrichment* (8th edn, Sweet and Maxwell 2011) 82; Lodder (n 20) 14.

neither benefit nor value passes from person to person. Nor indeed can they be returned or given up. The benefits of our actions are not fruits of our bodies or our labour, presumptively ours unless and until we choose to part with them. Though I can choose to whose benefit I direct my actions, there is no sense in which your benefit—the very improvement made to your life and prospects—could instead be mine or someone else's. If we spoke of 'preference satisfaction' or 'improved quality of life' in place of 'benefit' and 'value', the point would be plain.

None of this means that the law could not make our consent a condition of others benefiting from our actions, so as to entitle us to demand that these benefits be paid for where this consent is lacking. Though benefits cannot be given back, they can be offset. Any advancement of your goals and wants can be countered by taking steps that set them back in equal measure. So by requiring that you pay me for the services I mistakenly performed for you, I can ensure that whatever benefit you took from them is met by a corresponding handicap, depriving you of means you could otherwise employ in satisfaction of your preferences and towards your chosen ends. But in so doing the law would not be solving some problem of allocation, in the same way as the rules of private property are directed towards the allocation of assets and entitlements. For there is nothing here that requires allocation, indeed nothing which is capable of allocation and (re)distribution, nothing that could be yours, rather than mine. Besides, so long as I am and remain free to decide how I act, what reason is there to give me any additional control, or veto, over the benefits others may gain from my choices and actions? Perhaps I wouldn't have acted in this way had I known it would advance your plans, serve your interests. But what good comes from engaging the state's coercive machinery to assist me in removing this benefit from you? There are better things for a legal system to be doing.

VIII Beyond Enrichment

It is doubtful whether there is any injustice in you benefiting from my actions and choices without my consent, all the more doubtful that such injustice is sufficient to merit legal redress. This reflects the position long taken by the common law, rejecting any suggestion that the mere fact that a defendant benefited from the claimant's actions without the latter's consent entitles the claimant to restitution of that benefit. So in *Victoria Park Racing v Taylor* the claimant owned land it used as a racecourse, putting on race meetings for profit.[28] The defendants set up a platform on neighbouring land from which the races could be viewed, and they broadcast reports of those races, from which they in turn profited. The result was that attendance at the races dropped, as did the claimant's takings. The claimant sought to stop the broadcasts. The claim failed. So long as the defendants kept off the claimant's land, they were free to observe what went on there, to pass this information on to others, and to make money doing so.

The claimant there sought an injunction, not restitution. But there's no question that the result would have been the same had it sought instead to recover the gains the defendants had made. As Dixon J observed:[29]

> [C]ourts...have not in British jurisdictions thrown the protection of an injunction around all the intangible elements of value, that is, value in exchange, which may flow from the exercise by an individual of his powers or resources whether in an organization of a business or undertaking or the use of ingenuity, knowledge, skill or labour.

In *Victoria Park Racing*, the claimant unsuccessfully pleaded that it held copyright in the information broadcast by the defendant and, more broadly, we might say that intellectual property regimes presuppose that there is no general interest in the benefits others may derive from our actions. For the role of such regimes is to mark out situations where I can indeed demand that others refrain from taking advantage of my ideas and labours. Establishing copyrights, patents, and the like is significant precisely because we ordinarily have no such right that we alone profit from our actions.

That's not to deny that there are circumstances in which the law does and should require a defendant who has benefited from a claimant's services to pay for those services, even where there is no effective contract that provides for this payment. But traditionally recovery depended on establishing more than the bare facts of the defendant's enrichment and the claimant's lack of consent. So the old form of action by which the claimant sought payment

[28] *Victoria Park Racing and Recreation Grounds Company v Taylor* (1937) 58 CLR 479.
[29] Ibid 508–09.

for work done for the defendant—a *quantum meruit*—included an allegation that the work was done at the defendant's request. Proceeding on the (unsound) assumption that all enrichments, as a matter of logic, fell to be treated in the same way, this requirement of request was explained away by unjust enrichment lawyers as going only to the element of enrichment: services benefit only those who would want to have that work done, so showing that the defendant requested it establishes his benefit.[30]

But these cases support an alternative reading. That the defendant requested the claimant provide the relevant service tells us that the work was done not only with the defendant's consent, but with his encouragement. Save where it is made clear that the services are to be provided free of charge, the work will be done on the understanding that it is to be paid for. At this point we are getting very close to something that looks a lot like an agreement or contract. Indeed in many of these cases there *is* a contract, but one that has since been discharged. In others, the parties' clear agreement is denied contractual effect through a failure to meet some condition of validity. Loath to breathe any life back into the idea of quasi-contract, unjust enrichment lawyers promptly concluded that, to make sense of these cases, we had to leave behind not only the law of contract, but also any attempt to explain the parties' rights and liabilities by reference to their agreement.

But this was too quick. In some cases, the conclusion that there was no binding agreement was precipitous. Contract doesn't exhaust the field of legally enforceable voluntary obligations and so the formal conclusion that there is no contract is not yet conclusive of there being no binding agreement between them.[31] Moreover, in those cases where there *is* a contract, it has too readily been assumed that its termination means that that contract then falls away as a possible ground of claims and liabilities. The power to terminate is itself typically given by the contract. It would be surprising if the parties were entitled to provide for termination but not for the consequences of termination.[32] More generally, the absence of any subsisting contract

[30] See eg Birks (n 23) 111–13; Burrows (n 23) 41.

[31] See eg Samuel J Stoljar, 'The Great Case of *Cutter v Powell*' (1956) 34 *Canadian Bar Review* 288; Joseph M Perillo, 'Restitution in a Contractual Context' (1973) 73 *Columbia Law Review* 1208; I M Jackman, *The Varieties of Restitution* (The Federation Press 1998) 70–90; Steve Hedley, 'Implied Contract and Restitution' [2004] *Cambridge Law Journal* 435.

[32] See further 6.III, 6.IV.

providing for payment means, at most, that any promise the defendant made to pay for the work is not per se enforceable. Accordingly, if he is nonetheless to be held liable to pay, we need to say more than that this is what he promised to do. But it doesn't follow that the parties' agreement, and in particular the fact the work was done with the claimant's encouragement and on the shared understanding that it was to be paid for, then has *no* bearing on their respective rights and liabilities. That their agreement isn't binding does not mean that we must proceed as though there was no agreement at all. And so, though the defendant's promise to pay may not be enforceable in and of itself, it may nonetheless be reasonable to require payment precisely because this is the fairest way of allocating the risks and rewards of a transaction which the parties entered into on the understanding they would be shared.[33]

Since, in these cases, we are not seeking to enforce the parties' agreement, this way of thinking can be extended to cases in which there is no agreement, perhaps no direct communication between the parties at all, but where the defendant nonetheless knows that the claimant is providing him with the services in the expectation of payment and the defendant chooses to proceed on that basis. This is true of those cases in which the defendant's liability is said by some to be based on his 'free acceptance' of the service. No doubt payment can be justified on other grounds and in other circumstances too. That the work was done at the defendant's behest may alternatively justify payment in order to make good the claimant's reliance losses. The same may be true where the claimant acts in aid of the defendant in circumstances that preclude their first contracting in respect of those services.

This is only a sketch of the sorts of considerations which might go to support claims in some services cases and much more would need to be said to provide a full account of the conditions in which such claims may reasonably lie. The key point for now is that in all these cases the claimant's right to payment turns on more than the mere fact that the defendant benefited from the claimant's labours without his consent. That these cases are concerned with something other than non-consensual 'transfers of value' is also suggested by the measure of the payments ordered, which don't appear to be assessed by reference

[33] See too Dietrich (n 1) 151–56; Dan Priel, 'In Defence of Quasi-Contract' (2011) 75 *Modern Law Review* 54, 71–76.

to the defendant's gain, but instead require him to pay a reasonable price for the services; a rather different idea, one which can support a substantial award even where the defendant makes no gain at all.[34]

In recent years, however, English courts have offered their support to unjust enrichment lawyers' reimagining of the services cases.[35] In *Cobbe v Yeoman's Row*, Cobbe did work securing planning permission in furtherance of a property development deal with the defendant landowner.[36] The failure to put their agreement into writing meant there was no contract, and the defendant reneged on the deal. Cobbe sought, *inter alia*, payment for his work under various headings: unjust enrichment, *quantum meruit*, failure of consideration. Lord Scott, giving the lead judgment, held that these all amounted to much the same thing: 'The amount of the quantum meruit for Mr Cobbe's services would, in my opinion, represent the extent of the unjust enrichment for which the defendant company should be held accountable to Mr Cobbe.'[37] But alongside this it was also said that this award should reimburse Cobbe for the expenses he incurred doing the work and for the time and trouble this took, all of which sounds rather less enrichment focused.[38] *Benedetti v Sawaris* is less equivocal.[39] There, the Supreme Court was again faced with the question of how to assess a *quantum meruit* award, here for work the claimant did in assisting the defendant in a corporate takeover. This time Lord Clarke was able to say that it was 'common ground that the correct approach to the amount to be paid by way of quantum meruit where there is no valid and subsisting contract between the parties is to ask whether the

[34] See eg *Menetone v Athawes* (1764) 3 Burr 1592; *Planché v Colburn* (1831) 8 Bing 14; *Sabemo Pty Ltd v North Sydney Municipal Council* [1977] 2 NSWLR 880; *Batis Maritime Corporation v Petroleos del Mediterraneo SA (The 'Batis')* [1990] 1 Lloyd's Rep 345 (QBD); Watts (n 1) 72–79; Beatson (n 22) 34–38. Cf John P Dawson, *Restitution without Enrichment* (1981) 61 *Boston University Law Review* 563, 577–85. That these awards are not distinctly gain-focused is also suggested by their name: *quantum meruit*, as much as he deserves.

[35] In those jurisdictions in which unjust enrichment has met with a cooler reception, the common law position remains by and large unchanged: see eg *Lumbers v W Cook Builders Pty Ltd* [2008] HCA 27, (2008) 232 CLR 635. This refusal to throw off centuries of precedent has baffled some unjust enrichment advocates: see eg Burrows (n 23) 40–41. But it's the High Court of Australia which has the better of this argument: see too Joachim Dietrich, '*Quantum Meruit* for Services Rendered in a Three-Party Context: (Implied) Contract, Restitution, or Unjust Enrichment?' [2009] *Restitution Law Review* 98.

[36] *Cobbe v Yeoman's Row Management Ltd* [2008] UKHL 55, [2008] 1 WLR 1752.

[37] Ibid para 42.

[38] Ibid paras 42, 45 (Lord Scott), 93 (Lord Walker).

[39] *Benedetti* (n 25).

defendant has been unjustly enriched and, if so, to what extent'.[40] This was then played out in the detail of the judgments, each addressing squarely the question of how the defendant's gain was to be identified and measured.

These cases mark a shift in approach. But it is one made with little argument, indeed little recognition that any change is being made. Instead the textbook line is incorporated by reference: these awards always were addressed to the benefit the defendant took from the claimant's services but this truth was obscured by the old forms of action and the spectre of quasi-contract. Any change then is a change of presentation, not of substance. And where we do find argument, it is the familiar appeal to 'symmetry' or 'logic' that requires all enrichments to be dealt with in the same way. But, as we've seen, there is no symmetry between services and asset transfers, no logic that requires or supports their like treatment. The change in approach seen in these cases is unsound.[41]

It was also, for the decisions reached in these cases, unnecessary. In both *Cobbe* and *Benedetti*, the work the claimant did was at the defendant's request and with his agreement. In both cases, there was no effective provision made for what payment the claimant was to receive for his services, yet the services were provided on the clear and shared understanding that they were to be paid for. In such circumstances, one might think there is nothing for the court to do but to fix a price. One might also think that the price should be fixed at the going rate for such services, save where the evidence suggests that the parties themselves would have set a different price.[42] This is what the courts did. Lord Reed in *Benedetti* stated that a court can't 'make the parties contract for them'.[43] Yet it's clear courts can make provision for payment of a reasonable sum where a contract is silent on this point.[44] Is what the courts did here any different? The problem facing the claimants was, it was

[40] Ibid para 9. Cf paras 175–76, 178 (Lord Neuberger PSC).

[41] On this point, compare *Blue Haven Enterprises Ltd v Tully* [2006] UKPC 17, where the claimant did work developing land he mistakenly believed was his but which in fact belonged to the defendant. A claim for restitution was denied on the basis that, though the defendant was clearly enriched, he had neither encouraged the work nor refrained from asserting his title to the land while the work was proceeding. No equivalent requirement of encouragement or acquiescence applies in the asset transfer cases.

[42] See too *Way v Latilla* [1939] 3 All ER 759 (HL).

[43] *Benedetti* (n 25) para 99.

[44] See eg Sale of Goods Act 1979, s 8(2); Sale of Goods and Supply of Services Act 1982, s 15(1); Edwin Peel, *Treitel: The Law of Contract* (13th edn, Sweet and Maxwell 2011) 1143–44.

thought, not simply that their contracts were incomplete but that there was no contract at all. For Lord Reed, 'in the absence of a contract, neither party's intentions or expectations [could] be determinative of their mutual rights and obligations'.[45] But this assertion has little going for it. Intentions and agreements are given legal recognition beyond the law of contract, so we can't take the finding that there is no contract as meaning that the parties' intentions and expectations should not be recognized or given effect. Of course, it matters why no contract is found. Sometimes there is good reason to decline to enforce the parties' agreement, sometimes there is good reason to make such enforcement dependent on their meeting other conditions, such as requirements of form. But if the parties' intentions do give an answer, it is one the courts should adopt unless some such reason obtains.

In both *Cobbe* and *Benedetti*, there were agreements, albeit incomplete. Indeed in *Cobbe* there was near-full agreement: the claimant was going to obtain planning permission and pay the defendant £12 million; in return the defendant would convey the land to him for development. Each would then get a share of the profits from that development. However, since the parties had chosen not to put their agreement into writing, the statutory requirement that such contracts be written meant the claimant couldn't hold the defendant to it. But while the statute meant that the claimant had no claim to the land, it didn't demand that he receive nothing for his work. Given too that there was no agreement or understanding that the claimant was to go unremunerated, this leaves us with a voluntary arrangement whereby the claimant did work for the defendant, work which it was understood was to be paid for, but no effective contractual provision fixing a price. In *Benedetti*, the court found that there had in fact been a contract that provided for payment for the claimant's services, but that this had then been abandoned. There was some support for the view that a second contract might be found, albeit one which did not specify what sum the claimant was due.[46] But on any view the work the claimant did was with the defendant's agreement, and again done on the understanding it was to be paid for.

No doubt, the less complete an agreement is, the more work the court has to do filling in the gaps and the less secure it will be in its conclusions that a given determination accords with the parties'

[45] *Benedetti* (n 25) para 99.

[46] Ibid paras 85 (Lord Reed JSC), 177 (Lord Neuberger PSC). Cf para 9 (Lord Clarke JSC).

broader intentions and interests. At some point, the gaps become so great or so many that attempts to piece together what the parties did intend or would have intended become exercises in fashioning a fair solution for them. We might doubt whether this point was reached in either *Cobbe* or *Benedetti*. Even when that point is reached, there's no reason to think that the sole consideration relevant to determining what each is, in justice, due is the gain each has made. In any case, the inquiry into the defendant's enrichment, which the courts then conducted, soon took them back to the sorts of questions they would have had to ask had they considered that the claim turned, in the first instance, on the parties' agreement.[47] So in both cases the defendant's enrichment could only be considered an unjust enrichment in light of the agreed terms on which the services were provided. In *Cobbe*, the failure of consideration was the defendant's failure to perform his side of their agreement. In *Benedetti*, the defendant's enrichment was unjust precisely because the claimant did the work, and the defendant accepted it, on the basis that it would be paid for. In both cases, it was held that the relevant enrichment was not the full measure of profit the defendant derived from the claimant's labours but only the value of the services themselves.[48] This value was, in the first instance, their market price, or, in other words, the price that those in the same position as the parties were in would be expected to agree to. It is sometimes claimed that, behind the references to implied and quasi-contract, the courts were applying ideas of unjust enrichment long before its recognition as a legal category or concept. It is tempting to say that here, under the guise of unjust enrichment, the courts are applying implied contract thinking long after its rejection.

IX A Unity of Rationale

Unjust enrichment lawyers have long identified unjust enrichment as a ground of rights and liabilities independent of contract and tort. It was their commitment to this claim which caused them to abandon understandings of unjust enrichment which capture all cases

[47] See too Peter Jaffey, 'Unjust Enrichment and Contract' (2014) 77 *Modern Law Review*, 983, 987–92.

[48] *Cobbe* (n 36) para 41 (Lord Scott); *Benedetti* (n 25) paras 14 (Lord Wilson JSC), 182 (Lord Neuberger PSC).

to which the law responds by imposing a liability which is, in one way or another, gain-based.[49] It would have been possible to go the other way: to keep using 'unjust enrichment' in such a way as maps the parameters of the law of restitution and to acknowledge that, so understood, unjust enrichment is not in fact a distinct source of rights and liabilities. The difference is one of presentation, not of substance. But having taken this step, the hunt was on for some other feature that gave unjust enrichment its focus and content. One answer, increasingly common, is that the law of unjust enrichment is directed to defective transfers of value. One problem with this answer is that it mis-describes the cases it is intended to capture. As we have seen, cases of pure services involve no transfer: the value or benefit the recipient gets is not something the provider had previously. But this is no less true in those cases in which there is a transfer, where some asset passes from claimant to defendant. Here too the benefit, the value, the defendant obtains from his receipt and use of the asset lies in the goals its advances, the interests it serves, which explains in turn why assets, like services, have different values to different people. And so value is no less abstract, no more capable of allocation and transfer, when it results from the transfer of some tangible asset. The transfer of a thing of value is no transfer of value.

Perhaps this doesn't matter. When some unjust enrichment lawyers talk of transfers of value, it is possible that they are looking only to describe those situations in which one person's benefit comes about through another's actions or resources.[50] It may be useful, for some purposes, to collect all these cases together under a single heading. If 'transfers of value' doesn't do the trick, we don't need to give up on the idea, only to find a better name for it. But whatever we choose to call it, this body of cases so collected reveals no common rationale, no common ground of liability. The reasons that support claims in cases of mistaken payments and other asset transfers don't extend to those in which the defendant benefits from the claimant's services. If unjust enrichment lawyers, having already cut out restitution for wrongs and cases of contractual restitution, want to maintain that unjust enrichment identifies a single, unitary ground of rights and liabilities, defining a body of like cases and claims, they should cut out the services

[49] See 2.III.

[50] See eg Andrew Burrows, *A Restatement of the English Law of Unjust Enrichment* (Oxford University Press 2012) 45.

cases too. It is sometimes said that this would impair the unity of the law of unjust enrichment.[51] But there's nothing to stop those who wish to throw the services cases in with the cases of asset transfers from doing so. We could, if we wished, designate this the law of unjust enrichment and this body of law will indeed have a unity. It just won't be a unity of rationale.[52] By contrast, if we want the law of unjust enrichment to identify a body of cases that has a material, rational unity, then that unity is impaired not by the exclusion of the services cases, but by their inclusion.

[51] See Burrows (n 23) 30.

[52] See 1.I.

5

Consent

I Authority and Consent

Wherever a claimant is empowered to determine the disposition of a particular asset or other advantage, decisions as to how that asset or advantage is to be used and exploited are, in the first instance, his to make. Where someone else receives, or exploits, or is put in a position to exploit that asset or advantage, the first question then is whether this was authorized by the claimant. If it was, we have good reason to leave the defendant with whatever access and to uphold whatever entitlement to that asset or advantage the claimant intended for him. If it wasn't, then the same considerations gives us reason to take this power as remaining in the claimant and to assist him in taking steps to put him back into a position whereby he can continue to exercise that power or, at the very least, to give him access to equivalent resources or advantages.[1]

What counts as proper authorization, therefore, matters. The authority a claimant may be accorded over a particular asset or opportunity will typically, perhaps invariably, have its limits. Some choices won't be his to make. For those choices that do fall within the scope of that authority, there is sometimes good reason to require that they be manifested in a particular form or accompanied by some further act before they will be given legal effect, and so to deny such effect to clear and reasonable choices that do not meet these further requirements. Nonetheless, within these parameters, the existence and content of any such authorization is settled by what consent the claimant has in fact given.

[1] See chapter 7.

The presence of consent will often be clear; so too its absence. A claimant who has his goods snatched from him gives no consent to the thief's use or enjoyment of them, and the law has had no difficulty in concluding that, while the goods may now be in another's possession, title remains in the claimant. Cases such as these have tended to make their way into accounts of the law of unjust enrichment, if at all, only at the margins, only by analogical extension from their core case of mistake. Yet these may better be regarded the true central cases of unjust enrichment, offering the clearest examples of this ground of liability. Nevertheless, these accounts were right to see in the cases on which they focused—cases of mistake, coercion, failed conditions—a common concern with the claimant's consent to the relevant disposition and, in so doing, to recognize that the class of non-consensual transfers and enrichments extended beyond cases of taking or of another's mismanagement (eg bank errors, misapplications by custodians). For, notwithstanding the claimant's participation in the transfer and though this transfer was not, in all respects, unchosen, these 'unjust factors' support the conclusion that his consent to that transfer was, in one way or another, insufficient to count as a true, effective exercise of his authority.

But having made it this far, these accounts didn't take the next step of asking what good or value supported the priority thereby accorded to the claimant's choices, and so what reason we have for ordering restitution in such cases. Often the mere fact that the claimant did not consent to the defendant's enrichment was treated as reason enough for its reversal. A question invited, though rarely addressed, by these accounts was why, if factors such as mistake really did negate a claimant's intentions when disposing of his assets, title was nonetheless held to pass. After all, for these accounts, the rules of title were key: only where title passed, or where the claimant did not seek to rely on any subsisting title, did unjust enrichment have a role to play in explaining a defendant's liability. One answer would have been to take no stand on these rules, to say they are what they are, and that unjust enrichment simply describes an alternative *technique* for reversing non-consensual transfers. In this way, the law of unjust enrichment would exist as a supplement to the rules on title, much as equity supplemented the common law.[2] But taking this line would require the

[2] This analogy is also drawn, but its implications not drawn out, in Lionel Smith, 'Property, Subsidiarity and Unjust Enrichment' in David Johnston and Reinhard Zimmermann (eds), *Unjustified Enrichment: Key Issues in Comparative Perspective* (Cambridge University Press 2002).

abandonment of any claim that unjust enrichment delineated any distinctive *ground* of liability.

Those who did address this question took a different line. They said that title passed because this was indeed what the claimant intended: that his mistake affected only his intent to benefit the defendant, not his intent to pass title;[3] or, less implausibly, that 'vitiation' of consent or of intention was a matter of degree and that, while (most) mistakes may suffice to vitiate the claimant's intention to benefit, they aren't sufficient to vitiate his intent to pass title.[4] The truth of these claims is hardly self-evident, but they tended to go by without argument or defence. What was needed, yet what these accounts failed to provide, was a careful examination of how these various vitiating factors operate: how—in what sense, to what degree—they qualify or undermine a claimant's choices and intentions; how they truly support the claimant's contention that his apparent consent was not *true* or effective consent. Only through such an examination will we be in a position to tell whether the form of recovery imposed by the common law, with its particular combination of rules of title and liability, can indeed be traced back to the way these factors impact on a claimant's choices.

II Mistakes

We can start with mistakes. Within accounts of the law of unjust enrichment, mistakes are said to support recovery on the basis that they 'vitiate' the claimant's intention to benefit the defendant.[5] What this means is unclear. It is sometimes said that whether a mistake vitiates a claimant's intentions (or renders a disposition 'non-voluntary' or some equivalent expression) can be determined only once we know

[3] See 3.VIII.

[4] See Graham Virgo, *The Principles of the Law of Restitution* (2nd edn, Oxford University Press 2006) 153, 159–60, 585; *Barclays Bank Ltd v W J Simms Son & Cooke (Southern) Ltd* [1980] QB 677 (QB) 689. Cf Peter Watts, 'Restitution—A Property Principle and a Services Principle' [1995] *Restitution Law Review* 49, 52.

[5] See eg Peter Birks, *An Introduction to the Law of Restitution* (rev edn, Clarendon Press 1989) 100–01, 147; Andrew Burrows, *The Law of Restitution* (3rd edn, Oxford University Press 2011) 87; Charles Mitchell, Paul Mitchell, and Stephen Watterson (eds), *Goff and Jones: The Law of Unjust Enrichment* (8th edn, Sweet and Maxwell 2011) [1-22], [9-21]; Virgo, ibid 139, 159.

how the law responds to mistakes of that kind.[6] On this basis, one's intentions are vitiated only where and only because the law determines that they shall not be given effect. But to say this is in truth to deny that mistakes vitiate intention at all. Rather one's intention is vitiated by the law's response to that mistake and vitiated only in the sense that one's disposition does not take effect as (mistakenly) intended. The proposition that mistake vitiates intention ceases to be a claim about why mistakes ground restitution and instead simply restates the fact that they do.

By contrast, if the idea that mistake vitiates intention is to tell us anything about why it is that mistaken claimants are entitled to restitution, then vitiation must describe not how the law responds to mistakes but how mistakes affect the substance or quality of a claimant's intentions. The suggestion then is that mistaken beliefs in some sense defeat or negate the choices made and intentions formed in reliance on them. But this seems an odd claim. A person's intentions—as with all states of mind—are matters of fact.[7] Either the claimant had a particular intention at a particular point in time or he didn't. If he did, then to proceed as though he didn't is fiction; if he didn't, there is nothing to defeat or negate in the first place. Occasionally the idea that mistaken transfers are not truly or properly intended is challenged along just these lines. Where a claimant's intention to pay the defendant is formed on the basis of a mistake, the resulting payment is, so it is said, no less intentional, no less intended.[8] Say I mistakenly believe that this is money I owe you. My intention, when paying the money over, is to transfer that money to you outright. Of course, I wouldn't

[6] See eg Birks (n 5) 100: 'The notions of voluntariness and non-voluntariness in parting with wealth are controlled by the cases. You cannot conclude in favour of restitution just by looking at the story of a transfer from P to D and deciding as though it were a question of fact, that P did not mean D to have the given item of wealth.'

[7] This purely factual or descriptive understanding of intention is sometimes doubted. So it might be said that whether a defendant intended to kill requires a judgment as to whether 'killing' is the same as 'causing death' and, if not, what sorts of causings of death are to count as killings; so too a judgment as to when life starts (conception, birth, etc): cf Victor Tadros, *Criminal Responsibility* (Oxford University Press 2005) 218–21. No doubt to know whether I intend to kill we need answers to these questions, and, for some purposes at least, this requires normative argument. But the fact that how we describe or assess a certain intention will sometimes involve a normative inquiry doesn't mean that the question of what I intend (however we describe it) or whether I have a particular intention (once defined) is anything other than a question of fact.

[8] See eg P J Millett, 'Restitution and Constructive Trusts' (1998) 114 *Law Quarterly Review* 399, 401–02; William Swadling, 'Explaining Resulting Trusts' (2008) 124 *Law Quarterly Review* 72, 92–93; William Swadling, 'Policy Arguments for Proprietary Restitution' (2008) 28 *Legal Studies* 506, 529.

have intended this had I known the money wasn't owing and I don't 'intend' that you have that money *now*. Yet none of this challenges the reality of my intention to pay that money at the time I paid it over. And therefore, so the argument goes, whatever reason we may have to require you to repay that money, it cannot be that my payment, and the benefit it gave you, was not intended.

The challenge fails. I can demand restitution of the money I paid you and I can do so on the basis that your receipt and retention of that money is not what I intended. But to explain why requires a fuller, truer account of the operation and effect of mistakes than unjust enrichment lawyers have given. Getting a clearer sense of how mistakes ground recovery will also help us determine when they should ground recovery. Restitution has long been granted for some mistaken dispositions, yet for just as long there has been uncertainty as to how far these claims should extend. Unjust enrichment lawyers have, on the whole, pushed to expand the class of mistakes from which relief may be sought. The courts, however, have been more hesitant, reckoning that some limit must be placed on such claims, but without any real confidence about where the line should then be drawn. Until we make better sense of the claim that mistaken transfers are not intended and have a firmer grasp of the grounds of their reversal, this confusion will continue.

III Intentions and Plans

All intentional action is directed towards the achievement of some end or set of ends. An agent identifies a state of affairs he wishes to see realized and formulates a proposal or plan of action for its realization. His acts are the implementation of that plan, his attempt to secure his chosen objective. So my writing these words in this sentence is one step of the broader project of writing this book. My writing the book is in turn a means towards a collection of further ends: communicating certain ideas, pursuing my career, meeting my obligation to the publisher, etc. All these things—all aspects of these connected plans and proposals, all my chosen ends and my chosen means to those chosen ends—I direct my actions to and so intend.[9]

[9] See generally John Finnis, 'Intention and Side-effects' in R G Frey and Christopher W Morris (eds), *Liability and Responsibility: Essays in Law and Morals* (Cambridge University Press 1991).

Intentions are often distinguished from motives, but the contrast is at best misleading. Sometimes motives are identified with one's ulterior purposes in acting in a given way. What was his motive for killing her? To secure the inheritance. Here one's motives are straightforwardly one's (further) intentions: he intended to kill her and (thereby) to inherit the fortune. At other times, motives are identified not as states of affairs an agent seeks to bring about through his actions, but as a particular category of emotion or desire which induced those actions. What was his motive for killing her? Greed (or revenge, or jealousy...). Here the agent's motives are not themselves his intentions, but they are only correctly identified as *that agent's* motives by virtue of his intentions, the ends to which his actions were directed. So there is no opposition between intention and motive. When it is said that motives are generally irrelevant in criminal law, that only intention matters, what is meant is that it typically doesn't matter what (say) the killer intended *beyond* killing his victim, what further state of affairs he sought to bring about by bringing about *this* result.

The way that individual actions are intended as elements of a particular plan, which are often themselves just steps in a set of broader, longer-term projects, explains certain features of what actions we designate as intended. Intended action is only intended (as it is often put) 'under a description'.[10] The same action can be described in various ways, bringing out different features of the agent's conduct, its circumstances, and consequences. Only under certain descriptions will that act be intended; under others it will not. What distinguishes those descriptions under which an action is intended is precisely their place in the relevant plan or proposal. For instance, in writing these sentences, this book, I hope and intend that the arguments they contain convince all who read them. I know, however, that they won't, that the book's arguments will convince some, but confound or cut no ice with others. And so by making these arguments I am, at one and the same time, through the very same choices and actions, convincing and confounding. But while the convincing is intended, the confounding is not.[11]

[10] G E M Anscombe, *Intention* (2nd edn, Basil Blackwell 1963); Donald Davidson, 'Actions, Reasons, and Causes' (1963) 60 *Journal of Philosophy* 685; G E M Anscombe, 'Under a Description' (1979) 13 *Nous* 219.

[11] Davidson's example (Donald Davidson, *Essays on Actions and Events* (2nd edn, Clarendon Press 2001) 53): 'A man moves his finger, let us say intentionally, thus flicking the switch, causing a light to come on, the room to be illuminated, and a prowler to be alerted. This sentence has the following entailments: the man flicked the switch, turned on the light, illuminated the room, and alerted the prowler. Some of these things he did intentionally, some not.'

This example distinguishes different consequences of my acts: some aimed at and so intended; others, though perhaps foreseen and accepted, not. But the same point extends to the circumstances in which I act. Across the corridor Kenneth is having a nap. So I am writing these words as Kenneth has his nap. But while I intend to write these words, it's not my intention to write them *as Kenneth sleeps*. It is no part of the plan of action I am putting into effect or of the state of affairs I seek to bring about through my actions that Kenneth be asleep at this time. If Kenneth wakes up, or if he is simply pretending to sleep, my intentions are in no way frustrated. Whether he or anyone else is awake or sleeping, now or at any other time, is neither here nor there. (And so just as it is not my intention to write these words *as Kenneth sleeps*, so it is not my intention *not* to write these words *as he sleeps*. Many of these formulations are ambiguous. For instance, 'I don't intend to φ given/if C' (where C is some circumstance or contingency) could mean either 'I do not intend to [φ given/if C]' (meaning: my intention to φ is not specifically an intention to φ in the event of C) or 'If C, I do not intend to φ'. In the former, C is not factored into my proposal one way or another. In the latter, my intention to φ is conditional on C not obtaining. Context and inflexion will typically make clear which is meant.)

So the same act can, without contradiction, be both intended (under certain descriptions) and not intended (under others). This will be the case wherever there are consequences to my actions that I did not aim at bringing about. It is also true wherever there are circumstances in which I am acting which are not (we might say) incorporated within my proposal, within my plan of action. In many instances, the circumstances in which an agent acts don't figure at all in his proposal. This is true of the example just given. Any number of people will be sleeping or waking as I write this, but who is asleep and who awake is simply immaterial to what I intend to do. On some occasions, however, there are circumstances or contingencies that are factored into my proposal. I want to kiss Erika. But I only want to kiss her if she herself wants to be kissed. My intention to kiss Erika is formed on the understanding that this is indeed what she wants. Here Erika's consent is an element of my proposal, factored in as a condition of my intention to kiss her.

Where, as here, my intentions are explicitly conditional on some state of affairs obtaining, then, unless I reopen my earlier decision and revise my intentions, they remain conditional when I go on to act on them. To say that my intentions are conditional is not to say that I am in some way undecided. On the contrary: I have resolved to act where the relevant condition obtains. So conditional intentions are, by their nature, no less firm and are no more requiring of pre-implementation revision or supplement than intentions to which no such explicit conditions attach.[12] In the same way, when this intention is then acted on, it doesn't at that point become unconditional. Satisfied that Erika is happy to be kissed, I kiss her. But my intention remains to kiss her only if—or, now, only because—she consents.

IV Conditions

The intention of the claimant in the unjust enrichment lawyer's central case of the mistaken liability payment is conditional in just this way. Payments, like countless other actions, can be nominally unconditional. By this I mean that I can intend to pay you a sum of money while attaching no conditions to this plan of action. The fact that I have identified no such conditions needn't mean that my intention is an intention to pay you *come what may* or *in any event*. It is likely that few, if any, intentions are truly unconditional this way. The failure to identify any explicit conditions to which the payment is subject doesn't mean that the payer positively intends to pay, whatever may happen (even if the banks fail, even if the payee murders my family...). Not only are contingencies such as these not considered and so not factored in when my proposal is devised, it also seems clear that, even when I state that my intentions are unconditional, I don't (at least ordinarily) mean to suggest that my intention is to perform even in the face of such emergencies.

In any case, it is clear that intentions to pay can be, and often are, conditional, my intention to pay you an intention to pay only if or where a certain contingency obtains. Often these conditions are formulated explicitly: I intend to pay you £100 if (or when) you pass your exams, if you ask me to, if it rains tomorrow, etc. The conditionality of these intentions may, but need not, express any uncertainty about whether the relevant contingency will be met. I may have no

[12] See further J P W Cartwright, 'Conditional Intention' (1990) 60 *Philosophical Studies* 233; John Finnis, 'On Conditional Intentions and Preparatory Intentions' in Luke Gormally (ed), *Moral Truth and Moral Tradition: Essays in Honour of Peter Geach and Elizabeth Anscombe* (Four Courts Press 1994).

doubt whatsoever that you will pass your exams, yet my intention to pay you when you pass them is nonetheless conditional on this happening. (Just as a man's intention to kiss his wife on their wedding day is conditional on her consenting, even though the possibility of her not consenting never crosses his mind.) I intend to pay only where and because you have passed you exams, your success the reason and the trigger for my payment.

As in these examples, my intention to pay is shown to be conditional through the relevant 'if...' clause. But such conditions can also be identified where this is a necessary implication of the plan of action of which my intended payment is part. This is the case where my payment is intended to discharge a debt. The intention to discharge a debt is an intention to pay (only) such money as is truly owing to the payee. It is then a condition of my intention to pay you—that is, my intention to pay you this money in order to discharge my indebtedness—that this money is indeed due. This is true when I first resolve to pay you, and it remains true when I then act on that intention and pay that money over. So when I do pay, the payment is indeed intended, but not intended unconditionally. I intend to pay you the money I owe, I don't intend to pay you money I don't owe. Or to put it another way: my payment was intended *as the payment of a debt*, but it was not intended *as a gift* or *as the payment of money not owing*. If, therefore, it turns out that I am mistaken in thinking I owe you this money, I can say that I paid you on a condition that has failed and that I had no intention that you should have the money in these circumstances.

It's possible to believe that money is owing but to intend that the recipient should have that money even in the event that it is not in fact due. If so, though my assumption remains that the money *is* due and though I pay you believing I am discharging a debt, my intention is not conditional on that money being due (and indeed it would be misleading to say that my intention is simply to pay off a debt). But this isn't what most mistaken payers have in mind or intend. Nor does the fact that I give no thought to the possibility that the money isn't owed mean that my intention to pay off that (assumed) debt amounts to an intention that you should have that money in any event. These are plainly different intentions, different states of mind. And, once more, nothing changes when this intention is put into action and the money is paid over. At the point of handing it over, there is no abrupt revision of my initial intentions, no last-minute resolution that you should have the money even if it turns out not to be due. I simply act on my original intentions as they apply to the facts as I, wrongly, believe them to be.

So those who have treated mistakes as instances where the claimant can be said not to have intended the payment have the better of the argument with those who insist such payments are nonetheless intended. For, though it is indisputable that mistaken payers do have an intention to pay their payees, intending title to that money to be transferred to them, and though it is this intention they are seeking to put into action when they make their payments, this was only ever an intention to pay money that was due. The payment of money in excess of what, if anything, was owing, was and is unintended.

Nonetheless, the standard account of mistakes doesn't come through unscathed. Absent an intention that you should have the money come what may, my intention to *pay off a debt* is, from the word go, an intention that you should have such money as you are due *but no more*. Accordingly, where it turns out that I am mistaken and the money I pay you is not owed, my intention that you should have that money is not defeated by my mistake, for there is no applicable intention to defeat. So the significance of my mistake here is not that it in some way compromises my intentions: it doesn't, and indeed doesn't need to. If I now seek to recover that money from you, I don't need to call these intentions into question. I'm not saying that I have changed my mind or that my intentions at the point of transfer should be disregarded. On the contrary: since my intention is to pay the money I owe you, that intention does not extend beyond your receiving the money you are in truth owed. Since the money I in fact paid is not money you are owed, the only condition on which I ever intended that this money should be yours is not met. As such, the money you now hold is money that, in these circumstances, I do not, and never did, intend you to have and empowering me to recover that money ensures that my intentions are in fact upheld.[13]

So we should reject the idea that mistakes vitiate intention and with it the suggestion that such vitiation is a matter of degree, with some mistakes having a greater vitiating effect than others. Rather mistakes are significant in these cases for they go to the conditions in which the claimant intends the defendant to receive and retain the

[13] This answers the concern raised in Andrew Botterell, 'Property, Corrective Justice, and the Nature of the Cause of Action in Unjust Enrichment' (2007) 20 *Canadian Journal of Law and Jurisprudence* 275, 286.

relevant asset or advantage. These conditions set the extent, the limits of the claimant's intention to confer title to that asset or the relevant advantage on that defendant: if they are met, this transfer is intended, if not, it isn't. Intentions are, in this way, binary. So there is no question of some mistakes being more destructive of a claimant's intentions than others. No intentions are destroyed (or vitiated or defeated or nullified...) in any manner or in any degree at all.

No doubt mistakes can differ in degree in other respects. Overpaying you by £1,000 is a bigger, more costly mistake than overpaying you by £1. Some mistakes do more damage to the goals to which the relevant plan of action is directed. Forgetting my passport does more to stymie my holiday plans than forgetting my toothbrush, for while having to buy a replacement toothbrush may be an inconvenience, my holiday cannot go ahead if I am without my passport. It is with these sorts of considerations in mind that the law identifies certain mistakes as 'fundamental': mistakes that go to the root of a particular transaction, which make it 'essentially different to the thing as it was believed to be'.[14] It may sometimes be reasonable for the law to draw such distinctions, to identify certain mistakes, by virtue of the gravity of their consequences or their impact upon the parties' broader aims and actions, as meriting special treatment. For instance, it may be that, in the law of contract, a reluctance to encourage parties to seek to shift risks properly allocated to them and a concern with the costs of declaring partially executed contracts void means we have good reason to allow parties to have contracts set aside on the grounds of mistake only where the consequences of not doing so are great. Similar considerations may extend beyond the law of contract to other sorts of transactions and dispositions.

But these differences in gravity of consequence and in treatment don't correspond with differences of intent and intendedness. I have no intention—none at all—of setting out without either my passport or my toothbrush. I no more intend to overpay you by £1 than by £1,000. The justifications, such as there are, for the law's different treatment of different mistakes are to be found not in that agent's intentions, but in the various other concerns and interests implicated in such cases. So if the common law's approach to mistaken transfers—sometimes holding title to pass, sometimes not—is

[14] *Bell v Lever Brothers Ltd* [1932] AC 161 (HL) 218 (Lord Atkin).

reasonable, this is not because my transfer is any more intended in the one set of cases than it is in the other. The partial effect given to my transfer in the standard cases of unjust enrichment—whereby title to the asset passes, but I am permitted to recover its monetary equivalent—is not attributable to my partial consent to that transfer. There is a sense in which my mistake as to your identity (a mistake typically thought to prevent title passing) is more far-reaching, more complete than my mistake in thinking I am obligated to make the transfer. In the latter case, I have a real, though conditional, intention to transfer the asset to you; in the former, I do not intend *you* to have the asset at all.[15] Nonetheless, where it turns out that I owe no such obligation and so where this condition fails, I no more intend that the asset be yours in these circumstances than I do when I make a mistake as to your identity or indeed than when you simply snatch the asset from me.

V The Diversity of Mistakes

What is true of mistakes as to liability is true wherever a claimant's intentions are similarly conditional, wherever his chosen ends and his chosen means to those ends depend on a particular state of affairs obtaining. So we see the same thing where a mother, wishing to provide equally for her two daughters and having already made appointments totalling £8,600 from a trust fund to her younger daughter, appoints £8,600 to her elder daughter, forgetting that the latter had been appointed half the fund at an earlier date.[16] Just as a claimant seeking to pay off a debt intends only to pay such money as is truly owing, so the mother, aiming to ensure that each daughter receives the same sum, intends only to appoint such funds as truly required to put her daughters on an equal footing. Here too then the payment is conditional, intended only on the basis and only to the extent

[15] It may be that the defendant's identity—ie that he is indeed the person to whom the claimant intends to make the transfer—is a condition of every transfer, such that one might call it fundamental to or constitutive of the idea of transfer (see David Fox, 'The Transfer of Legal Title to Money' [1996] *Restitution Law Review* 60, 64–67). But this doesn't mean that other conditions, not essential to the very idea of transfer but nonetheless attached by *this* claimant to *this* transfer, are not every bit as basic to his intentions when making that transfer, nor that, where *these* conditions fail, the transfer is any less unintended.

[16] *Lady Hood of Avalon v Mackinnon* [1909] 1 Ch 476 (Ch).

that the younger daughter had indeed been paid more. Paying the elder daughter a greater share of the fund than had been or would be received by her sister was never intended.

Forgetting the earlier appointment in favour of the elder daughter was, on the face of it, careless. Often, perhaps more often than not, there is more mistaken claimants could have done to establish whether the relevant condition was met before going ahead with the transfer. On occasion, the failure to check whether that condition obtains may indicate that the transfer was not in fact conditional, that the claimant's intention, in truth, was to make the transfer in any event. But where the claimant's intention to make the transfer really is conditional, it is not made any less conditional by his failure to take reasonable steps to verify that this condition obtains. So if I fail to check that I do indeed owe you this money and simply assume that it is owed and pay accordingly, I can still say that I intended you to have only that money which you were in fact due. If it turns out the money I paid was not due, my belief that I owed you this money is no less mistaken by virtue of the mistake being (to this extent) self-inflicted. So the rule that mistaken payments may be recovered even where the claimant's mistaken belief was negligently formed is a sound one.[17] In so far as our concern is to see that my intentions—and hence my authority in relation to dispositions of that money—are respected, it makes no difference how I came to make this mistake, and hence how it is that the money ended up in your hands.[18]

It is sometimes suggested that forgetting a particular fact is not the same as being mistaken, and that forgetful claimants are better classed alongside the ignorant, who have no belief one way or another on a particular matter.[19] Those who nonetheless treat cases of ignorance and forgetfulness as mistakes sometimes identify them as 'tacit'

[17] *Kelly v Solari* (1841) 9 M & W 54. It is sometimes said that if the claimant's negligence is no bar to his bringing a claim in respect of some such mistaken transfer, then his (or for that matter the defendant's) negligence should likewise have no bearing on what he may then recover (such as in determining who should bear the losses entailed by a defendant's change of position: see eg *Dextra Bank & Trust Co Ltd v Bank of Jamaica* [2001] UKPC 50, [2002] 1 All ER (Comm) 193, para 45). *Non-sequitur*. See further 8.III.

[18] See too *Restatement (Third) of Restitution and Unjust Enrichment* (American Law Institute 2011) § 5, Comment *f*: 'the role of restitution for mistake is to protect property against inadvertent dispossession. A claim in restitution is not affected by the claimant's negligence, because rights of ownership are not dependent on the owner's degree of care.'

[19] *Barrow v Isaacs & Son* [1891] 1 QB 417 (CA) 420 (Lord Esher MR); Duncan Sheehan, 'What is a Mistake?' (2000) 20 *Legal Studies* 538, 541–43.

or 'passive' mistakes, in contrast to the 'active' mistake of one whose positive beliefs turn out to be incorrect. It's doubtful that these distinctions stand up: the mother who makes the transfer to equalize her daughters' shares necessarily acts on the mistaken belief that the elder daughter has so far received less. This is true whether she positively misconstrued the earlier dispositions, forgot, or simply never knew about them.

In any case, even if these distinctions—between mistakes, forgetfulness, and ignorance, between active and passive mistakes—do hold good, they are, for present purposes, worth drawing only if they have a bearing on how these cases fall to be treated. Some do indeed contend that it is only in cases of mistake, or in cases of 'active' mistake, that a claimant should be entitled to restitution.[20] Discussion at times proceeds as if the issue here is merely conceptual or terminological: as though the remedies available to (actively) mistaken claimants should be extended only to those who can likewise claim to have been truly mistaken when making the transfer. So we find discussion of what a mistake *really* is, whether to forget a particular fact is to be mistaken about that matter, whether you can be mistaken if you have doubts, and so on. Since the term 'mistake' carries shades of meaning, these questions receive conflicting or inconclusive answers. This resort to ordinary language is in any case unhelpful. What matters is not how far the language of 'mistakes' might extend, but how far the reasoning which supports restitution in cases of clear mistakes extends to these other cases too. There is no reason to assume that these reasons are co-extensive with linguistic convention.

The textbook writers have, on the whole, favoured extending recovery to all cases of causative mistake and ignorance.[21] If imperfect information vitiates a claimant's intentions in the core case, so, presumably, it must in others. The courts, however, have never fully bought in to this and, over the years, have tried out various approaches designed to restrict restitution to a narrower class of mistakes. To date, none of these has stuck, each appearing, in the end, arbitrary. Nonetheless, the intuition that the law should stop short of (presumptively) granting

[20] See eg *Pitt v Holt* [2013] UKSC 26, [2013] 2 AC 108, para 108.

[21] Those (more or less) supportive of presumptive recovery for all causative mistakes include: Burrows (n 5) 214–17; James Edelman and Elise Bant, *Unjust Enrichment in Australia* (Oxford University Press 2006) 173–5; Virgo (n 4) 157 (cf 165); *Goff and Jones* (n 5) [9-107]–[9-112].

restitution wherever a claimant can identify some factor about which he was mistaken or ignorant and which would have made a difference to his decision to make the transfer is, I suspect, sound.

In the cases we have been considering until now, the mistake is as to some fact or state of affairs that is essential to the transfer achieving its intended object. The transfer is conditional upon the existence of that state of affairs precisely because that transfer is itself intended as one element of a broader proposal that presumes or applies only where that state of affairs obtains. Not all mistakes are like this. I own some shares which I'd like you to have. I want nothing in return and set no conditions on your receipt or use of them. I transfer the shares to you, triggering an unanticipated and significant tax liability.[22] If I had known I would be opening myself up to this liability, I wouldn't have made the transfer. But this liability in no sense thwarts my plans in making the transfer: you get the shares I wanted you to have, just as I wanted you to have them. My intention wasn't that you should get the shares only if no liability would attach to me in the process: the transfer was not part of some tax mitigation scheme, the possible tax implications of the transfer were simply not factored in to my proposal. My aims in making the transfer were, therefore, achieved. They simply had an unwanted, unintended side effect.

So this case is different to the mistaken liability payment with which we started. There my objective was to pay off a debt, an objective that is achievable only if the money I pay you is in fact owing. As we have seen, in this case, my intention is, all along, only to pay you what you are owed, for you to have only so much as—and hence no more than—you are due. When it turns out that this money is not in fact due, I can appeal to this intention in support of my claim that the money should now be returned. Not so here. True, the tax liability *was* unintended and, while I intended the transfer, I didn't intend a transfer *that would trigger such a liability*. But while we can say that there is here a contingency to which my intention to make the transfer did not extend, we can't say that the tax liability defeats, or is any way incompatible with the proposal, and so the intentions on which I acted when making that transfer. Accordingly, if I bring a claim to have that transfer reversed, I can't appeal to what I did intend, only to what I didn't. For all I can say in truth is that there was here a gap in my intentions, in the proposal on which I acted, for they didn't factor

[22] Cf *Pitt v Holt* (n 20).

in the tax implications of my transfer, and that, *if I had*, I'd have revised my proposal accordingly, intending the transfer only on the condition that no such liability would attach.

So we can distinguish mistakes that defeat or undermine one's intentions and the proposal they put into action from those which merely reveal gaps in those intentions and proposals. In both cases, we might say that the mistake identifies a condition to which the claimant's intention to make the transfer does not extend. But these intentions are conditional in different ways. In the latter case, in respect of the relevant contingency, the claimant has, in truth, no intention one way or another: the proposal he acts on simply doesn't address this eventuality. But in the former, the relevant contingency *is* factored in, in so far as it is addressed in or entailed by the proposal on which he acts, by the ends to which his actions are directed, in the way that my liability to pay you is necessarily factored in to my intention to pay you the money I owe. (There may be cases where it is unclear into which of these two categories a particular contingency, and so a particular mistake, falls. To the extent that our proposals, our plans of actions, are indeterminate, so may be the contingencies to which they are subject.)

Should both sorts of mistake suffice to ground a claim for restitution? The change of position defence means, at least in principle, that we can extend unjust enrichment's reach without fear of causing harm to those on the receiving end of these transfers. You get a defence if, and in so far as, my claim would leave you worse off than if I'd not made the transfer. But (so it might be thought) if, or to the extent that, it would not, no injustice is done to you if my claim succeeds. Yet the fact that the you will be left no worse off than had you not received the shares is not itself a reason for taking them from you. Allowing me to recover in cases such as this would, no doubt, serve my interests, giving me greater opportunity to ensure that the dispositions I make of my assets advance my chosen goals and accord with my preferences. However, we would be doing this by giving me what is, in effect, a second bite of the cherry. My initial proposal was implemented and the transfer took effect as I intended. My complaint now is that, had I known more or known better, I would have intended something different, adopted a different plan of action. This is in contrast to the case of the mistaken liability payment, where I'm asking for no second chance, where allowing me to recover itself upholds the proposal on which I acted, giving effect to my intentions when paying you.

So there is a case for limiting restitution for mistakes which is grounded not in unelaborated fears of 'too much restitution', nor in concern for a defendant's security of receipt—which is implicated no more and no less by one class of mistake than by another—but in what these different mistakes reveal about the content and extent of a claimant's intentions when making a transfer. For it is only in those cases where the mistake goes to some element on which the claimant's intended course of action is dependent or to which his proposal is otherwise subject, as is the case where I am mistaken as to the existence of the debt I intend to discharge, that a claimant can appeal to the reality of his intentions in support of his claim to have that transfer reversed.[23]

VI Uncertainty and Risk

This approach to mistakes can also explain why no claim should lie where a claimant makes a payment in—as it is sometimes put—'submission to an honest claim'.[24] You think I owe you £1,000. I have my doubts, but it suits me to put the matter past us and pay up. It turns out the money was not due and, had I known this for sure at the time, I wouldn't have paid you. Yet my payment wasn't conditional on the money being owed. On the contrary, I knew it might not be, but I paid nonetheless so as to bring the matter to an end, a state of affairs realized by that payment but which would be thwarted were I now to seek or be granted recovery. So despite my mistake in thinking

[23] This approach would, for what it is worth, deny restitution in most of the hypothetical test cases proffered by those doubtful of the wisdom of extending recovery to all causative mistakes: see eg Andrew Tettenborn, *Law of Restitution in England and Ireland* (3rd edn, Cavendish Publishing 2002) 76: 'I give £1,000 to my niece as a birthday present, not realising that she has just married a man I privately detest'; Sonja Meier and Reinhard Zimmermann, 'Judicial Development of the Law, Error Iuris, and the Law of Unjustified Enrichment—A View from Germany' (1999) 115 *Law Quarterly Review* 556, 562–63: the claimant pays the defendant, unaware that he is an enemy of a close relative of the claimant's or the claimant pays on a misunderstanding of his financial position (cf *Deutsche Morgan Grenfell Group Plc v Inland Revenue Commissioners* [2006] UKHL 49, [2007] 1 AC 558, para 87 (Lord Scott)). Though in these cases the payment wouldn't have been made had the payer not been mistaken, the proposal on which the payer was acting and the ends he was seeking to secure in making the payment do not incorporate or depend upon the correctness of these assumptions.

[24] Gareth Jones (ed), *Goff and Jones: The Law of Restitution* (7th edn, Sweet and Maxwell 2007) [10.52]–[10.56]. See eg *Maskell v Horner* [1915] 3 KB 106 (CA) 118 (Lord Reading CJ).

the money was likely due—an 'active' mistake indeed—we have good reason, in the very same respect for my intentions and for my authority over the money I paid as justifies restitution in the standard case of the mistaken liability payment, to leave this payment undisturbed. No special defence, no appeal to distinct policies in favour of ending disputes and litigation need be invoked.

It is sometimes suggested that where, as here, I pay doubting whether I am truly liable to make that payment, I can't claim to be mistaken as to my liability.[25] This matters, so it is thought, because while mistake is a 'vitiating factor', doubt isn't. The blanket opposition of mistake and doubt is unwarranted. That I doubt that I am right doesn't mean I am not mistaken if I turn out to be wrong. Indeed if doubts precluded mistakes, then any suspicion that I may be mistaken would, by that very fact, rule out any possibility of my being mistaken. Say I know I owed you money but can't remember if I have already paid. I conclude, however, that it's more likely than not that I haven't already paid. If it turns out that I have already paid, my conclusion that I haven't is mistaken and, though we might say I was right to have my doubts, these doubts mean I was no less mistaken to think that the money was owing.

So much seems to be accepted by most unjust enrichment lawyers. Yet it is also assumed that there comes a point at which a claimant's doubts are so great that he can no longer plausibly be regarded as making a mistake. The question then is what degree of doubt is compatible with being mistaken and hence (on this view) being entitled to recovery if these doubts turn out to be well-founded. This view might be challenged. If I doubt whether I have paid you already, I believe it could be true that I have paid, could be true that I haven't. But only one of these things can be true: either the payment has already been made or it hasn't. If it turns out I have paid previously, the thought that I might not have done and hence that the money may still be owing is mistaken. Since doubt entails taking as credible two or more contradictory propositions (eg I have paid; I haven't paid) and since, therefore, not all of these propositions can be true, I must be mistaken about the credibility of at least one of those propositions. On this view, doubt is not incompatible with mistake, but entails it. So, we might say, even if I am almost certain—'99 per cent certain'—that I have paid, I am

[25] *Kleinwort Benson Ltd v Lincoln City Council* [1999] 2 AC 349 (HL) 410 (Lord Hope): 'A state of doubt is different from that of mistake'. Cf *Deutsche Morgan Grenfell Group Plc v Inland Revenue Commissioners* (n 23) para 26 (Lord Hoffmann).

mistaken in thinking there is even a '1 per cent chance' that I haven't. And so, if I then pay you, again, on the basis that there is a chance that the money is still owing, with no intention that the money should be yours at all events, but simply intending to discharge the debt if it turns out to be due, my payment is caused by that mistake.[26]

In any case, the practical, normative question of which claimants should be entitled to restitution is not to be settled by linguistic convention, so here too the question is not whether the concept or term 'mistake' can be stretched to those who pay with doubts, but how far the reasons for granting restitution to the plainly mistaken apply also to the doubting. In the easy case, where I pay under no doubt as to my liability, and so where I am revealed to be wholly mistaken when it is revealed that the money is not owed, my recovery of that money is attributable to my intention that the money should be yours on the condition that—and hence only if—it is indeed due. Are my intentions any different where I pay you, uncertain as to whether this money is truly owing? This depends. I could intend you to have the money come what may. This, as we've just seen, is the case where I pay to put an end to any dispute over whether the money is owing, and hence where, even though I may not believe the money is due, I intend you to have the money and move on. But that may not be the reason I pay you. Say instead I dispute your claim to this money; indeed, say I'm certain that I don't owe it you. Nonetheless, it makes sense for me to make the payment pending resolution of this question. Here, when I hand you the money, I am not intending to draw a line under the matter. On the contrary, my intention is that, if and when it is established that the money is not due, it should be returned to me. If the money is indeed not due, I can't plead any mistake. I was right all along. But on the central question—whether I intend the money to be yours to keep in the event that it turns out not to be due—my intention matches that of the mistaken payer. In both cases, my intention is that you only ever get to keep such money as is truly owing to you. And so, here, as with the standard case of mistake, allowing me to recover the money accords with my intentions and respects my authority over the disposition of my money.

The common law reveals no little confusion here. The orthodox rule states that payments made under protest, even where accompanied with

[26] Cf Ewan McKendrick, 'Mistake of Law—Time for a Change?' in William Swadling (ed), *The Limits of Restitutionary Claims: A Comparative Analysis* (United Kingdom National Committee of Comparative Law 1997) 232–33.

the express proviso that the payer doesn't intend to forego his right to the money if it is revealed not to be owing, are irrecoverable unless the payer can establish that he paid under duress.[27] The reason typically given is that such payments are 'voluntary'. This, however, misses the point. These payments are indeed voluntary, in the sense that the claimant made the choice to pay, and did so without mistake or coercion. But this hardly goes to the payer's claim, which is that he, nonetheless, had and has no intention that the defendant should, in these circumstances, get to keep it. By treating these payments as voluntary *and hence final*, we treat those who pay intending that the defendant keep the money only if it is due— intending that it be returned should it not—as equivalent to those who intend to pay up and move on. Yet there is no equivalence here, no comparability between those who pay to bring the matter to an end and those who pay intending to keep it open.

The rule denying recovery is sometimes explained on the basis that a claimant who pays with (significant) doubts as to his liability to make the payment is a risk-taker.[28] The idea is typically taken to speak for itself and so little effort is made to explain what risk-taking precludes recovery or why it does so. Perhaps the case which best fits this description is again that where I pay up, accepting that the money may not be due, but wishing to see any dispute ended and so intending that you should get the money come what may. To say that I take the risk that the money may not be owing is here to say that I consent to you having the money even if it isn't. But, as we have seen, this can't be said where I pay with the expressed intention that you should get to keep the money only if it is indeed due. What risk do I take here? The risk, perhaps, that you will be unwilling or unable to pay me; so too that a court might refuse to assist me in its recovery. But neither of these provides us with a reason to defeat my intentions and deny my claim. If I make the payment, again intending that you keep the money only if truly due, but without making clear that this is what I intend, perhaps I run the risk that you will misunderstand me and believe that my payment is unconditional and final. But if you do misunderstand, you have the protection of change of position; if you don't, it's again unclear why this risk-taking should defeat my claim.

[27] *Brown v M'Kinally* (1795) 1 Esp 279; *Maskell v Horner* (n 24). Cf *Woolwich Equitable Building Society v Inland Revenue Commissioners* [1993] AC 70 (HL).

[28] See eg *Deutsche Morgan Grenfell Group Plc v Inland Revenue Commissioners* (n 23) para 27 (Lord Hoffmann).

The risk-taking argument, such as it is, trades on the implication that I am trying to avoid the consequences of my choices and actions, to have the best of both worlds. I face a particular choice. One option carries dangers but also benefits. I take that option, swayed by those benefits, but when the dangers eventuate, I want to be rescued from them. But while again this captures those who intend to end the matter but then seek repayment when it's revealed the money wasn't due, it hardly captures those who never intended to part with their money in any event, intending to pay only such money as is due. True, those who pay knowing the money may not be due may forego opportunities to establish whether that money is due before making their payment. This decision may or may not be reasonable. Yet even where I would have done better seeking clarification as to my liability before paying up, my subsequent wish to have the money repaid is not an attempt to shake off the consequences of my actions, unless we take my choice not to dispute your claim to the money before payment as a choice to put it beyond dispute. But that's not my choice. My intention was, all along, to keep my options open. Of course, the effect of the common law rule is to take away this option once I pay. As such, *knowing the rule*, my choice to pay becomes a choice to pay come what may, and I thereby take the risk of the money being irrecoverable, even if it is later shown not to have been due. But the rule can't be called in aid of its own justification.

Absent some concern which justifies overriding the claimant's intentions, we have no reason to deny restitution to those who pay when doubting whether they are truly liable to pay, so long as their intention, at the point of payment, is that the defendant should get to keep the money only if it is indeed due. Paying when unsure of one's liability to make the payment is not tantamount to intending that the recipient should have the money come what may. Nor is it, in any meaningful sense, to 'take the risk' of the money not being due, unless we have already concluded that any payment, once made, is final.[29] A rule, such as the common law's, which treats all such payments as

[29] See too *Sebel Products Ltd v Customs and Excise Commissioners* [1949] Ch 409 (Ch). The claimant disputed a tax demand, but paid up, with its action challenging the validity of that demand pending. When the tax demand was declared invalid, the claimant was allowed to recover the money on the basis it had no intention that the defendant should keep the money even if it turned out not to be due and, since the defendant knew that the claimant had paid on that basis, an agreement to repay the money could be implied. The finding of a contract, compelled by the general rule denying recovery, has been criticized. But the result is correct and the analysis of the payer's intentions sound.

'voluntary' and final, whether or not the payment was made to bring the matter to an end, is not one which respects and reflects a claimant's intentions when making the payment and can be supported, if at all, by a concern to see such disputes resolved.

VII Misprediction

Unjust enrichment lawyers distinguish mistakes, where an agent errs on some matter of past or existing fact, from 'mispredictions', where his failure is in misjudging or not anticipating some future contingency. The courts, taking their lead from the textbooks, have embraced this distinction, and this terminology, denying restitution for mere mispredictions.[30] Here too we find analysis of linguistic convention passed off as normative argument. It hardly matters whether it is or is not a misuse of language to describe those who mispredict future events as mistaken. We may, on occasion, be faced with some statutory provision making reference to 'mistakes' and so need to consider what this might be taken to cover. But, in general, time spent addressing this question is time wasted.

The general denial of recovery in cases of misprediction is sometimes supported on the basis that incorrect information can vitiate a claimant's intention when making a transfer only if it is incorrect at the point of transfer.[31] Since the falsity of a misprediction comes only later, it involves no defect or impairment in the decision the claimant made at the time. Once we see, as we now have seen, that recovery for mistakes is not itself grounded in any vitiation of the claimant's intentions, this argument falls away. The case for allowing me to recover when I pay you by mistake is not that my intentions were vitiated, but that they were conditional. What is defective is not my intention that (say) you should have such money as you are due, but rather my understanding of the facts. This defect is relevant so far as it tells the story of how I came to make the payment notwithstanding the failure of this condition. But what matters is not how the asset got there, but that I had and have no intention of you getting to keep it in the

[30] *Dextra Bank & Trust Co Ltd v Bank of Jamaica* (n 17).

[31] See eg Birks (n 5) 147; Weeliem Seah, 'Mispredictions, Mistakes and the Law of Unjust Enrichment' [2007] *Restitution Law Review* 93, 103–04.

circumstances which now obtain. Allowing me to recover that money then recognizes and upholds the conditional nature of my intentions.

The conditions attached to transfers may describe existing or future contingencies. So I may pay you intending thereby to discharge a debt I believe I have already accrued or I may pay you intending that payment to meet a liability I expect to accrue to you. In both cases, I pay with the intention that the money should be yours to keep only if this is, or becomes, money you are due. In both cases, my intentions are respected if I can recover in the event that this condition is not met. The structure of intentions and of the ways plans of actions can be subject to conditions gives no support to any difference of approach between mistakes and mispredictions.

An alternative approach is say that restitution for mispredictions is denied because the claimant is a risk-taker. Since future contingencies cannot, by their very nature, be established at the date of transfer, the claimant necessarily makes the transfer uncertain as to whether that contingency will obtain. By proceeding to make the transfer regardless—rather than, say, sitting and waiting to see what will happen—he takes and accepts the risk that it will not.[32] As before, the idea of risk-taking is bandied around with little care taken to explain quite what risk is being run or what reason this then gives to deny recovery. When I pay you on the assumption and basis that some event will come to pass, one could, perhaps, say I take the risk that things might not turn out as anticipated. So what? The intended implication, it seems, is that by choosing to part with my money before the event, I take the risk not only that the relevant contingency won't obtain, but also that I will then be unable to recover the money I paid. But this begs the question. If I didn't intend to part with the money out and out, intending you to keep it any event, this isn't a risk I have run—let alone accepted—unless the law makes it a consequence of my payment that I won't be able to recover the sum if the relevant condition isn't then met. Whether the law has good reason to preclude me from recovering the money in these circumstances is the very question we are looking to answer.

Indeed, the same accounts which hold that the future's inherent uncertainty makes me a risk-taker where I pay you on the basis that some event will come to pass then go on to say that I avoid the charge of risk-taking, and so *can* recover, just so long as I tell you about this

[32] Birks, ibid 147.

condition when I make the transfer. If that condition does indeed fail, I can recover by virtue of there having been a 'failure of basis' or 'failure of consideration'.[33] But simply communicating this to you will often make it no more likely that the relevant condition will be satisfied. If the risk I run is the risk that the future will not turn out as anticipated, I don't avoid that risk by letting you know that this is what I anticipate. Of course, by my telling you this, you know from the word go that my intention is that you get to keep the asset only if this condition is met, and so you know I'm going to want the asset back if it isn't. One risk I do reduce then is the risk of you disposing of the asset in the meantime or resisting my claim to recovery on the basis that it would be unjust to have it taken from you. But, once more, these are the sorts of concerns addressed by the change of position defence. The bare possibility that you might not be in a position to make restitution isn't enough to support a bar on all such claims. (Compare this to the case of mistakes, where my transfer is likewise conditional, but no suggestion is made that you must know of this condition for me to recover.)[34]

Where I do inform you of the condition to which the transfer is subject, my intention in making the transfers is said to be qualified. So it is. But the qualification comes not by my telling you this, but by the presence of this condition in my chosen plan of action. My intentions don't change by voicing them. What I intend is the same whether or not I tell you, and in so far as our concern is to give effect to my intentions, we have no reason to make recovery depend on your awareness of that condition. However, in keeping with the arguments made in the context of mistakes, recovery in the event of mispredictions can reasonably be limited to those cases where the claimant intends the defendant to keep the payment only if a certain condition is met. So, on this basis, it shouldn't be enough that some or other event comes to pass which enables me to say: 'Had I known *this* would happen, I wouldn't have made the transfer.' That I am in financial difficulties now is no reason to allow me to claw back all the gifts I've made over the years, even if it really is true that I wouldn't have indulged in such acts of generosity had I known I'd need the funds later on. Instead

[33] Ibid 147–48.

[34] That the basis of a particular transfer or enrichment is shared is, however, relevant in so far as these claims are concerned not with undoing unauthorized transfers and enrichments, but with setting a price for requested services or otherwise filling gaps in incomplete agreements: see further 4.VIII, 6.III, 6.IV.

we should be looking for cases where my intentions, explicitly or by implication, really are that you should get to keep the payment or the asset I transferred only if some state of affairs continues or comes about. This may be clearest where I make this clear to you at the point of transfer but is not limited to those cases.

Here too then, it is doubtful that risk-taking identifies any valid concern that can be invoked to deny restitution to those who can truly say that their intention was that the defendant should not have the relevant asset in *these* circumstances. Perhaps there should be further limitations on recovery in cases of misprediction. If so, they will need not merely to be grounded in considerations other than respect for the claimant's intentions, but sufficiently strong to override that consideration. So it may be thought to be for the better that gifts are not made with strings attached, or that such strings should at least be made known to the recipient. It may be that the good of gift-giving is compromised by enabling donors to exercise this sort of on-going control over their donees' freedom to use and enjoy what they've been given, or that the difficulty or inconvenience of unwinding such dispositions years later gives us reason to leave them undisturbed. Or say a couple buy a house together but split up a few years later. The house is in their joint names but one says that his intention when contributing the greater part of the purchase price was only ever to fund a shared home, that he never intended the other to have the benefit of his contribution unless they were living there together happily. Nonetheless, it may sometimes be reasonable to limit his claim to some lesser share to ensure a division of assets that allows each of the parties to rebuild their lives apart.

VIII Coercion

Coercion is often lined up next to mistake as a factor that vitiates a claimant's intention when making the transfer. We have seen already that the idea of vitiation fails to capture what it is about mistaken transfers that supports their reversal. It fares little better when we look at coerced transfers, though this time for different reasons. In cases of mistake, the claimant's allegation is that his intention to confer this enrichment on this defendant was conditional on the relevant state of affairs existing, and so recovery of that enrichment upholds the intention on which he acted when making the transfer. If enrichments conferred as a result of coercion are also, in an applicable sense, non-consensual, they seem to be non-consensual in a different way. For here there is, on the face of it, no condition that goes unsatisfied, no sense in which the claimant can say that he intended something different. You threaten my life unless I give you the money in my wallet. I hand it over, you take it and run, my life is spared. My handing over of the money was intended as my chosen means to my chosen end of saving my life, the end indeed secured by my actions. As the means to this end, we shouldn't say that my intention to hand you the money is vitiated—whatever this means—unless we are also to say, implausibly, that my intention to save my life is likewise vitiated.

Perhaps I can still say that I didn't intend the money to be yours.[35] I intend to hand you the money, but the intent to pass title involves more than this: an intention not simply that you take possession of the money (sometimes not even this), but an intention that the money should then be at your free disposal, yours to keep and use as you like. Do I intend this too? Why would I? My aim is to avoid the harm; I do this by handing over the money. I need have no intention regarding the money beyond this. In so far as I do, what reason do I have for intending you to keep the money, rather than, say, intending to take whatever steps I can to recover it once the threat is averted? My lack of any intention to pass title is wholly compatible with my awareness that I am unlikely ever again to get my hands on the money. I can intend what I know to be all but impossible, fail to intend what I know to be inevitable. The suggestion that I *surely* intend the necessary (let alone likely) consequences of my actions—and so that I *surely* intend the money to be yours—is a simple, though common, mistake.[36]

[35] Cf *United Australia Ltd v Barclays Bank Ltd* [1941] AC 1 (HL) 29 (Lord Atkin).

[36] We see this mistake, for instance, in the heavy weather criminal lawyers make of the (wholly sound) decision in *R v Steane* [1947] KB 997 (CA). Steane was charged with 'doing acts likely to assist the enemy, with intent to assist the enemy'. The relevant acts were radio broadcasts of German propaganda that Steane claimed he conducted in the face of threats to him and his family. The jury was directed that if his acts did assist the enemy then, unless the duress was so great as to preclude him forming any intent at all, he must have intended this assistance as the natural consequence of these actions. His conviction was quashed on appeal. If, as Steane alleged, his aim was simply to save himself and his family, then though he clearly intended the broadcasts—his chosen means to that end—there was no reason for him to go on to intend that those broadcasts would indeed assist the enemy, and this is true even if he knew for sure that those broadcasts would indeed assist them. (Or, in other words, though he intended his actions under the descriptions 'saving my family' and 'broadcasting these messages', it doesn't follow that he also intended them under the description 'assisting the enemy', even if it were true that by broadcasting these messages he knew he was also assisting the enemy.)

This is enough to ground a claim to restitution. Those that suggest that coercion 'vitiates' intention have a different idea in mind however. For the common view is that your threats mean that, even so far as my intentions *do* extend, my (intended) actions are not (fully) voluntary and so my transfer is not *truly* consensual. If so, my claim to recovery needn't turn on the difference between my intending you have the money and my intending that you keep it, but can be grounded in my lack of consent that you have the money *at all*. Quite what this means, however, is hard to pin down. Your threat to my life curtails my reasonable options, my continued existence essential to any plans, any interests I have. So my decision to hand over the money does not so much advance my interests as ensure that I retain interests to advance. But the same is true if my life is threatened by illness and I must spend that money to be cured. While the stakes, and the motivational pressure, are the same in both cases, my choice to spend my money on the cure shouldn't be considered anything other than truly voluntary. (Or, if this doesn't seem clear enough, imagine I have the cure to hand already. When I take it, do I do so in any sense involuntarily or non-consensually?) So the fact that I have just one viable option is not enough to call into question my consent to that option. What then is different where the danger comes from your threat? One difference is that when you threaten me, you wrong me, and so the curtailing of my options comes not from simple bad luck but by you setting yourself against my interests. This gives reason enough to grant me restitution, reason enough to view your retention of that gain as unjust. But the reasons given by your wrongdoing are not reasons for taking my transfer to be less than fully consensual (though it may still be) and apply only where I seek restitution from you or your confederate.

No doubt we have good reason to treat choices made under pressure differently to those that are not. Pressure can limit one's options. An option that would ordinarily be unreasonable may become reasonable when deprived of alternatives. Pressure can also limit one's opportunity to weigh up one's options and one's capacity to pick well between them. Getting it wrong is made more likely the less time one has to make a decision and the more unexpected the choice. It is, at least in the main, for these reasons that coercion—and sometimes other sources of severe pressure—can justify or excuse choices and acts that are, or would otherwise be, wrongful. So the choice, say, to steal is more reasonable when the alternative is (through coercion or necessity) death than it is when the alternative is paying, or simply making do without the object of one's cravings, the choice to do wrong more understandable when made in the face of immediate and unexpected danger. In these instances, coercion makes a difference by virtue of its impact upon our reasons for action: the reasons we have and the reasons on which we in fact act. But the question for the law of unjust enrichment is not whether the claimant acted reasonably but whether his choice to make that transfer, reasonable or not, should be recognized as effective to dispose of that asset and his title to it. The issue here then is not so much whether we can endorse or understand the claimant's choices as whether we should treat them as *his* choices, giving them the same respect and effect as we give his choices generally.

The idea that choices can be more or less voluntary and so, in this sense, more or less *chosen* is nonetheless one in common currency. The appeal of this idea might be best seen by an analogy. If you grab my hand and physically manipulate me into signing my goods away, I give no consent to any such disposition. This is true whether the named disponee is you or someone else. When you put a gun to my head and tell me to sign or you'll shoot, you invade my autonomy and overtake my interests in much the same way. My actions are chosen by you, directed towards interests that are yours rather than mine. Should the effectiveness of my disposition turn on your decision to manipulate me one way rather than another? If the analogy holds, we have reason here too to treat my apparent disposition as no true or effective disposition.

To this we might add that the principal good that comes from a system of private property is the good of the increased options opened up to individuals and groups by according them this sort of access to and control over resources, providing them additional means they can apply in the pursuit of their projects and interests. The point of giving effect to an owner's intended dispositions is precisely to support him in this pursuit. However, where a disposition is the result of coercion, the owner's interests are advanced only in the avoidance of a threatened setback to those interests, and not by misjudgment or ill fortune, but another's design. Indeed we might say that the system of private property opens up this particular opportunity for extortion, that according individuals these powers also exposes them to their being exploited in this way. As such, the reasons for adopting a system of private property and for supporting the intended dispositions of individual owners within such a system are also reasons for refusing to endorse dispositions secured through coercion, dispositions which are, by virtue of their impulsion, set against the goods private property exists to promote.

More broadly, a system of private property, like a system of contract, will assist us as private individuals and groups in the pursuit of our various projects only if we in fact exercise these powers wisely. If we don't, the options contract and property give us will turn out simply to provide additional means of self-defeat and self-harm. So we would do well to deny ourselves the power to contract if, in the main, we couldn't be relied upon to make choices in our own interests, binding ourselves to arrangements that do us more harm than good. Similarly, even if we get more of these decisions right than wrong, and so even if the powers accorded by property and contract do in fact end up serving our interests, we would still have reason to curtail those powers where there is a likelihood of their being used self-destructively. It is this concern which grounds rules of incapacity; so too the imposition of cooling-off periods in relation to certain types of dealing. In these cases, the reason for treating the transaction as ineffective, or at least revocable, is not that it isn't truly intended—typically it will be—but the significant danger that, though intended, it will not in fact serve the agent's interests.

We might then see a parallel between these rules and those allowing parties to avoid contracts and transfers made under duress. Here too the transaction is (we may, for now, assume) intended but, again, we have reason to think that this is unlikely to be in my interests, save in the narrow sense that my immediate interests were better served by acceding to the demand than by resisting. And, again, this reason for treating my disposition as ineffective and for allowing me to recover applies whether the beneficiary is you, who issued the threat, or some unwitting third party.

6

Basis

I Obligatory Transfers

It is a good answer to a claim in unjust enrichment that the relevant asset or enrichment was conferred in performance of a valid legal obligation.[1] I contract to buy a painting from you. I believe the painting to be a Manet and I contract and pay in this belief. It turns out to have been painted by someone else. If this doesn't invalidate the contract, I cannot recover the money from you by showing that I paid on the mistaken assumption that I was getting a Manet in return. Sometimes this point is made by saying that the law of unjust enrichment is subsidiary to the law of contract.[2] Presumably the same goes for all those other bodies of law from which obligations to transfer assets may arise. But without some account of why unjust enrichment should be subsidiary to all these various categories and ideas, subsidiarity doesn't explain why claims in unjust enrichment give way in the presence of such obligations but merely restates that they do. One explanation sometimes offered is that the claim in unjust enrichment is denied on the basis of circularity: it is senseless to require a claimant to confer

[1] See too Daniel Friedmann, 'Valid, Voidable, Qualified, and Non-existing Obligations: An Alternative Perspective on the Law of Restitution' in Andrew Burrows (ed), *Essays on the Law of Restitution* (Clarendon Press 1991); Robert Stevens, 'Is There a Law of Unjust Enrichment?' in Simone Degeling and James Edelman (eds), *Unjust Enrichment in Commercial Law* (Thomson Reuters 2008); *Deutsche Morgan Grenfell Group Plc v Inland Revenue Commissioners* [2006] UKHL 49, [2007] 1 AC 558, paras 84–85 (Lord Scott).

[2] Ross Grantham and Charles Rickett, 'On the Subsidiarity of Unjust Enrichment' (2001) 117 *Law Quarterly Review* 273; Steve Hedley, 'Unjust Enrichment: A Middle Course?' (2002) 2 *Oxford University Commonwealth Law Journal* 181, 190.

an enrichment which he could at once claim back; all the more so if, having recovered the gain, he became obligated, once more, to confer it (and so on).[3] But if the problem is merely one of circularity, it could just as well be solved by denying the initial obligation to make the transfer as by denying the transferor a claim in unjust enrichment. At most we might say that a choice needs to be made; the choice to dispense with the claim in unjust enrichment is as good as any other and so, once chosen, we should stick with it.

In truth any other choice would be unreasonable and any claim in unjust enrichment is rightly foreclosed by the determination that that, or some such, transfer was obligatory. By designating an action as obligatory, it is made non-optional. When I have an obligation to transfer a particular asset to you, the option to deal with that asset in some other way is one no longer open to me. So the answer to my complaint that I did not properly authorize and so did not truly choose that transfer is that the law gave me no choice *not* to make that transfer. These obligations are effectively superimposed on my holdings, *pro tanto* limiting my power to deal with my assets as I choose. If I am under an obligation to give you this laptop, I am no longer at liberty to dispose of it elsewhere. If I am under an obligation to pay you £1,000, though this obligation doesn't attach to any specific fund or moneys I presently hold, when the time for payment comes, I must find that sum from the resources at my disposal. If I don't, and you obtain judgment against me, that judgment will be enforced by the sale of my assets. Indeed obligations such as these presuppose some such set of private holdings; my obligation to transfer this laptop or pay this money assumes that I have, or ought to have, such items to dispose of to you.

Providing me with a claim in unjust enrichment would, therefore, controvert the determination that the transfer is indeed obligatory, and would in turn contradict the all-things-considered judgment of principle that supports and is reflected in that determination.[4] Of course, that determination may be unreasonable, and a claim in unjust enrichment provides one means by which it may be challenged. But if that challenge is successful, the proper conclusion is that what was

[3] Andrew Burrows, *Understanding the Law of Obligations: Essays on Contract, Tort and Restitution* (Hart Publishing 1998) 21. Cf Andrew Burrows, *The Law of Restitution* (3rd edn, Oxford University Press 2011) 328–29.

[4] See too Friedmann (n 1) 247–48.

initially designated obligatory is held, on further reflection, not to be obligatory. Unless and until that obligation is set aside in this way, the determination that the claimant is under an obligation to make the transfer pre-empts any possible claim in unjust enrichment, for that obligation denies, or at least qualifies, the very freedom to determine that asset's disposition which unjust enrichment claims seek to vindicate. To put it another way: my title to my assets provides only a presumptive authorization to deal with those assets as I choose, one that may, and in practice will, be subject to various limitations. Some of these will be voluntarily assumed, many others not. Of the latter, some can be seen as constraints which are inherent to the regulation of private property (eg I am limited in my use of my land by my obligation not to interfere unreasonably with my neighbour's use and enjoyment of his land), while others are simply instances of more general prohibitions and obligations (eg I mustn't batter you even with my own cudgel).[5] All these combine to mark out the scope of an owner's all-things-considered authority over the disposition of his assets and, with it, the range of choices and determinations to which the law of unjust enrichment attends and which unjust enrichment claims serve to protect.[6]

The grounds of obligations to transfer assets are, of course, diverse and so there are diverse reasons why an owner may be denied the choice to deal with his assets as he wishes. The reason contractual promises restrict my freedom to deal with the assets I've contracted to give away is different from the reason tax liabilities restrict my freedom to deal with the assets from which those liabilities are to be met. But while different obligations have their different grounds, we don't need to work through these reasons one by one to see why, in every case, the conclusion that the transferor owes such an obligation rules out any possibility of his claiming in unjust enrichment.[7]

[5] See generally J W Harris, *Property and Justice* (Oxford University Press 1996) 32–38.

[6] It is for this reason and in this sense that title can be said to provide the holder with what is merely a baseline or default set of powers and privileges: see 3.V.

[7] It is sometimes said that the rule that there will be no claim in unjust enrichment where the claimant was obligated to confer that enrichment is not absolute (see eg Lionel Smith, 'Demystifying Juristic Reasons' (2007) 45 *Canadian Business Law Journal* 281). But the supposed counter-examples are all instances where the relevant obligation was, in the end, cancelled or denied, or where recovery was grounded in something other than the claimant's lack of true consent to the disposition. See further 6.IV.

II Facts and Grounds

Where a transfer is made in performance of a valid legal obligation, that obligation is sometimes said to provide a justifying ground or legal basis for the transfer. So when I pay you for the painting, the contract provides a basis for the payment such as enables you to resist any claim I may bring in unjust enrichment. This idea can be extended beyond obligatory transfers. Just as my contractual obligation grounds your entitlement to keep the money I pay you under that contract, so we might say that my flawless intention to give you the same sum of money as a gift likewise provides a justifying ground or basis for your receipt and retention of that money. So understood, to say there is a basis for the defendant's enrichment is to say that it is an enrichment he is entitled to retain, while to say that there was no basis for a given transfer or enrichment is to identify it as one which, at least presumptively, calls for reversal.

All of this is unobjectionable so far as it goes. Asking whether there was a ground or basis for the defendant's enrichment is then just another way of asking whether his enrichment is an *unjust* enrichment, one that he must give up. The question is the same whichever way we ask it. Nonetheless, it is often thought that the difference here is not simply one of expression but one of substance, and that an inquiry into the basis for the transfer relieves us from any need to inquire into positive reasons for restitution, or at least from any inquiry into the sorts of 'unjust factors' (mistake, coercion, failed conditions, etc) which are conventionally treated as necessary conditions for unjust enrichment liability. Neither is true. Take any standard case of unjust enrichment. Some asset is now in your hands that was previously in mine. I can't get it back without the law's intervention. Should it intervene? Only if there is good reason to do so. One might choose to frame this inquiry in terms of whether there is a basis for the transfer, asking whether the initial transfer was (in this way) legally effective rather than what might ground its reversal. But, however my claim is presented and whatever formulae are adopted for its resolution, the question the court must answer is whether it should grant me restitution, and that question cannot be answered—or can't be answered well—without some consideration of what good reasons for restitution there are.

Now the consideration courts in practice give to reasons for restitution may be largely superficial and unreflective. Far more often than not, the court won't be invited and won't be required to conduct any inquiry into unjust enrichment's first principles. Instead cases are argued and decided on the (typically unspoken) premiss that they should be resolved, so far as possible, in accordance with the rules and rulings set down in the authorities. Where the law is settled, a judge will then have little to do but establish the facts and apply that settled law to them. So if I bring a claim alleging that I paid you money I mistakenly believed you were due, the judge charged with deciding our case won't need to consider what goods and values may be served by ordering restitution. The law, on this point at least, is clear: if the facts are as I allege, I recover. And, while the reasonableness of a given ruling and so of holding that a given gain ought, or ought not, be given up is never solely a function of its compatibility with past official rulings and statements, it is often reasonable for courts to proceed in this way, deferring to the standards expressed and applied by other officials.[8]

Often then, courts need do no more than ascertain what has happened and fit those facts within some established formula for recovery. These formulae will commonly make no direct appeal to the basic reasons that support recovery. Indeed they work best where they don't. The law's success at solving practical problems is dependent on the clarity and determinacy of its directives. Of course, we want the law to be not only clear but sound, and so the law falls to be measured not simply—indeed not primarily—by its clarity but by its reasonableness, by the fairness and justness of the answers it gives. Sometimes sound direction and decision-making require a sensitivity to the varied factual conditions in which such decisions have to be made which cannot be accommodated within any fully determinate general rule formulated *ex ante*. Nonetheless, all else equal, the law does its job better where it states clearly what it requires of us and when. It is better then that the law directs me that I can't drive down this road at more than 30 mph or that road at more than 40 mph, than were it simply to tell me not to drive too fast or at such speed as would pose an unreasonable risk to those in my vicinity. The same is true of the law of unjust enrichment. Its principal addressees are officials charged with resolving these claims and they are better served by rules that specify the circumstances in which such gains are to be given up than by, say,

[8] 1.VI.

the bare instruction to order restitution wherever it would be unjust for the defendant to retain his enrichment.

This job is done, in large part, by the unjust factors. These are not themselves reasons for restitution, but instead statements of the factual conditions in which unjust enrichment claims will lie. So identifying mistake as an unjust factor tells us nothing about what good reasons there are for granting restitution in cases of mistaken transfers. But what it does tell us is that, where the transfer is prompted by some qualifying mistake, recovery presumptively follows. This leaves various questions unanswered. Having identified mistake as an unjust factor, we still need to know whether any mistake will do, what sort of connection must exist between the mistake and the transfer, in what circumstances the recipient may be able to resist the claim notwithstanding the mistake, and so on. All these questions can be answered only by further consideration of the reasons which support and otherwise bear on these claims. At other times, it may be that we cannot establish whether a given unjust factor is present without some such evaluation. Not every case of pressure is a case of duress, and what distinguishes duress from other examples of pressured transfers seems to be, at least in part, the unreasonableness of the coercer's actions. So, unlike mistake, what constitutes duress isn't a pure question of fact. Nonetheless, here too the identification of unjust factors contributes to the translation of general reasons for restitution into concrete practical determinations, assisting in the specification of the circumstances in which transfers will, or ought to, be reversed.

The law of unjust enrichment imposes liability on defendants for certain gains they have derived from their claimants. Wherever there is a law of unjust enrichment, there is a body of law that addresses the question of which of these gains are to be given up. We can approach this question, if we choose, by employing the notion of a justifying basis. This may indeed bring into sharper relief certain factors bearing on the reasonableness of these claims. So by framing the inquiry in this way we may well be more likely to be attentive to the fact that no claim should lie where the transfer was obligatory. But in the end we will always be led back to the factual circumstances against which such claims are set and in which such liability is to be imposed. So too we can choose not to call mistake and duress 'unjust factors' and, more broadly, we may make little effort to classify or systematize the factual conditions in which unjust enrichment claims arise. But however we frame this body of claims and the practical questions they raise, we will be able to describe the factual circumstances in which such claims lie and some such account of those circumstances will remain essential for anyone wanting to know what the law is.

So one may choose to say that when I pay you in the mistaken belief I owe you this money, this mistake defeats the proposed basis of my payment, which in turn is what triggers your liability. But this doesn't mean the mistake ceases to be a factual condition of my claim, nor that I am thereby spared having to plead and prove these facts if my claim is to succeed. And so, even if we start off by asking whether there was a basis for the claimant's transfer, we will in no time need to ask what facts provide or defeat such a basis. There is then no opposition between an inquiry into the basis of the transfer and one that looks to the presence of particular factual conditions in which liability will arise. Accordingly, there is no true alternative to an inquiry into such unjust factors. An unjust factor is simply a description of (some salient aspect of) the factual setting in which the transfer was made and which, by virtue of a relevant reason for restitution, supports a claim to its reversal. Since every unjust enrichment claim will arise out of some or other combination of facts, every real or imaginable instance of unjust enrichment liability is explicable through the notion of unjust factors.

A transfer without basis, without more, describes neither a set of facts on which unjust enrichment liability will arise nor a reason or principle which justifies the imposition of such liability. The statement that there is no basis for a particular transfer identifies that transfer as one which the law takes to be in some way ineffective. But it says nothing about the reasons for this ineffectiveness, nor the circumstances in which this conclusion does or ought to obtain. Instead 'absence of basis' inhabits a middle ground between the real-world facts from which unjust enrichment claims arise, the rules by which those facts are identified as supporting these claims, and the reasons or principles which justify those rules and hence the recognition of such claims on such facts. Because of this, an inquiry into whether there is a basis for the transfer is no alternative to, and no substitute for, an inquiry into either the facts upon which unjust enrichment claims will arise or the reasons that ground them. And so, even if we choose to conceive of these claims through the frame of transfers without basis, we will still need to ask when and why unjust enrichment liability arises. The answer to the 'when?' question will, in the end, be a set of various fact combinations (or, as we may call them, unjust factors).

The answer to the 'why?' question will be a set of reasons or principles. These questions are best addressed and answered directly, not by interposing the further question of whether there exists a basis for the transfer between them.[9] And, even if we do, the answers we give them should be no different.

So why is it so often thought that an inquiry into basis provides a true alternative to examination of unjust factors and for the positive grounds for restitution they identify? The thinking is this: take a case where I pay you believing I am obligated to do so. The basis of my payment is, we might then say, the validity of that obligation. If that obligation is cancelled or turns out not to exist, the basis of my payment fails and, if the basis of my payment has failed, your liability to make restitution arises automatically. By contrast, if liability requires the identification of an unjust factor, there's a further question to ask. The invalidity of the obligation means that it sets no bar to my recovery, but we still need to go on to ask if there is positive reason to require you to repay.[10] Of course, on both approaches, liability follows if certain factual conditions are met and so, either way, we can set out what these factual conditions are, and an account of these conditions will be needed if we are to know when these claims are to succeed. The difference is simply that, on the former approach, the conditions of invalidity are also the conditions of unjust enrichment liability.

The real question then is whether the factors that result in the avoidance or cancellation of a purported obligation should in all cases be regarded as unjust factors for the purposes of the law of unjust enrichment. This would in turn be true if the reasons for ordering restitution in such cases are continuous with the reasons for avoiding or denying the obligation to make the transfer. If they are, an inquiry into the transfer's basis does indeed relieve us of any need to inquire further into grounds of restitution. But this will only be because the inquiry into basis fully addresses these grounds. Either the considerations relevant to the question of whether restitution should be ordered are already factored in to the determination of whether there is a basis for the transfer or they are not. If they are, then to ask whether there is such a basis is to ask, inter alia, whether it is reasonable to require the defendant to make restitution of his gain. If they're not, taking restitution to follow

[9] See too Peter Birks, 'No Consideration: Restitution after Void Contracts' (1993) 23 *University of Western Australia Law Review* 195, 232–33.

[10] See eg Peter Birks, *Unjust Enrichment* (2nd edn, Clarendon Press 2005) 114–15.

automatically from the finding that there is no basis for the transfer is a mistake, since we thereby exclude from consideration some reasons that properly bear on the availability of such claims.

The latter appears the more likely. That it is reasonable to deny any obligation on the claimant to make the transfer doesn't mean that it is reasonable to assist him in recovering gains conferred on the basis that such an obligation existed. If the law wishes to discourage a particular kind of activity, it may sensibly decline to offer any assistance to those who engage in it.[11] Hence the law won't recognize any obligation on me to pay the hitman I've hired. Nor, however, should it assist me in recovering the money I paid over to him if he doesn't do the job. As such, there may be occasions where treating the voidness of that obligation as itself sufficient to trigger unjust enrichment liability operates unreasonably. Enrichments conferred in performance of a valid legal obligation cannot be recovered. But it doesn't follow that enrichments conferred performing void or cancelled obligation are recoverable. Valid obligations provide a bar to recovery. But the absence of a bar is not itself a reason for restitution, nor need it always be accompanied by such a reason.[12]

III Contract, Breach, and Termination

In the context of contractual obligations, the denial of unjust enrichment claims is often explained on the basis that the law of unjust enrichment should not be allowed to subvert the allocations of risk provided for in the contract. This way of putting it is somewhat misleading. The risk of the painting not being a Manet in our initial example is not one that we sought to allocate, since it's not a risk which either of us considered. The idea that it was a Manet never crossed your mind; the idea that it wasn't never crossed mine. We simply contracted in respect of the painting in front of us and you are obligated to transfer it, I to pay, whoever painted it. Of course, the effect of that contract is to require me to pay either way, so we can say that the contract means I bear the risk of it not being a Manet. But

[11] See eg *Berg v Sadler and Moore* [1937] 2 KB 158 (CA).

[12] See too Kit Barker, 'Responsibility for Gain: Unjust Factors or Absence of Legal Ground? Starting Points in Unjust Enrichment Law' in Charles Rickett and Ross Grantham (eds), *Structure and Justification in Private Law* (Hart Publishing 2008) 57–60; *Atlantic Coast Line Railroad Co v Florida* (1935) 295 US 301, 309–10 (Cardozo J). Cf Stevens (n 1) 33.

then saying the contract allocates this risk is no more than a roundabout way of saying my obligation to pay isn't dependent on the painting being a Manet, and the proposition that unjust enrichment mustn't upset the contractual risk allocation just another way of stating that no such claim will lie where the payment is obligatory. Risk allocation is here a consequence of contractual obligation, not its basis.

The risk allocation account may also appear at odds with the clear refusal to allow claimants to sue in unjust enrichment whenever the defendant fails to perform in full. We contract that you will do some building work for me. I pay, but the work you do is defective. I can sue you for damages for breach but, without more, have no right to demand repayment of the money I paid. Yet it seems I can say that I paid you only on the basis that you would do what you promised, and so my consent was conditional on obtaining your full performance. Moreover, if we ask whether the risk of your non-performance is allocated by the contract, the clear answer seems to be that it is and that it is allocated to you. (It's you who has to do the work and who has to cover my losses if you don't.) How then does allowing me to recover the money upset the contract's risk allocation? Once more we get a clearer answer by attending to our respective contractual undertakings and obligations. Though the risk of your non-performance isn't mine to bear in that it is your obligation to perform and I can obtain damages if you don't, your (full) performance is not a condition of the validity of my own obligation to perform. Or to put it another way: your breach does not, without more, entitle me not to perform, nor does it, again without more, undermine the validity of our contract as a whole. So the money I have paid you remains money paid in performance of an obligation that was and remains valid.

The thought that the real concern here is with not upsetting the contract's risk allocation is sometimes thought to suggest that there should be no blanket rule precluding unjust enrichment liability in respect of obligatory payments and transfers. For if our concern is with the contract's allocation of risk, then the objection to claims in unjust enrichment extends only so far as such claims would indeed upset this allocation. Where they wouldn't, there should be no bar.[13] And indeed

[13] See eg Burrows, *The Law of Restitution* (n 3) 327–30; Charles Mitchell, Paul Mitchell, and Stephen Watterson (eds), *Goff and Jones: The Law of Unjust Enrichment* (8th edn, Sweet and Maxwell 2011) [3-16]–[3-22]. Cf Jack Beatson, 'Restitution and Contract: Non-Cumul?' (2000) 1 *Theoretical Inquiries in Law* 83.

it is sometimes said that the cases do reveal examples of the law unjust enrichment reversing transfers made in performance of valid contractual obligations. This is, I think, a misunderstanding, though one which is unsurprising given the confusion in the orthodox analysis of these cases.

The orthodox understanding goes like this. There can be no claim in unjust enrichment for the recovery of payments and other transfers made under a contract so long as that contract remains on foot. This poses no obstacle if an apparent contract turns out to be void, nor if a contract that is voidable is then avoided. However, the mere fact that one party breaches the contract doesn't cause that contract, and hence the parties' obligations, to fail. Accordingly, the rule that there is no unjust enrichment liability within a subsisting contract means that a claimant who doesn't receive the performance he was due under the contract is not entitled, without more, to restitution of his own performance and must make do instead with a claim for specific performance or damages. However, the position changes where the defendant's breach is such as to give the claimant the option to terminate the contract. If he then exercises the option, the contract falls away and the way is cleared for each party to seek restitution of the benefits they have thus far conferred under the contract. Hence, though the case law is not without complication, we find that, once a contract has been terminated for breach, the courts have allowed parties to recover money paid and other benefits provided under the contract to date.[14] The same goes if the contract is discharged other than through breach, for instance as a result of frustration.[15]

One difficulty with this account is in seeing why termination makes a difference to the possibility of claiming in unjust enrichment. The courts have made clear that termination operates prospectively and not retrospectively.[16] The parties do not have to go on performing but all rights and obligations accruing prior to termination are unaffected. This rule is one that unjust enrichment lawyers have not sought to challenge. But if this is right, it appears that termination does nothing to change the positions of the parties in respect of the benefits already conferred under the contract. These benefits were conferred in performance of an obligation which was valid at the time and which

[14] See eg *Rowland v Divall* [1923] 2 KB 500 (CA); *Dies v British and International Mining and Finance Corporation* [1939] 1 KB 725 (KB).

[15] See eg *Fibrosa Spolka Akcynja v Fairbairn Lawson Combe Barbour* [1943] AC 32 (HL).

[16] *Johnson v Agnew* [1980] AC 367 (HL) 392–3; *Hurst v Bryk* [2002] 1 AC 185 (HL) 193–94.

remains valid now. And so, just as the validity of those obligations precluded any claim in unjust enrichment before termination, their continuing validity should likewise preclude any such claims after termination. Indeed there are cases which do and say just this.[17]

This account reveals a basic confusion. Unjust enrichment claims are denied unless the contract is first terminated, yet termination leaves untouched the obligations under which the relevant benefits were conferred. If those obligations barred restitution before termination, they should bar restitution after termination too. The rule that termination releases the parties only from obligations that have not yet accrued was not always so well settled.[18] At one time, termination was taken to work like rescission, wiping out the contract in its entirety and not simply for the future.[19] So understood, there's no difficulty in seeing how termination of a contract opens up the possibility of recovery of gains conferred in its performance. Perhaps the rule allowing for restitution upon termination is simply a relic of this time, a hangover from a way of thinking elsewhere rejected. The reason the courts went on to reject this understanding of termination was to ensure that, by terminating, the claimant wasn't thereby deprived of his claim on the contract. If termination operated to rescind the contract *ab initio*, the claimant's only option would be to seek restitution and reimbursement for his performance to date. But in moving to ensure the contract was kept open for the recovery of damages, they appeared not to recognize that they were thereby undermining the basis for claiming in unjust enrichment.

Might it be possible to say that the availability of these claims shows that, whatever the courts may say, termination *does* operate retrospectively? We could instead think of the power to terminate as giving a claimant not simply a choice between continuing with performance as before and prospective release, but also, as a further alternative, the option of rescinding the contract *ab initio*, so opening up the possibility of recovering money paid and assets transferred in performance. So the claimant would then have three options, not two: carry on regardless, put a stop to performance from this point on and sue for

[17] *Bank of Boston Connecticut v European Grain and Shipping Ltd (The Dominique)* [1989] AC 1056 (HL). Cf *Chandler v Webster* [1904] 1 KB 493 (CA).

[18] *Henty v Schröder* (1879) 12 Ch D 666 (Ch); *Horsler v Zorro* [1975] Ch 302 (Ch).

[19] See eg *Giles v Edwards* (1797) 7 Term Rep 181; *Hunt v Silk* (1804) 5 East 449. Cf *Boston Deep Fishing and Ice Company v Ansell* (1888) 39 Ch D 339 (CA) 365 (Bowen LJ).

existing breaches, or go back to the positions the parties were in at the outset. But though this then accommodates some features of the case law, it misses others. For one thing, this would rule out any possibility of the defendant seeking restitution of payments he has made under the contract so long as the claimant seeks to keep the contract sufficiently open to sue for damages for breach.[20] It would also mean that a claimant wanting restitution would have to give up the benefit of arbitration clauses within the contract,[21] and could, more generally, use the third option of rescission to avoid any liabilities of his own under the contract.[22]

There will be occasions where restitutionary recovery doesn't contradict the idea that termination operates only prospectively. The origins of the law on termination lie in cases where a defendant's performance was a condition of the claimant coming under an obligation to perform.[23] So we may structure our contract such that you come under an obligation to deliver the painting only once I pay you. Your obligation to hand the painting over is then dependent or conditional on my payment. If I fail to pay, this condition is not met and you are not required to perform. Here then, my breach operates not to kill off your obligation so much as to ensure that it doesn't come to life. It follows that if you give me the painting without receiving payment, you are not acting in performance of any present obligation and hence, though the contract remains live, you should be entitled to recover the painting or its value in unjust enrichment. But this sort of case is exceptional. Far more often restitution will be sought of payments and transfers that were indeed due at the time under the contract. So if I pay up front, as agreed, and you then fail to deliver the painting, I can ordinarily recover the money on the basis that there's been a total failure of consideration. Yet my obligation to pay wasn't conditional on you delivering the painting. On the contrary, I first had to pay for your obligation to accrue.

Nonetheless, it is sometimes suggested that the same line of argument can be extended to these cases too. Though my obligation to

[20] Cf *Dies* (n 14); *Rover International Ltd v Cannon Film Sales Ltd (No 3)* [1989] 1 WLR 912 (CA).

[21] Cf *Heyman v Darwins Ltd* [1942] AC 356 (HL).

[22] Cf *Hurst v Bryk* (n 16).

[23] See Tariq A Baloch, *Unjust Enrichment and Contract* (Hart Publishing 2009) 97–111; *Hurst v Bryk* (n 16) 193 (Lord Millett).

pay isn't conditional on your performance in the sense that you don't need first to perform for my obligation to arise, it is said that it may nonetheless be conditional in the further sense that, unless you do then perform, your right to the money falls away.[24] Accordingly, my payment was obligatory at the time, but your breach removes any right you have to retain it and I can turn to the law of unjust enrichment for its recovery. This looks like a retrospective cancellation of my obligation, but this is not brought about by my termination of the contract, but follows simply from your breach without more.[25] My decision to terminate goes only to the further question of whether we need to go on performing, thus preserving the idea that termination operates only prospectively. And if this is true, termination should not be seen as a condition of my claim to recover the money I've paid. Indeed, it follows that there may be times when I am entitled restitution where your breach accords me no power to terminate or where I haven't exercised that power. Moreover, my obligation—and hence your right to retain the benefit of its performance—may be conditional on events other than your performance, and so there may be circumstances in which I am entitled to restitution in the absence of any breach. More generally, there is then no objection to unjust enrichment liability within a subsisting contract so long as the obligation under which the benefit was conferred has been set aside.

IV Agreements, Undertakings, and Gaps

This approach avoids some of the more glaring failings of the orthodox account and does a better job of accommodating features of the case law that are simply missed or rendered anomalous by that account. But it also gives us reason to doubt whether these claims have much to do with unjust enrichment at all. Indeed, whether we endorse this approach or the orthodox textbook account of termination, we may question whether any appeal to unjust enrichment is needed to make sense of the law here. The power to terminate the contract following

[24] J Beatson, *The Use and Abuse of Unjust Enrichment: Essays on the Law of Restitution* (Clarendon Press 1991) 46–61, 75–77; Stevens (n 1) 24–30; Baloch (n 23) 107–08, 157–64. Cf *McDonald v Dennys Lascelles Ltd* (1933) 48 CLR 457, 477 (Dixon J); *Fibrosa* (n 15) 65 (Lord Wright).

[25] See too Beatson, ibid 53–54.

breach will itself be rooted in the express or implied terms of that contract.[26] If it is the contract that grounds the power to terminate, so the contract should be the first stop when looking to account for the consequences of exercising that power. Indeed, one might go further and propose not only that the contract *may* provide for the consequences of termination, but also that it cannot but provide, expressly or impliedly, for at least some of those consequences. The power to terminate is a power to bring about certain changes in the parties' legal relations and so cannot be understood except by reference to those changes. Accordingly, to agree that breach of a certain term gives the power to terminate is necessarily to agree that breach of that term should give the claimant the power to bring about the set of legal consequences that attend termination.

Which consequences? At least presumptively, the ones found in the cases generally. These are the standard consequences of termination and so the consequences which, absent any indication to the contrary, we can reasonably presume the parties intend when they provide for the power to terminate. These consequences include the option to seek restitution of payments and other transfers made under the contract and indeed recompense for work done on the contract thus far, again save where and to the extent that the parties themselves have provided that no such claims will lie. So if we agree that your failure to deliver the painting gives me the power to terminate our contract, we are thereby agreeing, inter alia, that in that event you lose whatever right you had to that money and I am entitled to restitution.

This conclusion is strengthened if we the take the view just discussed that these restitutionary claims turn not on termination but on the failure of conditions the parties have themselves attached to their respective obligations. On the orthodox view, it might be possible to claim that the only necessary consequence of termination is to bring the contract to a halt, relieving the parties of any obligations to perform which are not yet due. The law may then add the further consequence that each party be entitled to restitution in respect of benefits conferred thus far. But the idea of termination—ie (on this view) the idea of prospective discharge—is intelligible without this addition. So one might say that when the parties provide for termination, all they need be providing for is the discharge of their future obligations. If so, any further rights and obligations the parties acquire

[26] See *Moschi v Lep Air Services Ltd* [1973] AC 331 (HL) 350 (Lord Diplock).

upon termination, such as any claims for restitution, require further justification. This is where, on this orthodox view, unjust enrichment comes in: though it is the contract which determines the availability of termination and opens up the possibility of then recovering those benefits, it is some principle of unjust enrichment which grounds these claims (just as the parties' undertakings determine what amounts to a breach of contract but may fail to specify what claims attend that breach).

If, however, we take these claims not to depend on termination, but instead to respond to instances where a condition to my performance or to your retaining the benefit of my performance is not met, then restitutionary liability requires no such additional justification. For to make, say, your performance a condition of your right to retain the benefit of my performance can only be to make that benefit recoverable in the event that this condition is not fulfilled. By agreeing to the condition, we agree to restitution in the event the condition fails. In other words, a payment made under a contract is either made out and out—meaning that the money is the recipient's to keep come what may—or it isn't, in which case its retention is conditional on some or other state of affairs obtaining.[27] Whether or not the payment is made out and out is for the parties to decide and so is settled, in the first instance, by the terms of their agreement. If we agree that it's not to be made out and out, we are thereby agreeing that the money is to be retained only in certain circumstances, and by agreeing this we agree to its return if those circumstances don't come about.

Of course, there will be times where the parties' express and implied undertakings fail to specify fully the conditions which attach to their respective performances or (on the orthodox view) fail to identify the full range of circumstances in which the power to terminate will arise, and with it the claims and liabilities will follow from the defendant's breach. Say you deliver the painting later than we agreed; a clear breach of contract. We want to know whether I have the option of recovering the money I have already paid you under the contract or whether I am limited to my claim in damages. We could have provided that timely delivery was a condition of you keeping the money. Alternatively, we could have provided that the price was payable even if delivery was late and I could recover only compensation for the loss

[27] See too *Fibrosa* (n 15) 67–68 (Lord Wright), 74–75 (Lord Roche).

this caused. But we did neither: we didn't attend to this question, or perhaps we did but couldn't reach agreement.

Still the question needs an answer. How gaps like these should be filled is far from straightforward.[28] Where the parties' agreement runs out, it will usually be reasonable still to prefer solutions which are consonant with, or at least do not undermine, what they did agree and accord with their broader objectives when entering into this agreement. Beyond this, it may be better to see losses shared or, if not shared, to be borne by the party better positioned to have avoided them or to bear them now. At some point there may be no option but simply to say that the loss should lie where it falls. Is unjust enrichment a relevant consideration here? Only in the loose sense in which we might ask whether a given solution produces a reasonable allocation of benefits and burden between the parties. But there is no role here for unjust enrichment in the sense unjust enrichment lawyers intend. I made a payment as obligated under our contract. The question is whether that obligation—meaning, in this context, your entitlement to the money I paid you—was conditional on your timely delivery of the painting. Only if it was is there any possibility of your enrichment constituting an unjust enrichment. Yet this is the very question we're seeking to answer, the very gap in the contract we're looking to fill. Moreover, once we do fill that gap, however we fill it, we don't need to turn to the law of unjust enrichment to explain why my payment is or is not recoverable. For though, as we have seen, restitution need not follow automatically from the invalidity of the obligation under which the transfer was made, in these cases the very point of taking the obligation to be conditional is to ensure that the payment is recoverable in the event of that condition failing. If unjust enrichment doesn't explain the condition, it doesn't explain my recovery.

None of this is to say that the law of unjust enrichment has no application to parties within a contractual relationship. Where a payment or other transfer is made which is plainly outside the scope of any of the parties' contractual obligations, there's no need to go hunting around for some implied contractual undertaking to make restitution. If I mistakenly pay you more than the agreed price, we have a clear case of unjust enrichment. So there should be no

[28] For discussion of this question, see Charles Fried, *Contract as Promise: A Theory of Contractual Obligation* (Harvard University Press 1981) 57–73.

assumption that the contract regulates all dealings between the parties. But the contract does have the first word on all matters that do fall within the scope of the parties' respective undertakings. If the contract states that, say, payments will be recoverable in the event of the breach of a particular term, then recovery of those payments in that event are straightforward claims on the contract. A provision that makes performance of that term a condition of the payee's right to retain that money is exactly equivalent.

Similar provision can be made for contingencies other than breach and in respect of obligations other than the payment of money and other asset transfers. In anticipation of the football World Cup, you engage me to write a volume celebrating an England victory, to be ready to hit the shelves within weeks of this remarkable triumph. For this to happen, you need me to start writing now, covering the build-up to the tournament, player profiles, and so on, meaning I'll need only to fill in the details of the tournament itself for the book to be ready. My payment is to be by royalty fixed as a percentage of the total takings from sale of the book. But, of course, we don't know whether England will win, so we make it a term of the contract that it will be terminated if England lose. And so we go on to provide that in that event I am to be paid a fee for the work I have done up to that point. We may ourselves specify the precise figure or we might simply provide for payment of a reasonable sum, to be fixed by a court if need be. Any claim I then bring for such payment is again a straightforward claim on the contract.

Imagine now that we make no express provision for payment in the event of termination. England lose, you cancel the contract, and I seek payment for the work I've done. Your termination, discharging our future obligations, doesn't determine whether payment is due. We could have agreed that I'd be paid only in the event of publication, such that I shoulder the risk of the book not being published and my work being in vain. The first question for the court is whether our failure to provide expressly for payment is to be read as our agreeing to my not being paid in this event. If so, my claim will fail. But if not, and so if the court concludes that it was always intended that I be remunerated for my work, it will succeed. This will be the case whether or not you can be said to have been enriched by the work I had done to this point. Again what matters is, in the first instance, what we agreed. And here too, where that agreement runs out, the focus doesn't shift to the law of unjust enrichment but to determining how the gap in the parties' agreement can reasonably be filled.[29]

In any case, as we have seen, there is reason to doubt that the considerations which, outside contract, support restitutionary liability where the claimant pays the defendant by mistake or on some condition which fails extend to cases where the defendant benefits from the claimant's work.[30] But while there is no general parallel or symmetry between asset transfers and other enrichments, a symmetry of sorts emerges where the parties seek to recover in respect of their performance under contracts now terminated for breach or frustration precisely because these claims are better viewed not as instances of unjust enrichment liability at all, but rather as contractual claims, grounded in the parties' own undertakings and the law's broader support for them.

V Contract and Unjust Enrichment

Unjust enrichment lawyers have been quick to pounce on attempts to extend contract beyond those cases and claims that really can be resolved by reference to the parties' genuine agreement. To say that these claims are contractual is said only to obscure their true basis or rationale. No doubt once we move beyond the parties' true choices and expectations, we need to say more to explain why a particular implication or ruling is reasonable. But these lawyers have been too quick to assume that, at this point, the significance of the parties being in a contractual relationship is exhausted. For this overlooks the possibility that these relationships can have a normative significance beyond their agreed terms, and so the fact that these parties brought themselves together into some such voluntary association may be material to their mutual claims and responsibilities even where the agreed terms of their association are silent. There is here a grey area at the edge of contracts, where the parties' choices and undertakings run out but still cast a shadow, shaping their dealings and what may reasonably be required of them. The error made by unjust enrichment lawyers is to conclude that, if we can find no relevant undertaking, we are left only with norms which take no force from and operate wholly

[29] Cf Beatson (n 24) 78–94.

[30] 4.VII.

independently of the parties' choices and undertakings—that the only true contractual norm is 'keep your promises'—an error compounded when they turn instead to a principle of unjust enrichment which, on their accounts, denotes no identifiable norm of justice whatsoever.

For much the same reason, we shouldn't assume that the conclusion that the parties' contract is unenforceable or void means that their respective claims and liabilities are to be determined on the basis that no such relationship existed between them. Reasons for denying transactions the legal effect the parties intended for them vary. Sometimes, as in cases of illegality, the aim is to discourage, or at least not to support, some activity involved in, or connected to, the performance of that agreement. At other times, the concern is with safeguarding the position of one or both of the parties, as with contracts entered into by minors. In neither case will the reasons for denying the agreement full contractual effect necessarily extend to denying it *any* effect. So if we want to see that children and the mentally incapable aren't exploited, then we have reason to deny them the contractual capacity we accord to those of full age and competence. But this needn't mean we have reason to deny all effect to the agreements they enter into. We may object only to the contract being enforced against, but not by, the weaker party. We may have reason to invalidate or refuse to enforce these agreements only in so far as they are in fact exploitative. To the extent that they are exploitative or otherwise work to the weaker party's disadvantage, we might reasonably choose to amend the parties' agreement to achieve a fairer distribution of benefits and burdens. That we consider the other party to have secured an unduly high rate for his services may be reason to refuse him payment at that rate but not payment at the market rate instead.[31]

The legal effect given to voluntary agreements and arrangements need not be all or nothing, but may vary in degree.[32] Legal systems may reasonably choose to give recognition to agreements for some purposes but not others. Indeed we see this in the basic distinction between contracts that are void and those that are merely unenforceable. In so far as they refuse to give effect to agreements, legal systems may, and sometimes do, adjust the terms of those agreements so as to avoid some threatened harm or evil. There is a good in giving people

[31] See eg Sale of Goods Act 1979, s 3(2).

[32] See too Steve Hedley, 'Implied Contract and Restitution' [2004] *Cambridge Law Journal* 435, 440–43, 447.

the power to enter into binding arrangements with one another. Sometimes that good comes into conflict with other goods and values. Where it does, it may be reasonable to deny some arrangements, intended by the parties to be legally binding, full contractual effect. But even in these cases, the good of enabling the parties to enter into such binding arrangements is not denied so much as weighed against and, to this extent, outweighed by these other considerations. And since this good is not denied here, it still goes to shape the law's response to these cases and claims and, in all cases, merits recognition and protection to the extent that it is not outweighed by or incompatible with those countervailing reasons.

So, once again, it is a mistake to think that the reasons for upholding the parties' agreement wholly fall away and that it is some principle of unjust enrichment which must be weighed against the policy concerns which ground the contract's invalidity. On the contrary: the considerations that ground liability in unjust enrichment apply only where the grounds for upholding the parties' own voluntary arrangements end. There is a role for the law of unjust enrichment in cases of void and unenforceable contracts. But it is a residual role, coming in only where the payment or transfer is one outside the reach of the parties' agreement or where the law, exceptionally, chooses to deny all effect and recognition to the parties' choices and undertakings.

7

Claims

I Restitution

The cause of action in unjust enrichment is often taken to support no response other than an order that the defendant make restitution of that enrichment. Indeed on many accounts this is true by definition. So where unjust enrichment is defined as 'the generic conception of all the events which give rise to restitution' or as 'a unifying legal concept which explains why the law recognizes…an obligation on the part of the defendant to make fair and just restitution for a benefit derived at the expense of a plaintiff', we can say the defendant has been unjustly enriched only where he comes under a liability to make restitution.[1] On these accounts there is what has been termed a 'perfect quadration' between unjust enrichment and restitution: every claim for restitution is a claim in unjust enrichment, every claim in unjust enrichment a claim for restitution.[2] But even for those who came to reject this position, unjust enrichment often remained defined by the restitutionary response it generated.[3] Unjust enrichment was now one principle or one class of event that triggered claims for restitution. And so, though there could be restitution

[1] See, respectively, Peter Birks, *An Introduction to the Law of Restitution* (rev edn, Clarendon Press 1989) 17 and *Pavey and Matthews Pty v Paul* (1987) 162 CLR 221, 256–57 (Deane J).

[2] Birks, ibid 17–18.

[3] See eg Peter Birks, 'The Law of Unjust Enrichment: A Millennial Resolution' [1999] *Singapore Journal of Legal Studies* 318, 328; Graham Virgo, *The Principles of the Law of Restitution* (2nd edn, Oxford University Press 2006) 9.

without unjust enrichment, it remained the case that there was no unjust enrichment without restitution.[4]

Moreover, even if the explicit definitional link between unjust enrichment and restitution is broken, that restitution is the only proper response to unjust enrichment might appear to be a matter of logic or necessary implication.[5] If an unjust enrichment is one which the defendant should not, in law and as a matter of justice, have received and should not retain, how else to correct that injustice than by restitution of that enrichment?[6] If unjust enrichment claimants want something more or something other than restitution, they need to show that they have suffered some other injustice.

But though the only claim unjust enrichment may support may be a claim to restitution, it's typically thought that there are different ways restitution can be effected. I pay you by mistake. You must make restitution. But does this require you to hand back the very cash you received from me or is it enough that you pay back any equivalent sum? Does my right to restitution extend to others who subsequently receive that cash from you? Often questions like these are packaged together by asking whether the claimant's right to restitution is proprietary (*in rem*) or merely personal (*in personam*). Accordingly, on these accounts, once the claimant's cause of action in unjust enrichment has been made out, we must still ask what sort of restitutionary claim or award he merits.[7]

Some think that the answer to this question too is fixed by the claimant's cause of action.[8] If we want to know the proper form and

[4] Cf Peter Birks, *Unjust Enrichment* (2nd edn, Clarendon Press 2005) 17–19. The view that unjust enrichment sometimes supports some response other than restitution is endorsed in Charles Mitchell, Paul Mitchell, and Stephen Watterson (eds), *Goff and Jones: The Law of Unjust Enrichment* (8th edn, Sweet and Maxwell 2011) [36-28]–[36-30]. However, the examples they give are of measures that prevent the defendant being unjustly enriched in the first place. No doubt a defendant cannot make restitution of an enrichment he does not, in the end, receive. But nor, by the same token, can such a defendant be said to be unjustly enriched.

[5] See eg Peter Birks, 'The Concept of a Civil Wrong' in David G Owen (ed), *Philosophical Foundations of Tort Law* (Clarendon Press 1997) 47–48. Cf Stephen A Smith, 'Unjust Enrichment: Nearer to Tort than Contract' in Robert Chambers, Charles Mitchell, and James Penner (eds), *Philosophical Foundations of the Law of Unjust Enrichment* (Oxford University Press 2009) 195–98.

[6] For one possible answer, see Nicholas J McBride and Paul McGrath, 'The Nature of Restitution' (1995) 15 *Oxford Journal of Legal Studies* 33.

[7] See eg Birks (n 4) 39; Sir Peter Millett, 'Restitution and Constructive Trusts' in W R Cornish, Richard Nolan, J O'Sullivan, and G Virgo (eds), *Restitution—Past, Present and Future: Essays in Honour of Gareth Jones* (Hart Publishing 1998) 208.

[8] See Robert Chambers, 'Two Kinds of Enrichment' in Robert Chambers, Charles Mitchell, and James Penner (eds), *Philosophical Foundations of the Law of Unjust Enrichment*

measure of restitution, we need to know the proper form and measure of the defendant's unjust enrichment. On this view, what look like distinct forms of restitutionary relief are simply the reflection of distinct forms of unjust enrichment. Sometimes the defendant is unjustly enriched by his acquisition of some asset. Where he is, restitution of that enrichment is restitution of that asset. At other times, the defendant's unjust enrichment lies instead in his receipt of 'abstract value', in the benefit he derives from some state of affairs the claimant brought about. Here restitution requires the defendant to give up something of equal value, such as achieved by a payment to the value of that benefit. In all cases, the correct response to an unjust enrichment is restitution of that very enrichment.

If there is a logic to this position, it is one the law has yet to embrace. The standard response to mistaken asset transfers is not to allow the claimant to recover the relevant asset. If I transfer some shares or a bike to you by mistake, you will ordinarily get an indefeasible title to those shares or to the bike and I must make do with recovery of their market value. One response might be to say that, though you are no doubt enriched by your receipt of the bike or shares and not simply by the receipt of their value, it is only the latter enrichment which the law takes to be unjust. But what reason is there for thinking that you are unjustly enriched only by your abstract enrichment? I make not two transfers here—the first of the bike or shares, the second of their value—but one. My mistake goes to that one transfer, one decision: to pass this asset to you. So there is no sense in which my intention to give you the value of the asset is compromised by my mistake but not my intention to give you the asset. Of course, it could be said that the combined effect of the rules of title and liability is to treat the transfer of the asset as effective, but not the transfer of value. But it doesn't follow that it is your receipt of the value of the asset alone which is unjust, that the reasons for requiring you to make restitution extend only to your abstract enrichment and not to your acquisition of that asset.

Here we see the same mistake of thinking that we can read off the nature of the injustice to which the law is responding from the response it adopts, that if the law is to protect a claimant's interests it

(Oxford University Press 2009); Robert Stevens, 'When and Why Does Unjustified Enrichment Justify the Recognition of Proprietary Rights?' (2012) 92 *Boston University Law Review* 919, 925–29.

must protect them in full. The good of protecting a particular claimant's interests will often come up against other goods and values that would be compromised were the law to intervene on the claimant's behalf. Sometimes these competing considerations will outweigh or override those in favour of allowing his claim. At other times, they may be insufficient to deny the claimant all legal redress but still justify placing a limit on what he may recover. In such instances, there is good reason for the law to protect the claimant's interests only in part. And so reasons for restitution vie with reasons against restitution, with considerations that support denying or limiting such claims. Accordingly, it may sometimes be reasonable to give a claimant who has unjustly enriched a defendant something other, indeed something less, than restitution of that enrichment. The thesis that the distinct forms of restitution map onto distinct forms of unjust enrichment therefore fails. It fails not because enrichments do not come in different forms—they do—but because it wrongly assumes that the only legitimate response to unjust enrichment is restitution of that enrichment in kind.

II Objectives and Rationales

Once we see that it is a mistake to think that the form and measure of a claimant's restitutionary award must mark the extent of the defendant's unjust enrichment, a broader challenge to orthodox accounts of unjust enrichment is opened up. As we have seen, the impetus for academic interest in the law of unjust enrichment came from the observation that there exists a body of laws and doctrines, operating (at least in the main) independently of contract and tort, which have the common effect of removing some gain made by the defendant. One criticism made of these accounts was that they failed to explain why we should take the defendant's gain as key to these cases.[9] If I pay you £100 by mistake, you are up £100 but I am down by the same sum. If you must repay me £100, this removes your gain but also makes good my loss. So why is this better seen as a case of unjust enrichment rather than, say, unjust loss or deprivation? The standard response was to show that sometimes the claimant's loss and the defendant's gain

[9] See eg Steve Hedley, 'Unjust Enrichment as the Basis of Restitution—An Overworked Concept' (1985) 5 *Legal Studies* 56, 61–62.

come apart and, where they do, it is the latter the law takes as its measure.[10] But this did nothing to undermine the broader challenge the critics posed. That the effect of an award is to remove a gain, or for that matter to make good a loss, doesn't mean that this is its purpose. Since interests need not be protected in full or not at all, the rationale of an award cannot be worked out simply from its measure.

The claims that follow mistaken and other unauthorized asset transfers find their basis in the claimant's interest in that asset, the interest that was, prior to its transfer, given legal recognition by the claimant's title to the asset. One aspect of this interest is the control it gives to the owner over others' access to the asset and so to the benefits they may derive from this. But ownership interests are not simply interests in pre-empting others' beneficial use or in harvesting the benefits others may take from that asset but are, more fully, interests in the continued use of that asset, in the on-going deployment of that resource to the owner's chosen ends. It is (as we might put it) not the benefit you get from my asset that grounds my claim to restitution but the fact that it is *my* asset. In the first instance then, it makes no difference to my case what value you place on the asset, and you provide no reason to escape liability by showing you get no benefit from its receipt. Now, sometimes this interest of mine cannot be fully protected without doing harm to interests of yours. Because of this, there is, as we shall see, good reason for a rule which denies the claimant recovery where and to the extent that this leaves an innocent defendant disadvantaged as a result of his receipt, a rule which has the effect of capping the sum recoverable by the claimant to the measure of the defendant's surviving gains.[11] There will, therefore, be times when we need to inquire into whether and by how much the defendant has been enriched. But it does not follow that, at this point, my claim becomes a claim directed instead to the reversal of this benefit, of some transfer of 'abstract value'. Though the degree and mode of protection it is accorded may vary, the interest my claim serves does not.

In truth these cases are ill characterized as cases of unjust enrichment. To the extent that they are concerned with gains, they are concerned with losses too. Indeed, we might say, with losses first. These claims arise to secure or to protect the claimant's interest in the asset,

[10] See eg Peter Birks, 'Unjust Enrichment—A Reply to Mr Hedley' (1985) 5 *Legal Studies* 67, 73.

[11] See 8.II.

an interest that anticipates its receipt by the defendant. So it is true to say that the defendant is liable on account of what he received. But he is liable for what he received because it was something to which the claimant was already, in this way, entitled. In any event, the correspondence of loss and gain, such as there is, in these cases is no more than the upshot of transfer, of the same thing being given and received (whether or not there exists any correspondence in the values the parties attach to that thing). So, though the effect of these claims and the orders they support is often to remove some enrichment from the defendant and though their proper measure is often the measure of the defendant's gain, it is better to see these cases as concerned, in the first instance, neither with gains nor with losses, but with entitlement to the very thing received. The object of these claims and orders is, nonetheless, rightly described as restitution. But this is restitution not in the sense in which this term has been co-opted by unjust enrichment lawyers, with its exclusive focus on the defendant and the removal of his gains, but in its original sense of restoration, of returning something to a claimant that is rightly his.[12]

III Specific Recovery

If some asset of mine ends up in your hands without my consent, my interest in determining how that asset is to be used, including what use you and others may make of it, grounds my claim for restitution. Likewise it is this interest that determines what counts as true or sufficient restitution, which establishes not just why you are liable but, all else equal, what you are liable for. An owner's interest in his assets is given legal recognition through a set of claims, powers, and privileges relating to the application of those assets. This interest receives its fullest protection in cases of mistaken and other unauthorized transfers where the claimant owner's position as holder of this set of claims, powers, and privileges is left unchanged by the fact of its receipt by the defendant; where, in other words, he is taken to be, in substance if not in form, no less an owner now that the asset is in someone else's hands. Where or in so far as this interest entitled him,

[12] Cf Birks (n 4) 281–83.

before transfer, to immediate possession of the asset, this means entitling him to demand that it be given up to him now.

The common law, however, grants this form of relief only exceptionally. So, as we have seen, title to the asset is typically held to pass to the defendant notwithstanding the claimant's lack of proper consent and, even where title does not pass, the claimant often has no right to the return of the asset itself. On the standard view that claims in unjust enrichment are not concerned with protecting a claimant's interest in his assets, the denial of specific recovery is unsurprising. But the problem this view faces is why the claimant gets to recover anything at all. If we take the claimant to have made a true and effective exercise of his power to dispose of his asset, this interest provides not only no reason for restitution but a reason *against* it.[13] It might be thought that the rule that title passes pre-empts any claim to recover the asset. But there's nothing incoherent in an approach that provides that, in these cases, title goes with possession but that the claimant may then take action to recover possession and title.[14] The rule that title passes does not, therefore, rule out specific recovery.[15] The real significance of the passing of title is not what it tells us about the respective rights and liabilities of the parties to the transfer but what it tells us about their rights and liabilities vis-à-vis others not party to the transfer. For now, I am addressing only claims against the immediate recipient.

The common law's preference for money awards over specific relief is systemic. We see it too in the adoption of damages as the primary remedy for breaches of contract. There the preference for damages is often explained on the basis that it provides a less intrusive and less costly means of protecting the claimant's interest in performance. Ordering the defendant to perform will typically involve a greater interference with his liberty than requiring him simply to pay compensation to the claimant. Damages awards encourage a clean break between the parties, reducing the chances of further disputes and litigation. They can also be more easily enforced: if the defendant doesn't

[13] 3.VIII, 4.I.

[14] Indeed it is sometimes claimed, rather optimistically, that this is the approach English law in fact adopts in many cases of unjust enrichment: see eg Robert Chambers, *Resulting Trusts* (Clarendon Press 1997).

[15] More generally, having title or some other property interest (in the first of the senses of 'interest' described in chapter 3) is not essential to having a right that a defendant hand over that asset to you: see Ben McFarlane, 'Identifying Property Rights: A Reply to Mr Watt' [2003] *Conveyancer and Property Lawyer* 473, 474–76.

pay, his goods can be seized to generate the funds to pay the claimant, whereas where a defendant fails to comply with an order of specific performance the only option is sanction for contempt of court. But these concerns don't take us very far when it comes to restitution of misapplied assets. Being required to hand over an asset is ordinarily no greater an imposition on a defendant's liberty than having to pay its monetary equivalent and provides no less of a clean break. If assets can be seized to be sold, they can be seized to be handed over *in specie*. That there is no general principled objection to specific restitution is supported by the very different approach one finds in equity where, for assets held on trust, such orders are made as a matter of course.

Moreover, on the face of it, specific restitution has the advantage of avoiding some of the quantification difficulties that can arise with monetary awards. I mistakenly transfer my personalized car registration number to you.[16] I paid £15,000 for the number and would, if necessary, have paid significantly more. You have no interest in that particular number at all. You could sell it on but the market in such numbers is (we might imagine) unpredictable, such that it's impossible to say with confidence how much this number would fetch if put up for sale. What sum should be awarded? The number is one of a kind; there is no available substitute that is, to me, equivalent. So I am left worse off if I don't receive a sum assessed at the value I attach to that number. By contrast, you'll be left worse off if you are required to pay more than you would receive if you were to sell it. But we don't know what that sum is. On such facts, we can provide full protection to my interests while doing no harm to yours only by reassignment of the number to me.

These difficulties may be pre-empted if the court gives the defendant the option of surrendering the asset *in specie* or if giving back the asset is otherwise taken to discharge his liability to make pecuniary restitution.[17] If you were ordered to pay me whatever sum the court determined the registration number would likely fetch if put up for sale, any harm this would do you would be avoided if you could instead choose simply to transfer the number back to me, securing my interests in turn. Indeed, you have an incentive to return the asset whenever the costs of its retention exceed the benefits this brings.

[16] Cf *Cressman v Coys of Kensington (Sales) Ltd* [2004] EWCA Civ 47, [2004] 1 WLR 2775 discussed at 4.V.

[17] Cf Torts (Interference with Goods) Act 1977, s 3(2); *Cressman*, ibid para 37.

Whenever the sum you would have to pay me is greater than the value you can derive from that asset, including the net gains from its sale, you have reason to choose to give the asset up to me instead. In this way, an order to make pecuniary restitution may still lead, if this option remains open, to the ideal outcome of specific restitution. But only if the sum ordered is not set too low. If the value you attach to the asset is higher than the sum you are ordered to pay me, you have reason to pay that money and to keep the asset for yourself. If that sum is also below the value I attach to the asset, I will be left disadvantaged in turn.

The way a monetary award can best provide restitution is not, therefore, by identifying a sum equal to the value the defendant attaches to the asset, offsetting any benefit the defendant derives from having it at his disposal, but by steering the defendant towards making specific restitution. So long as the defendant retains the option of discharging his liability by making restitution *in specie*, it can do this not by taking the defendant's valuation of the asset as the upper limit of such an award, but as its minimum. Otherwise, monetary awards provide optimal protection for both parties' interests only where their valuations of the asset coincide or, more commonly, where there exist ready substitutes for the relevant asset available on the market. In these cases, an order to pay over the market price of the asset serves the claimant's interests without doing harm to the defendant (subject to any change of position), since the claimant can then use that money to obtain a substitute and the defendant can recover an equivalent sum by sale of the original asset.

IV Substitutes

As a matter of positive law, the defendant's liability to make restitution of a mistaken payment does not depend on the claimant establishing that that very money remains in the defendant's hands. Where the defendant has since spent that money, he can't of course return it *in specie*, but the court can simply order him to pay over an equivalent sum instead. If we see these claims as concerned with reversing a defendant's abstract enrichment, it's plain why the law should take no particular interest in what happened to the money after receipt. What matters is not whether the defendant retains this money but whether he remains enriched, better off all things considered. And so, save where his spending the money amounts to a change of position, his liability to make restitution of this enrichment remains after that money has gone.

But it is not the defendant's abstract enrichment which grounds these claims but the claimant's interest in the very thing the defendant received. So the fact that a claimant mistakenly enriched the defendant won't ground a claim to restitution unless the claimant can establish some such interest in the asset or advantage received by the defendant.[18] If he can make out such an interest, this alone provides a reason for restitution, irrespective of what, if any, value the defendant attaches to it. It doesn't follow that the defendant's liability should be dependent on his retention of the asset. But this does mean that we need to take a bit more care to explain when and how the claimant's interest in an asset may justify the liability of a defendant who no longer has that asset in hand.

Here is one way. Say I pay you £100 by mistake. You spend that money on a watch. You no longer have the money but you now have the watch to show for it. In some circumstances similar to these, the law allows me to recover the watch or its value. This process whereby a proprietary interest in one asset is taken to support some such interest in another asset acquired in exchange for it is known as tracing.[19] Occasionally claims to assets traceable in this way are said to be claims in unjust enrichment: you would be unjustly enriched were you able to keep a watch bought with my money.[20] Others have doubted whether claims to substitutes can fit within the orthodox unjust enrichment framework. These debates tell us little. Claims to substitutes have some similarities to claims in the standard cases of unjust enrichment, some differences. These similarities make it possible to find an analytical framework which covers them both, the differences makes it possible to find one which doesn't. The orthodox framework adopted by unjust enrichment lawyers left enough open that it could be understood and employed either way. If there is any

[18] 3.III.

[19] It is sometimes said that tracing describes only the process of identifying exchange products and does not answer the further question of what claims, if any, the owner of the original asset might bring in respect of the substitute: see eg *Foskett v McKeown* [2001] 1 AC 102 (HL) 128 (Lord Millett). I have my doubts over the utility of this distinction and I don't maintain it in the discussion that follows.

[20] See eg. Peter Birks, 'Property, Unjust Enrichment, and Tracing' (2001) 54 *Current Legal Problems* 231; Andrew Burrows, 'Proprietary Restitution: Unmasking Unjust Enrichment' (2001) 117 *Law Quarterly Review* 412.

substance to these analytic debates, the different positions must reflect some sense that the reasons for liability are, or are not, the same in both of these cases: if one thinks that claims to substitutes share the same rationale as claims in the standard case, then one will take the view that claims to substitutes are likewise claims in unjust enrichment; if one doesn't, then one won't. But given that the rationale for liability in even the standard cases of unjust enrichment is a question these accounts left largely untouched, there was little prospect that they would shed light on the question of how these reasons might (or might not) support claims to substitutes.

How then can we get from my interest in the £100 I paid you to an interest in the watch you bought with it? Ownership interests are interests in determining the use and enjoyment of some asset. These interests and the legal entitlements by which they are recognized and delineated typically extend to empowering owners to license others' use and enjoyment of the asset and to confer or create entitlements to such use. Moreover, owners are generally free to set the terms of such dispositions. So I may give you a copy of this book as a gift, asking for nothing in exchange. Or I may make its transfer conditional on you doing something for me, providing some other asset or service in return. Because of this latter possibility, my ownership of my assets provides me with a means to acquire other items of wealth through exchange.[21] In this way, so long as the asset has some value to others, ownership interests bestow on owners a potential for acquiring new assets and other forms of wealth. This potential, as one incident of ownership, is one the owner alone is entitled to take advantage of.

In the event that some asset of mine ends up in your hands without my proper authorization, you are now, as a matter of fact, in a position to exploit this potential. Of course, this aspect of my interest in the asset can be protected by requiring you to return it to me. I'll then be back in the position to set the terms of any disposition of the asset and so to obtain whatever items of wealth might be secured through such dispositions. Where, though, you have already exchanged my asset for some other—as where you spend the £100 I mistakenly paid to you on the watch—it's too late to demand that you return that first asset to me. In these circumstances, however, my interest in that asset—the

[21] See too John Finnis, *Natural Law and Natural Rights* (2nd edn, Oxford University Press 2011) 172; Ernest J Weinrib, 'Restitutionary Damages as Corrective Justice' (2000) 1 *Theoretical Inquiries in Law* 1, 13, 19; Birks (n 4) 82.

money I paid you—provides a ground for recognizing me as having an equivalent interest in the substitute—the watch you bought with that money. For the substitute is the product of the wealth-acquiring potential of that original asset and, since this potential, this means of acquiring other items of wealth, is mine and mine alone to take advantage of, taking the substitute to be mine ensures that it is me and me alone who derives any such advantage. In short: according me an interest in the watch is a way of giving (partial) effect to my interest in the money used to buy it since part of my interest in that money is in the purchasing power it provides.

This then is the truth in the suggestion that claims to substitutes can be said to vindicate or give effect to the claimant's interest—his property—in the asset he originally held.[22] For many unjust enrichment lawyers any such explanation appears incoherent. To say that a claimant has a proprietary right or interest is, for them, simply to say that he has a claim in relation to some thing that is good against an open-ended set of people. If I have a claim to the watch bought with my money and that claim is good not only against you but against others who may receive the watch from you, we can say I have a proprietary interest in that watch akin to the interest I held in the money previously. But this provides no explanation of that interest. Rather, my interest in the watch—how we get to this interest from my distinct interest in the money—is the very thing we are looking to explain. Property is, on this view, a category of (as some put it) legal response or (as we might say) bottom-line legal entitlement, not a cause of or reason for such entitlements. In this we see another example of the confusion caused by failing to attend to the two distinct senses in which the terms 'interest' is used.[23] If we take 'property' and 'property interest' simply to describe a form of legal response or entitlement, then it indeed makes no sense to identify property as the basis for such entitlements. But these terms are also used, indeed used more commonly, in a distinct sense, one that indicates a possible basis of or ground for claims relating to assets. Understood in this way, we

[22] Cf *Foskett* (n 19) 110 (Lord Browne-Wilkinson), 115 (Lord Hoffmann), 127, 129 (Lord Millett); Graham Virgo, 'Vindicating Vindication: *Foskett v McKeown* Reviewed' in Alastair Hudson (ed), *New Perspectives on Property Law, Obligations and Restitution* (Cavendish Publishing 2004); Ross Grantham and Charles Rickett, 'Tracing and Property Rights: The Categorical Truth' (2000) 63 *Modern Law Review* 905.

[23] 3.IV, 3.V.

might say that it is my interest in my assets which grounds my power to dispose of them as I choose, your duty not to interfere with them, and, as argued, my claim to their traceable substitutes. This way of speaking involves no category error.

There is a choice to be made as to how far we should go in protecting this interest. To deny an owner any interest in those assets acquired in exchange for his, as many jurisdictions do, is not to deny that his ownership interest makes him the person solely authorized to set the terms of its disposition.[24] Nor is according him such a claim the only way of protecting his interest in securing the wealth-generating opportunities that asset provides. We could instead provide him with funds that give him equivalent purchasing power or we could compensate him for the purchases he has missed out on, the opportunities he had lost, by being deprived of this power. But taking him to have an interest in the substitute is an effective way of ensuring both that his interest in that original asset is, to this extent, protected and that others do not get an advantage from the wealth-generating opportunities it brings.

V Enrichment

What if you retain neither the original asset I transferred to you nor any substitute? You give the watch you bought with the money I mistakenly paid you to a friend as gift. Or, say, you simply use the very money I paid you to pay a bill. Perhaps I can claim against the present holder of that money or the watch. But it seems there is nothing *you* can now do to give effect to my interest in their continued use and disposition. So, if the law is going to assist me in taking action against you, it must be on some other basis than that this will, in one way or another, secure my position as owner of the relevant asset. Here I'll consider two possible alternative bases on which an owner may seek to build a claim. The first looks to the advantages that the defendant

[24] Could an analogous argument be made for protecting my interest in determining how I apply my labour by granting me a presumptive interest in any assets generated or wealth created by my skills and efforts? Perhaps (cf 7.V). However, the rules of tracing, which do not factor in labour contributions, show that the common law (including equity) has not taken this step: see further Tim Akkouh and Sarah Worthington, '*Re Diplock* (1948)' in Charles Mitchell and Paul Mitchell (eds), *Landmark Cases in the Law of Restitution* (Hart Publishing 2006) 304–15.

derived and retains from his use of the claimant's asset. The second is directed to how the defendant's dealings with the asset impacted on the claimant's ability to secure for himself the advantages ownership provides.

It is sometimes said that ownership of an asset carries with it ownership of the benefits which derive from its uses. If it does—if, that is, my ownership interest accords me not simply authority to decide how that asset is used but priority over the enrichments created by or resulting from its use—I should be able to demand that any enrichments others take from my assets without my authorization be surrendered to me, on the basis that they are, in truth, mine.[25] You may remain enriched as a consequence of your use of my asset even where you retain neither that asset nor any substitute. So, if you spend the £100 I mistakenly paid you paying off your phone bill, this saves you from having to pay the bill from your own funds. Here your enrichment is a balance sheet gain, an increase in the stock of assets at your disposal. (An increase, that is, over what that stock would have been had I not paid the money to you.) At other times you may be enriched only abstractly: you come into possession of my bicycle, which you ride around for a few days. Later it is stolen from you, or perhaps you return it to me. Your use of the bicycle didn't save you any money, so you are not now wealthier by virtue of having had it at your disposal. But you got to use it for that time and so had the benefit of that use.

Does my interest extend this far? My ownership of my assets gives me control over their use. This in turn gives me (to this extent) control over what benefits others may derive from their use. But my right, in this way, to pre-empt others' access to the benefits that these assets may bring necessitates no right or claim to those benefits. And so just as my interest in choosing how I act need not extend to an interest in or claim to the benefits others may take from my actions, my interest in choosing how my assets are used need not bring with it any interest in or claim to the benefits derived from their use.[26]

So far as abstract enrichment (or value) goes, many of the points made when looking at cases of pure services apply again.[27] These

[25] For just such an argument, see Daniel Friedmann, 'Restitution of Benefits Obtained through the Appropriation of Property or the Commission of a Wrong' (1980) 80 *Columbia Law Review* 504.

[26] See too Sarah Worthington, *Equity* (2nd edn, Clarendon Press 2006) 108. Cf Peter Jaffey, *The Nature and Scope of Restitution* (Hart Publishing 2000) 149–51.

[27] 4.VII.

enrichments—the 'value transferred' by the receipt and use of assets—are no more than the satisfaction of individuals' preferences and wants. The benefit you get from using my bicycle is the contribution it makes to your goals and interests, to your quality of life. Whether and, if so, by how much you benefit from this use is a function of your priorities and circumstances. The uses you make of my asset are often uses I could have made. I could have been using my bicycle at the time you were riding around on it. Sometimes the use you make prevents or limits my future use. Perhaps there's no limit to how much my bicycle can be ridden, but if you use up my cake by eating it there will be nothing left for me. Here we have a difference from the services cases where what I do to benefit you does not ordinarily reduce my freedom of or capacity for action. But even where it could have been me rather than you who made use of the asset, the benefit—the value, the abstract enrichment—you take from its use is not something that could instead be mine. The contribution your use makes to your plans and interests is not the same contribution my use would have made to my plans and interests. There can, therefore, be no return or reallocation of these benefits, only offsetting, only the imposition of some measure which worsens the defendant's position, setting back his goals and interests, in equal measure to the advancement his use of the asset provided. So we can ensure that a defendant retains no such advantage from his use of the claimant's asset by requiring him to give up a sum of money equivalent to the value he places on that use. But the payment of such a sum from defendant to claimant involves no return or redistribution of this enrichment and so an order to make such a payment cannot be justified on the basis that the benefits of that asset's use are, like the asset itself, the claimant's unless and until he says otherwise.

Any system of private property must have rules determining what uses of an asset are reserved for its owner. So too it requires rules that direct the rest of us not to make unauthorized uses of others' assets, rules that thereby limit the benefits we are at liberty to take from those assets. Where a defendant's unauthorized use of a claimant's asset reduces the claimant's options, setting back his interests, there is reason for the law to intervene on the claimant's behalf to safeguard his position and secure those interests. The fact that this unauthorized use benefited the defendant may, as we shall see, make a difference to whether it is reasonable to require that defendant to make good any losses his use caused to the claimant. But there is no sense in saying that the benefits derived from such uses—as opposed to the use-privileges themselves—are included within the claimant's ownership interest such that they are presumptively his and so can be recovered from those who have 'taken' them without permission. And so, I suggest, the fact that the defendant did indeed benefit from the unauthorized use of another's asset does not, without more, provide sufficient reason for the state to take action at the claimant's behest to remove that benefit.

The 'without more' is important. The question is not whether claims directed to removing a defendant's abstract gains are possible, nor whether they are on occasion justified. No doubt they are. The question is how, and accordingly where, those claims might be justified. So it may be thought that those who knew they were making unauthorized use of another's assets without good cause should be prevented from keeping any gains derived from that use. This may then support empowering the owner to demand that the defendant give up the value of those gains to him. But while the fact that the asset was the claimant's and that the use the defendant made of that asset was without the claimant's authorization are necessary conditions of such a claim, they are not sufficient, and the reason for recognizing the claim here is not that gains deriving from the asset belong, simply by virtue of their provenance, to the claimant, but (something like) the good of ensuring wrongdoers don't profit from their wrongs and/or deterring others who would seek to do the same.

What if the defendant's receipt and use of the claimant's asset leave him not simply abstractly enriched but wealthier, his stock of assets increased? Here we have a gain that can intelligibly be allocated and so there is a question of whether that gain should remain with the defendant or be reallocated to the claimant. Often, though we can say the defendant is wealthier by virtue of his use of the claimant's asset, there is no identifiable item of wealth that we can identify as this gain. If you use the £100 I paid you to pay a bill, you avoid having to find that money elsewhere. By avoiding paying out of your own funds, you now have more money at your disposal. But typically it won't be possible to pinpoint any specific moneys you would otherwise have used to make the payment and so whose retention now constitutes your enrichment. Nonetheless an order that you pay over £100—any £100—sees that your resources, your stock, is not left enhanced by virtue of your use of my money.

There is good reason here for the law to make such an order. But I don't think that this reason is that my interest in that money carries with it an interest in whatever increases in others' wealth result from its use. To bring this out, take the following variation. You receive £100 from me by mistake, which you use to pay the bill. With the money you thereby saved, you buy £100 of lottery tickets, tickets you would not have bought had you had to go to your existing funds to pay the bill. These tickets make you £100,000 in winnings. Since you are now not £100 but £100,000 up, if I have an interest in whatever increased wealth you derive from the application of my assets, it seems I should now, subject to defences, be entitled to require you to pay over £100,000 to me.

You wouldn't have bought the lottery tickets if you hadn't received the £100 from me. So these winnings are causally attributable to your receipt and use of my £100. But you wouldn't have bought the lottery tickets had you not also had various other items of wealth at your disposal. That is, your decision to spend £100 on lottery tickets was made on the basis of the resources you had available to you. If you'd had £100 less, you wouldn't have bought the tickets, hence you wouldn't have bought them had you not received the £100 from me. But, by the same token, you wouldn't have bought them had your existing bank balance been £100 lower. In this way, your purchase of the lottery tickets is likewise causally attributable to the full extent of the funds to your name. Indeed, it may be we can go further still: you have a house, furniture, a car, various other possessions. If you did not already own these items, you would have prioritized their acquisition over the purchase of the lottery tickets. Perhaps, by choosing to buy a home years ago, you were in a position to take the benefit of the boom in house prices or you are in some other way wealthier than you would have been had you, say, continued to rent. In such ways, your purchase of the lottery tickets and so your £100,000 winnings are causally connected to your receipt and retention of these various items too. In turn, the acquisition of each of these individual items is itself attributable to countless other decisions you have made about how you should deploy the resources at your disposal at the time.

For this reason, if my ownership of my assets carried with it an interest in such increases in wealth as result from their use, this would still leave me some way short of being able to demand that you give up your £100,000 lottery winnings to me. For while these winnings can be connected back to your receipt and use of the £100 I paid you, they can likewise be connected to countless uses of any number of assets of your own. More than this: the lottery tickets you bought are not simply causally attributable in this way to the receipt and use of various other assets of yours as well as the £100 of mine, they are the direct exchange product of money which was unquestionably yours. We cannot therefore take my interest in the £100 I paid you as grounding an interest of mine in the lottery winnings which causally derive from the use of that money without, *pro tanto*, denying that your interest in the very £100 of yours with which those lottery tickets were bought grounds an interest in those tickets and hence in the winnings they generated. There is, as I've suggested, good reason to take ownership as encompassing an interest in the purchasing power that asset provides and, from this, in assets purchased with it, certainly better reason for seeing ownership interests as extending this far than there is to it extending to all assets whose acquisition is, in one way or another, causally attributable to its use.

So it makes a difference whether you buy the lottery tickets with the very money I paid you or with other funds at your disposal that we simply freed up by your receipt of my money. Only in the first instance should I have any claim to your winnings. We see the same differences in the rules of tracing which work on the basis of transactional and not merely causal links. To many unjust enrichment lawyers, this distinction has appeared arbitrary: why should it matter what money you used to buy the tickets? Surely you are unjustly enriched either way? On this way of thinking, the transactional links required by the rules of tracing should be viewed either as a proxy for establishing a causal connection (a proxy adopted because of the supposed evidential difficulties a direct inquiry into causation would raise) or as simply unfit for purpose.[28]

The mistake here is to think that these rules and the claims in whose service they operate are directed to enrichment or to the transfer or receipt of value. The truth is that this is not what these claims are about and that their rationale is instead to be found in the claimant's interest in the very asset received by the defendant: an interest which may reasonably extend to exchange products but not to abstract

[28] For the former view see eg Andrew Burrows, *The Law of Restitution* (3rd edn, Oxford University Press 2011) 120; Andrew Kull, 'Rationalizing Restitution' (1995) 83 *California Law Review* 1191, 1217–18. Cf Jaffey (n 26) 296–300. For the latter see eg Simon Evans, 'Rethinking Tracing and the Law of Restitution' (1999) 115 *Law Quarterly Review* 469. Cf Birks (n 4) 94–95.

enrichments or accretions of wealth resulting from that asset's receipt. The apparent arbitrariness and unfairness of granting me a claim to the full £100,000 if you use the money I paid you to buy the lottery tickets but not if you bought them with money of your own, which you would not have spent but for your receipt of the money I paid, is in truth just one example of the sort of differentiation entailed by any scheme of private property.[29] Oil is found under your land but not under my neighbouring land; the cellar holding both our books is flooded but only my books, stored below yours, are damaged. In these instances, that you gain and I lose may be thought similarly arbitrary, similarly unfair. But this sort of discrimination can be avoided only by rejecting any such difference between what is yours and what mine.

There may be exceptions, times where my property interest gives me a claim to wealth you've acquired (in one way or another) through your use of that item. It may be that some intellectual property rights work like this.[30] My right is not simply that you not exploit some idea or symbol without my consent, but that all wealth generated through its exploitation should come to me. Indeed, securing some such commercial advantage for the holder may be the point of some of these rights. But for the reasons given, it cannot, I think, be a general feature of ownership interests that they give owners an entitlement to other items of wealth which are secured through their use. We might put this another way: the proper scope of private property rights will be determined, in the first instance, by our reasons for recognizing those rights. These reasons may vary between different classes of item. But, whatever those reasons, the rights they support must be compossible—mutually and collectively compatible—such that my rights as owner of my assets square with your rights as owner of yours. This requirement of compossibility itself counts out any general rule that I may have a presumptive claim to items of wealth received or retained by you simply by showing that you hold them as a result of

[29] See too Lionel D Smith, *The Law of Tracing* (Clarendon Press 1997) 303–05; Lionel Smith, 'Restitution: The Heart of Corrective Justice' (2001) 79 *Texas Law Review* 2115, 2172–73.

[30] Do any intellectual property rights in fact work like this? If they did, we might expect the right holder to be able to demand destruction or delivery up of any infringing items held by a defendant and an account of profits generated by that infringement, regardless of fault on the defendant's part, subject (at most) to a defence change of position or some equivalent means of ensuring that blameless infringers are not disadvantaged. It's not clear that this package of remedies is presently attached to any intellectual property right in English law.

some use of items reserved for me. And, as such, I cannot make out a claim that you pay me £100 simply by showing that you are £100 richer by virtue of your unauthorized use of my asset.

VI Loss

One possible basis for claims following unauthorized asset transfers is that the defendant has something that the claimant can identify as properly his. But this works only where the defendant does indeed have something to which the claimant has some better claim. This is the case where the defendant retains the very asset originally held by the claimant, so too where he holds some other asset acquired in exchange for it. But this isn't true where all the defendant now 'has' is an enrichment causally derived from his receipt and use of the claimant's asset, whether this enrichment is mere abstract value or is marked by an increase in the wealth at the defendant's disposal. In these instances, any liability that attaches to the defendant must have some other basis. One such basis looks to the impact the defendant's actions had on the claimant's ability to secure for himself the advantages his ownership of that asset provides.

I'm sitting in the park, drinking a coffee and reading. You're playing football nearby. You kick the ball wildly. It lands square on the muffin I was about to eat. You are now under an obligation to make it up to me. So you might now buy me another muffin. But if the shop has now sold out, your obligation doesn't disappear. Your obligation is not conditional on your capacity to find and fund a replacement or on the possibility of fully restoring the *status quo ante*. You owe me compensation no less when what you damage can't be repaired or replaced. Some think that duties to compensate are nonetheless explained by the same considerations that grounded the duty for whose breach compensation is now sought.[31] On this view, though my muffin is squashed, whatever reasons you had not to squash my muffin now require you to make good the loss you caused by doing so. An alternative view is that duties of compensation in respect of wrongfully caused losses don't differ in their rationale from one wrong

[31] See eg John Gardner, 'What is Tort Law For? Part 1. The Place of Corrective Justice' (2011) 30 *Law and Philosophy* 1; Ernest J Weinrib, 'Two Conceptions of Remedies' in Charles Rickett (ed), *Justifying Private Law Remedies* (Hart Publishing 2008).

to another.[32] Instead, we might say, there is a good in seeing that victims of wrongs aren't disadvantaged by their interests being set back. Even if the specific interest harmed by the defendant cannot now be secured, there is reason to advance his wider interests to offset the harm the wrong did.

On either view I am entitled to compensation, on either view it is because I am (or was) owner of the muffin that marks me out as deserving of that compensation. But as this shows, the claims that my interest in my assets may support go beyond those that secure or facilitate my continued ownership of those assets. My muffin is lost, obliterated. Perhaps it cannot be replaced. Yet you still owe me compensation. Moreover, this is not a case where my claim is made against someone who now holds something of mine. I am not asking you to return my assets to me. You have nothing of mine in your possession. Rather my claim is that your actions have done me harm: setting back my interest in the use and enjoyment of my assets and the broader interests their use and enjoyment promotes.

Two features of this example may be thought to combine to substantiate my claim for compensation. First: your actions resulted in my muffin being squashed and thereby deprived me of the advantages (however small) I was positioned to secure through my ownership of it. If your actions made no difference at all to my ability to enjoy my continued ownership of my asset or to the advantages I could secure through this—if, that is, they caused me no harm—there is nothing for you to compensate me for. Second: the reasonableness of requiring you to compensate me for these harms is also influenced by your culpability in causing them. So the case for making you rather than me bear these losses is stronger where you were (and I was not) careless in bringing them about, stronger still where you acted with this design.

In many cases of unjust enrichment, we have the first of these elements but not the second. You spend the money I mistakenly pay you paying off your phone bill. The money is not, let us imagine, recoverable from the phone company. So your actions mean that the money is now lost to me. But you didn't know of my mistake and had no reason to doubt your entitlement to the money you received. Now there is nothing necessarily unjust or unreasonable in requiring the blameless to bear the costs of the harms they cause. The law often does. But strict

[32] Cf Charlie Webb, 'Justifying Damages' in Jason W Neyers, Richard Bronaugh, and Stephen G A Pitel (eds), *Exploring Contract Law* (Hart Publishing 2009).

liability for the harms we cause is not universal and it requires justification: why should blameless defendants be required to bear *these* losses, given that they are not required to bear others? Sometimes it is said that strict liability for harms depends on the defendant owing (what we might call) a strict duty not to cause that harm.[33] If this is right, you should be required to compensate me only if you acted in breach of duty by spending the money in the first place, notwithstanding that you were blameless in so doing. On this basis, the question we would need to ask is whether you were under a duty not to spend that money even though you had no reason to know the money was not (as we might say) yours to spend. My view is that you were under no such duty but that you should nonetheless now be required to repay me.

Why think that liability to compensate for the harms one has caused must follow from the breach of duties not to cause those harms? If you promise to insure me in respect of losses I might suffer in some activity, you come under a duty to compensate me if those losses come about, though you were under no duty to prevent them. Typically the losses I might ask you to insure me against will not be losses you cause. Presumably, however, the same goes even where they are. Your promise to insure me against losses you may cause doesn't thereby obligate you not to cause these losses. So it will sometimes be reasonable to require you to make good a loss even where you didn't act unreasonably in causing it (indeed where you did not cause it at all). More broadly, we shouldn't think that liability without fault must nonetheless be liability for wrongdoing. If there is good reason to require a defendant to compensate for a particular harm, we can ask whether these reasons also extend to requiring him not to cause that harm in the first place. Often they will. But at other times they will not, and so we should not assume that there are grounds for imposing strict liability for harms only where there are also grounds for recognizing an obligation not to cause those harms.[34]

[33] See eg John Gardner, 'Obligations and Outcomes in the Law of Torts' in Peter Cane and John Gardner (eds), *Relating to Responsibility: Essays in Honour of Tony Honoré on the Occasion of his 80th Birthday* (Hart Publishing 2001).

[34] See too Joseph Raz, *From Normativity to Responsibility* (Oxford University Press 2011) 259–60. Cf. Gardner (n 31) 34: 'Some transactions [including the standard cases of unjust enrichment: ibid 22] need not be wrongful in order to call for correction. They are wrongful only if they go uncorrected. ... By correcting one mitigates what would otherwise be a wrong to the point at which it is no longer a wrong, no longer a breach of obligation. One has an obligation to correct precisely because *otherwise*—in the absence of correction—one commits a wrong.'

Whenever some interest of the claimant's of sufficient importance to merit legal protection is harmed or threatened, there is a good to be done in the law taking steps to secure that interest or, failing that, to see that that claimant is not left disadvantaged through this harm. But often this good cannot be done without harming others' interests, interests that likewise merit legal recognition and protection. If you squash my muffin, this is a setback to my interests. This setback is one that can, in one way or another, be made up for by appropriate compensation. If, however, you are required to compensate me, then this will set back your interests in turn. So, either way, one of us will be left worse off. Here the fact that it was you who caused me this harm and that you were at fault in doing this makes it reasonable to shift this loss on to you. (In the same vein, if I am at fault too it will generally be reasonable for the loss to be split between us.) Where you are not at fault, there is nonetheless reason to require you to bear my loss where you have agreed to do so. No doubt it is reasonable to shift losses in other circumstances too, perhaps in many.

For now what matters is that whatever qualms we have about strict compensatory liability relate to the unfairness of subverting the defendant's interests to secure the claimant's. But when we go back to the example of the mistaken payment, we can see that this won't always be the case. Here, requiring you to make good my loss doesn't set back your interests. By using the £100 I paid you to pay your phone bill, you were able to save £100 of your own. If you now have to pay me £100 you are left in the same position you would have been in had I not made the payment to you, no better but no worse off. There is then no choice to be made between protecting my interests and protecting yours, for we can protect mine without harming yours. Nor are we shifting a loss from me to you so much as ensuring that no loss is suffered.[35]

This may seem too quick. If the law didn't intervene on my behalf, you would be £100 better off, so shouldn't we say that by requiring you to repay me you are indeed made to suffer a loss, that your interests *are* set back? True, your saving came about only by your use of the money I paid you, a use that was not properly yours to make. But, as we saw earlier in the chapter, the simple fact that you now have items of wealth at your disposal as a result of your unauthorized use of my

[35] See too Birks (n 4) 6–8.

assets gives me no interest in, and so no claim to, those items. So there is no doubting that the money you saved is indeed yours. Nonetheless, the question now is not whether I can claim any of that money as mine, but whether you can resist my claim that you make good the harm your spending of my money did to me on the basis that, by depriving you of this saving, this gain, your interests would be unfairly set back. And here it matters that this gain is one you would not have made but for your unauthorized use of my assets, indeed the very unauthorized use that caused me the harm I am now calling on you to put right. So, to the extent of this gain, requiring you to make good this harm leaves you worse off only by offsetting an advantage which ought not to have come your way, an advantage you made through (unknowingly) doing me harm. Again to this extent, this then pre-empts the principal objection to my claim that you should make good this harm.

So there is good reason for the law to require you to pay me £100 from your own funds, since this serves my broader interests in seeing that I am not disadvantaged by the loss of my £100 and does so without unfairly harming your interests. On the same basis, if, before I brought my claim, you spent £100 of your own on lottery tickets that gave you winnings of £100,000, my claim should again be to £100. Your winnings are not the traceable proceeds of my money, and the mere fact that you would not have made those winnings without your receipt of my money does not, for the reasons given earlier, give me any claim to them. Rather, my complaint is that your actions meant my money was lost to me, that you compromised my ability to apply that money to my own ends and in pursuit of my own interests, and that this loss should be borne by you and not by me. Since my loss here is the loss of that money—or the loss of that money and whatever additional advantages I would have gone on to derive from it had it remained at my disposal—I should recover no more than an equivalent sum plus interest. By contrast, if your lottery tickets had generated no winnings, and assuming still that you bought the tickets only because you thought you had spare funds on account of the money I had paid you, you should be able to resist my claim for repayment. Though here too your actions harmed me, depriving me of my ability to apply that money to my own advantage, I cannot get you to compensate me without harming you in turn, leaving you worse off than you would have been had I not paid the money to you.[36]

[36] See further 8.II.

VII Use

What about those cases where your use of my asset does not seem to cause me any harm? You come into possession of my bicycle, ride it for a while, then return it. The bicycle is in no worse a condition now than when it left my hands. I wasn't going to ride it for the time you were riding it, so haven't been frustrated in any intended use of it. In those cases where title to the asset is held to remain in the claimant, it is typical to award the claimant damages on the basis of what is sometimes called the user principle, with the award assessed by reference to the sum the claimant could reasonably have charged the defendant for granting him such use of his asset. But while few doubt that these awards are justified, there is no consensus on what this justification is.

One suggestion is that these awards are in fact compensatory after all, the relevant loss being that the claimant missed out on the chance to negotiate a fee for allowing the defendant to make use of his asset.[37] But this view now has few supporters. Damages are awarded whether or not the claimant would in fact have agreed to permit such use and they are set at what the court adjudges would be a reasonable fee for that use whether or not this is the fee the claimant would in fact have charged. And, so the argument goes, if the claimant would not in fact have licensed this use for this fee, he suffers no such loss by being deprived of the opportunity to bargain for it. An alternative is to see these damages as compensating the claimant not for any material loss but for his loss of rights.[38] By using my bicycle without my permission, you infringe my rights. This infringement, whatever material loss may follow from it, entitles me to damages, since in so acting you usurped my right that you not (on this occasion at least) use my asset without my consent.

The modern trend, however, is to see these awards not as compensatory but as restitutionary: aimed at removing the benefit the claimant derived from his unauthorized use of the claimant's asset.[39] Why

[37] See eg *Strand Electric and Engineering Co Ltd v Brisford Entertainments Ltd* [1952] 2 QB 246 (CA) 256 (Romer LJ); Robert J Sharpe and S J Waddams, 'Damages for Lost Opportunity to Bargain' (1982) 2 *Oxford Journal of Legal Studies* 290.

[38] See eg Mitchell McInnes, 'Gain, Loss and the User Principle' [2006] *Restitution Law Review* 76. Cf Robert Stevens, *Torts and Rights* (Oxford University Press 2007) 59–68. For the shortcomings of this argument, see Webb (n 32) 165–69.

[39] See eg *Attorney General v Blake* [2001] 1 AC 268 (HL) 278–79 (Lord Nicholls); *Sempra Metals Ltd v Inland Revenue Commissioners* [2007] UKHL 34, [2008] 1 AC 561, para 230

must the defendant make restitution? For some it is because his gains were made wrongfully, for others it is because the gains derived from an asset's use properly belong to its rightful owner. Either way, these restitutionary accounts face the challenge of having to explain why these awards don't extend to the full measure of the gains the defendant derives from his use of the asset. If your unauthorized use of my bicycle enables you to make a meeting you'd otherwise have missed, striking a deal you otherwise wouldn't have struck, securing profits you wouldn't otherwise have secured, you will typically be required to pay me no more than a reasonable fee for the use of the bicycle, keeping these profits for yourself. One answer is to say my claim extends only to the wrongful 'transfer of value', only to the benefit of your using my asset and not to whatever additional gains may have resulted from that use.[40] But, here as elsewhere, talk of transfers of value is senseless; the value or benefit you get from your use of the bicycle is nothing I had previously, indeed nothing I ever could have had.[41] Once we reject this idea, the intended distinction between gains that are received from the claimant and those that merely result from use of his asset looks arbitrary.

If my ownership of the bicycle carried with it ownership of the benefits of its use, I could make out a claim simply by showing that you benefited from riding the bicycle without my permission. Your gain would be rightly mine. But, for the reasons given earlier in the chapter, this idea—an idea denied, if only implicitly, by much of the case law—is one we should, I think, reject. Again, this doesn't mean that it is never reasonable for the law to require you to surrender your gains, indeed to give them up to me. If you used my asset knowing that or not caring if it wasn't yours to use, there may well be good reason to take action against you to ensure you don't profit from your wrongdoing, so too perhaps to discourage others who might otherwise be tempted to follow your lead. But elsewhere, where your use of my asset, though unauthorized, was without fault, any liability is

(Lord Mance); Peter Jaffey, 'Restitutionary Damages and Disgorgement' [1995] *Restitution Law Review* 30; James Edelman, *Gain-Based Damages: Contract, Tort, Equity and Intellectual Property* (Hart Publishing 2002).

[40] Edelman, ibid 70. If, however, the gains the defendant must give up are limited to those that can be said to have come from the claimant, then we might wonder whether these awards are in fact compensatory after all, with 'restitution' available only to the extent that it is matched by some such loss to the claimant.

[41] 4.VII, 7.V.

better seen as compensatory, aimed at ensuring I suffer no disadvantage from your actions.

How so? If the asset is returned undamaged and your use of the asset didn't interfere with my planned use, there is, so it is typically assumed, no loss to compensate.[42] But I don't want you riding my bike in the same way I don't want you sleeping in my bed, even on those nights I'm away from home, and it makes no difference if you leave my room tidier than I left it. If it's said I suffer no tangible or material loss here, the answer is that not all losses are, in this sense, material. (In the same way you can benefit from riding my bicycle or sleeping in my bed even if it leaves you no richer.) Perhaps, if I'd had the opportunity, I would have sought a fee for permitting you to sleep in my bed or ride my bike. If we'd have agreed on such a charge, the fact you went ahead and did so without seeking my permission lost me this money. Restitution lawyers have been quick to reject as a fiction the suggestion that damages can be recoverable on the basis of this lost opportunity to bargain unless the evidence shows that such a bargain would have been struck. No doubt, if we wouldn't have come to any such agreement, I can't claim that your actions left me out of pocket. But it is a mistake to think this means you've caused me no loss. If I wouldn't have let you sleep in my bed or ride my bicycle at any price, the proper conclusion is not that I am no worse off when you do so but that the value I place on your not sleeping in my bed or riding my bicycle is so great that no sum of money would make it worth my while. Or in other words—if it really were true that I would not have permitted you to use my asset in this way, even for all the money in the world—the measure of my loss is not zero but incalculably high.

So the real lesson of those cases where the claimant would have spurned the opportunity to charge the defendant for his use of the asset is not that any damages cannot be compensatory but that requiring the defendant to pay only a reasonable fee for his use leaves the claimant radically under-compensated. It doesn't follow that these awards should be higher. If you are required to compensate me, your interests are harmed to the extent of your liability. This is, as we have seen, unobjectionable so far as your use of the asset has left you better off. Beyond this, you can object that your interests are being sacrificed to advance mine. This

[42] Cf *Watson Laidlaw & Co Ltd v Pott Cassells & Williamson* (1914) 31 RPC 104 (HL) 119 (Lord Shaw).

objection cuts less ice where you were at fault. But even then it will often be unreasonable to require you to bear all my losses, however great. Indeed, the law rarely demands that wrongdoers make good all the harms they've caused. There are also problems of evidence. Once we move away from balance sheet losses and gains, the identification and quantification of loss and gain becomes more difficult and the risk of error increases. In such circumstances, a rule that fixes recovery at the fee that might reasonably have been charged (or which on the market would be charged) for the defendant's use of the asset is not without merit.

VIII Remote Receipt

The account given here in some places mirrors and in others differs from the English law of unjust enrichment as we find it today. One difference—a difference in part of presentation, in part of substance—is found in the distinction the positive law draws between cases where title passes and those where it does not. This distinction is typically assumed to mark a difference of rationale, the point at which a claimant can no longer base any claim on his pre-transfer interest in the asset received by the defendant. This, however, is to mistake a difference in the mode of protecting the claimant's interest for a difference in the interest the law is protecting.[43]

Whether title passes makes some difference to what a claimant may recover from his immediate transferee. For instance, where title passes, the defendant's liability typically won't extend beyond the market value of the goods he has received. By contrast, where title remains in the claimant, the defendant may also be liable to make good consequential losses the claimant has suffered on account of the defendant's actions, whether or not he had reason to know that those goods in fact belonged to the claimant. These differences of response reflect and are reflected in differences in classification. The cases where title doesn't pass are often channelled through the law of torts; the defendant, even when innocent, is characterized as a wrongdoer. Once classed as a wrongdoer, it is then a short step to holding that the defendant should meet the losses caused by his wrongdoing, whether or not these losses leave him in any way enriched.

[43] 3.VI, 3.VII, 3.VIII.

The application of tort law and tort reasoning to resolve these claims has been attributed to the common law's failure to devise a cause of action which simply and directly asserts the claimant's ownership of some asset now in the defendant's hands.[44] Without this, the courts were left with having to give effect to these interests only obliquely: the claimant required instead to allege that the defendant's actions constituted an unauthorized (and hence wrongful) interference with his ownership of that asset, an interference which merited compensation. Whatever their historical explanation, these rules do a rough justice and their reform has, on occasion, been mooted.[45] This chapter examines how these cases would be approached if addressed on their merits.

It is in relation to remote recipients and in cases of insolvency, however, that the rules of title have their principal impact. If some asset of mine comes into your hands in such circumstances that title to that asset remains in me, I have a claim against you and, so long as that title endures, against anyone else into whose hands that asset later comes. If you or one of these later recipients becomes insolvent while still holding the asset, my claim will have priority over those of other creditors. The position changes if title passes. Now, unless some new title (or other right *in rem*) arises in my favour, my claim will rank alongside other ordinary unsecured claims. Things are less straightforward in relation to remote recipients. Some contend that, unless the claimant can establish some such right or title to the asset received by a remote defendant, no claim should lie.[46] Others propose that there is a general rule limiting unjust enrichment claims to direct recipients but admit exceptions to this.[47] On either view, claims against a remote recipient are significantly limited, if they lie at all.

[44] See eg J H Baker, *An Introduction to English Legal History* (4th edn, Butterworths 2002) 399; Peter Birks, 'Property and Unjust Enrichment: Categorical Truths' [1997] *New Zealand Law Review* 623, 646; Andrew Tettenborn, 'Conversion, Tort and Restitution' in Norman Palmer and Ewan McKendrick (eds), *Interests in Goods* (2nd edn, LLP 1998) 826–27.

[45] See eg *Iraqi Airways Corporation v Kuwait Airways Co (Nos 4 and 5)* [2002] UKHL 19, [2002] 2 AC 883, para 79 (Lord Nicholls).

[46] See eg *Kleinwort Benson v Birmingham City Council* [1997] QB 380 (CA) 400 (Morritt LJ); Smith, 'Restitution: The Heart of Corrective Justice' (n 29) 2115.

[47] See eg *T F L Management Services Ltd v Lloyds TSB Bank Plc* [2013] EWCA Civ 1415, [2014] 1 WLR 2006, para 52; *Relfo Ltd v Varsani* [2014] EWCA Civ 360, [2015] 1 BCLC 14, para 69; Andrew Burrows, *A Restatement of the English Law of Unjust Enrichment* (Oxford University Press 2012) 7–8, 48–52; Virgo (n 3) 105–12.

Why treat remote recipients differently? One argument goes as follows: cases of unjust enrichment are cases of defective or invalid transfers. An unjust enrichment claimant can succeed against a defendant because it is *this* defendant who was at the other end of the transfer that the claimant now impugns.[48] And so, for a defendant to be liable in unjust enrichment, there must be some nexus of transfer between him and the claimant. Take the standard case of unjust enrichment: I pay you £100 by mistake, title passes, I sue you in unjust enrichment. There is clearly a transfer between the two of us and I can recover the money from you. But if you then go and pay that £100 to a third party, I cannot recover from him since, between me and him, there has been no transfer. Indeed, not only is there no transfer between me and the current holder of the money, but the transfer by virtue of which he got hold of this money was itself flawless: title passed to you when I paid you the money and so your payment to the third party looks like a valid exercise of the power of disposition your title gave you. The same goes *a fortiori* if you pay the third party not the money I paid you but £100 of your own funds which you would not have spent had you not received the money from me. Again, though the third party is enriched and though this enrichment was, in this way, a result of my initial mistaken payment, there's no transfer between me and the third party; the money he received was money to which you were, and so he now is, absolutely entitled.

But it's a different matter if title doesn't pass. Though there is no transfer between me and the third party, my subsisting title provides its own nexus between us, its own basis for my claim to restitution. The assumption here is that title and direct receipt of a defective transfer are independent bases for restitution. If, however, we ask why the direct receipt of my mistaken payment supports your restitutionary liability, we are led back to my interest in determining the disposition of the money, my mistake significant precisely because it signals a lack of true or applicable consent to any such disposition. And so there are not two grounds for restitution here but one, with this single ground for restitution realized through two different techniques. This shows too that it is not only where title is held to remain in the claimant that his interest in that asset may support a claim to restitution. Again, it is a mistake to confuse a claimant's title with the interest that title

[48] Smith, 'Restitution: The Heart of Corrective Justice' (n 29) 2155–74; Andrew Tettenborn, 'Lawful Receipt—A Justifying Factor?' [1997] *Restitution Law Review* 1.

recognizes and protects, a mistake too to think that legal protection of this interest begins and ends with the location of title.

There's no doubt that my interest in the money can support claims against remote recipients. This is clear from those cases where title doesn't pass. Moreover, we can see that the fact that the law holds title to pass does not mean that it takes me to have no interest in the money, nor that this interest does not merit some legal recognition and support. This is the lesson of the ordinary cases of unjust enrichment, where title passes but you must nonetheless make restitution. So there is nothing in the reasons that ground unjust enrichment liability that means unjust enrichment claims can extend no further than direct recipients. If these claims are to have a more limited scope as against remoter recipients, this will only be because there are other countervailing reasons, competing goods and values, which apply to restrict the protection the law should, all things considered, accord to the claimant's interest in the asset in these circumstances.

IX Following and Tracing

Restitution is rightly denied in many cases that are regarded as examples of remote receipt or indirect enrichment. Say once more I pay you £100 by mistake. Feeling richer, you give £50 to a friend, £50 which doesn't come from the money I paid you and which you would not have given but for your receipt of that money from me. The friend is up £50 as a result of mistaken payment. Can I require your friend to give up the £50 to me? Traditionally the common law has said no. However, the courts' commitment to this position looks increasingly shaky.[49] The framework first proposed by the textbooks and now adopted by the courts provides that, subject to defences, liability in unjust enrichment will lie where (1) the defendant is enriched; (2) the enrichment is at the claimant's expense; and (3) the claimant can identify some relevant 'unjust factor'. My mistake is as clear an unjust factor as we get; your friend is just as clearly enriched. The only

[49] See eg *T F L Management Services v Lloyds TSB Bank* (n 47); *Menelaou v Bank of Cyprus Plc* [2013] EWCA Civ 1960, [2014] 1 WLR 854. Cf *Relfo v Varsani* (n 47) paras 72, 78, 114. See too *Banque Financière de la Cité v Parc (Battersea) Ltd* [1999] 1 AC 221 (HL), a decision explicable only on the basis that unjust enrichment liability can be made out on the back of remote causal links alone.

possible query seems to be whether we can say your friend's enrichment came at my expense. But, taking those words at face value, it seems at the very least plausible to say it was, and so the denial of any claim on these facts begins to look questionable, an example perhaps of the sort of arbitrariness and injustice which resulted from unjust enrichment's sorry history of marginalization and misunderstanding.

In fact the key issue and key confusion concerns not the 'at the expense of' requirement but the element of enrichment. The fact that title typically passes has fooled many unjust enrichment lawyers into thinking that unjust enrichment claims are concerned only with the receipt of abstract value. Having taken this first step, the question then arises why those who are similarly enriched as an indirect result of a claimant's mistaken disposition should not be similarly liable to give up that enrichment. A few bit that bullet, arguing that causal connections should suffice.[50] Others, seeing that the cases rejected that approach, were faced with the challenge of explaining these restrictions on claims against remote recipients. One response was to conjure up a requirement of privity, another to insist that the logic of unjust enrichment, perhaps of private law generally, necessitated the bipolar relationship of transferor and (immediate) transferee.[51] But these attempted explanations are at best ad hoc, at worst untrue.

No claim in unjust enrichment should lie against remote recipients on the basis of mere causal connections, as in the case between me and your friend. But this is because mere causal enrichment is insufficient to ground restitutionary liability even in cases of direct receipt. If my ownership of my assets carried with it (presumptive) ownership of any benefits which result from its use, we would have here a reason for giving me a claim against those who benefit from the unauthorized use or application of those assets. But, as we saw earlier, there are good reasons to deny that this is an incident of ownership. And if the asset's proper owner has no such entitlement to the benefits his asset creates, the mere fact that some other person derives such a benefit

[50] See eg Stephen Watterson, '"Direct Transfers" in the Law of Unjust Enrichment' (2011) 64 *Current Legal Problems* 435; Birks (n 1) 89–98.

[51] For invocations of privity, see Virgo (n 3) 105–07; Andrew Burrows, *The Law of Restitution* (Butterworths 1993) 45–54. Cf Burrows (n 28) 69. For appeals to the logic of bipolarity, see Ernest J Weinrib, 'Correctively Unjust Enrichment' in Robert Chambers, Charles Mitchell, and James Penner (eds), *Philosophical Foundations of the Law of Unjust Enrichment* (Oxford University Press 2009) 37. Cf Smith, 'Restitution: The Heart of Corrective Justice' (n 29) 2155–75.

from that asset, whether directly or indirectly, gives us no reason to order that this benefit be given up to the owner. Here then the effect of unjust enrichment lawyers' reimagining of this area of law has been to cast doubt on the sound, if largely intuitive, decisions of the courts concerning the proper reach of these claims.

It is a different matter if the money you pay your friend comes out of the very money I paid you. Now I can say that the money your friend now holds is money that was mine at the outset and to the disposition of which I never properly consented. It is this argument which grounds my claim to restitution when you, my immediate transferee, are in receipt of the money, and that same argument is hardly defeated by a further transfer of that money to which I was not party and hence to which I gave no authorization. So it is, in the first instance, no answer at all for your friend to say that he got hold of this money through a transfer that was, between you and him, flawless. Any entitlement he seeks to assert through that payment depends upon your authority to confer such an entitlement on him, and it is precisely that authority which my claim denies.

Of course, the rule of positive law that says title passes to you in many of these cases appears to confer just this authority on you. (Why only 'appears to'? Because this rule, and hence this authority, may yet be undercut by the law requiring you or your disponee to give up the asset to me on demand.) But in so far as this rule does remove this authority from me and confer it on you, this can't serve to justify the entitlement to that asset which your transferee now claims on the back of that authority. The rule cannot justify its own application. In other words, what we would need to explain is why, in spite of my failure to authorize any such disposition, my title and the authority it confers should be taken to pass to you and hence, in turn, from you to the friend to whom you pay that money, with the consequence that he can resist my claim to restitution.

One suggestion, noted previously, is that title is held to pass in many of these cases precisely to ensure that the interests of third parties and creditors are not prejudiced by claims in unjust enrichment.[52] But in what sense are the interests of third party recipients prejudiced by these claims? They are clearly left worse off than they would be if these claims were not allowed. But that is true of all defendants in all

[52] 3.VI.

unjust enrichment claims. If I pay you by mistake, you cannot resist my claim by showing that you would be left poorer by making restitution than if you didn't. That's not to deny that your interests may yet be harmed by my claim. If you have arranged your own affairs, deployed your own resources on the understanding that the money you received from me was validly transferred and so now properly at your disposal, you may be disadvantaged if now called upon to make restitution. This is the basis of the defence of change of position.[53] But until this point—and even then only *pro tanto*—the only interest adversely affected by holding you liable in unjust enrichment is your interest in keeping for yourself an asset that by law was mine to deal with and dispose of. No doubt you may be able to show how giving you access to this asset would do you good. Perhaps allowing the asset to remain with you would do you or the community at large more good than were the asset to be returned to me. But again, arguments such as these are by and large foreclosed by the adoption of a regime of private property.[54] The mere fact that I am no longer in possession of my asset cannot be taken as an opportunity to reopen the question of entitlement to that asset without undermining the very scheme of entitlements that private property recognizes.

The same goes if the asset made its way from me to you not directly but indirectly, passing through another's hands first. Here too, if you gave value to acquire the asset, or if you've since changed your position, my claim for restitution may set back your interests. Where this is so, there will often be good reason to restrict my claim so as to see that you aren't disadvantaged. But that there will be times when ordering restitution risks doing unjustified harm to a remote recipient is no more a reason to impose a general bar on such claims than it is in cases of direct transfers, where such concerns are instead dealt with by affording the recipient a defence (a defence which, typically, extends only so far as the interest of his which merits protection). Cases of remote receipt will sometimes raise evidential difficulties, difficulties not found, or not found so often or acutely, in claims against immediate transferees. Is the money the defendant received the same money as first paid by the claimant? If not, can we identify a series of transactional links connecting the defendant's receipt to the initial mistaken transfer? But this should not obscure the fact that cases of

[53] 8.II.
[54] 4.III.

direct and indirect receipt are, at root, alike, the route by which the asset came into the defendant's hands, by itself, immaterial to the way these cases fall to be treated.

At present, English law goes both too far and not far enough in its response to cases of remote receipt: too far in its increasing willingness to hold indirect enrichees liable even where no series of transactional links connects them to the initial unauthorized transfer, and so where they have received no asset or advantage to which the claimant can establish any prior entitlement. At the same time, it doesn't go far enough by often denying claimants the opportunity to look beyond their immediate transferees to those into whose hands the asset or its substitute has later passed. For when title is held to pass, as it often is, and the claimant is accorded no other title or right *in rem* in its place, claimants aren't empowered to follow their assets through a chain of transfers and substitutions, claiming against those who have come into possession of those assets further down the line.[55] So where I pay you by mistake but title passes and no trust of that money is imposed in my favour, I am taken to have no claim against any further recipients of that money or of assets acquired with it. My claim to restitution begins and ends with you.

Since the difference between those cases where title passes and those where it does not lies, in the main, in the way in which I can say my payment was not intended, my ability to seek restitution from remote recipients then turns on the nature of the 'defect' in my consent to that initial transfer. Often it is thought that the cases in which title doesn't pass are those where my consent is wholly absent or where the defect in that consent is particularly severe, with title passing where the defect is slighter. One suggestion then is that my remedies are greater in those cases where title doesn't pass because the defect in my consent to the transfer is greater.[56] For reasons given earlier, the common view that these 'defects' in consent differ (relevantly) in degree is, I think, mistaken.[57] So when I pay you in the mistaken belief I owe you the money, my intention that you have that money is conditional on that money being due. I no more intend you to have money you are not due, and so no more intend you to have it in the

[55] Cf *Lipkin Gorman v Karpnale Ltd* [1991] 2 AC 548 (HL).

[56] See eg Peter Watts, 'Property and "Unjust Enrichment": Cognate Conservators' [1998] *New Zealand Law Review* 151, 154.

[57] 5.IV.

circumstances which in fact obtain, than I would were you simply to snatch the money from me. (Though the fact that I am responsible for the money now being in your hands rather than mine may yet make a difference to what I can reasonably require of you.)

In any case, even were we to say that some unintended transfers are more unintended than others, this wouldn't get us to the position English law has adopted. Say lesser mistakes deserve lesser protection. Still this wouldn't explain drawing a line between direct and remote recipients; why, that is, the success of my claim should depend on whether or not the asset you received first passed through the hands of an intermediary. That I made a mere liability mistake rather than, say, a mistake as to my immediate transferee's identity—a mistake typically taken to prevent title passing—doesn't give a recipient, direct or remote, any greater claim to that asset, any stronger reason to resist my claim to restitution. Again, if that recipient didn't give value and in the absence of some change of position, the only interest the defendant can set up to counter my claim is his interest in taking what the law had declared mine.

The reasons that ground restitutionary liability in cases of mistaken and other unauthorized transfers extend to direct and indirect transferees alike. Nor are there any general considerations that weigh only against claims brought against indirect recipients. Perhaps there is cause to be particularly attentive to the interests of those further removed from the initial misapplication; perhaps the security of receipt of those who aren't party to that transfer requires greater protection or more sensitive treatment. But in none of these cases is there reason to cut off liability automatically at the point of initial receipt. So there is good reason to treat a claimant's right to restitution as in all cases operating, at least presumptively, *in rem*, with the claims available against remote recipients mirroring those available against the direct transferee.

X Insolvency

An unjust enrichment defendant's insolvency presents what is at root just another instance of indirect transfer.[58] I pay you by mistake. With

[58] See too Andrew Kull, 'Restitution in Bankruptcy: Reclamation and Constructive Trust' (1998) 72 *American Bankruptcy Law Journal* 265, 279–80.

the money still in your possession, you are declared bankrupt. Your insolvency means that I am in a competition with your other creditors. You don't have the resources to meet all our claims in full, so the question that arises is how these resources are to be applied towards the satisfaction of our various claims. Among those resources is the money you received from me. To the extent that the claims of your other creditors are satisfied from that money—or, if what you received from me was not money but some other asset, from the proceeds of sale of that asset—these creditors end up as remote recipients: they receive, via you, the insolvent, the money I initially held and owned. As we've seen, remote recipients, at least in the first instance, fall to be treated no differently to direct recipients. We might simply add that, just as my interest in my assets justifies their return from a defendant into whose hands they have passed without my proper authorization, it likewise justifies the law acting to prevent others making unauthorized use or taking unauthorized possession of those assets. If we are to give effect to the claimant's interest in his asset, then that asset should not be made available to other creditors. Instead, the claimant should ordinarily be able to recover that asset or, where applicable, its proceeds of sale in full.

This also shows why the standard objections to according unjust enrichment claims this sort of priority in insolvency get things the wrong way around. So the principal reason given against extending this protection to more unjust enrichment claimants is that this would be unfair to the defendant's other creditors, who would be disadvantaged by this reduction in the funds available to meet their claims.[59] Now the mere fact that other creditors would indeed be left worse off indicates no injustice to them. After all, even if unjust enrichment claims are given no such priority, they nonetheless leave the defendant's creditors worse off, since this adds one more person to the list of unsecured creditors between whom the defendant's remaining funds are to be divided. Each additional claim leaves existing creditors worse off, but this doesn't mean that each new claim is an injustice to those existing creditors. The reason giving these claims priority is thought by some to be unjust is that it means these claimants aren't merely added to this list, they jump the queue. Unjust enrichment claimants would secure an advantage over other creditors, recovering in full

[59] See eg *Westdeutsche Landesbank Girozentrale v Islington London Borough Council* [1996] AC 669 (HL) 690 (Lord Goff), 703–04 (Lord Browne-Wilkinson).

while those others are left with an even smaller pool from which their claims are to be met. This appears at odds with the basic principle of *pari passu* distribution: all creditors should bear a proportionate share of the losses resulting from the defendant's insolvency.

Set up in this way, the onus seems to be on those who would accord unjust enrichment claimants priority to say what's special about these claims and claimants, and so why they deserve this elevation over other classes of creditor. Some have then sought to support priority on the basis that unjust enrichment claimants are (typically) unsecured creditors, others have contended that without such priority the defendant's other creditors would receive a windfall.[60] Though sound in part, these arguments were weakened by a failure fully to explore or to grasp the reasons for these claims and so were too easily dismissed by those who, with no grasp at all of these reasons, saw only their deficiencies.[61]

As between creditors who, for instance, seek compensation for losses caused to them by the defendant's breach of duty, the *pari passu* principle reflects the fact that none of them has any greater claim than the others to the assets held by the defendant. Since none can provide a reason why a particular asset should be made available to him, in satisfaction of his claim, in preference to other creditors, they must all take their fair, proportionate share of these assets and of the resulting shortfall. But this isn't true where the basis of a creditor's claim is not something the defendant has done, but rather some thing that he has, some asset in his hands that the claimant is asserting is properly his. Nobody doubts that the claimant deserves to recover his asset in priority to other creditors where he retains title to that asset. But it is thought that this basis for according him priority is lost where title is lost. Once again, however, this is a mistake, caused by the same failure to see that it is the same interest at stake where (as is more common) title passes.

When we do see this, we can then also see why, were the money I mistakenly paid you to be made available to your other creditors,

[60] See eg David M Paciocco, 'The Remedial Constructive Trust: A Principled Basis for Priorities over Creditors' (1989) 68 *Canadian Bar Review* 315; William Goodhart and Gareth Jones, 'The Infiltration of Equitable Doctrine into English Commercial Law' (1980) 43 *Modern Law Review* 489, 500.

[61] See eg William Swadling, 'Policy Arguments for Proprietary Restitution' (2008) 28 *Legal Studies* 506, 517, 525–27.

this would indeed be an unjustified windfall rather than, say, a fair reduction of the losses that those creditors would in any case suffer as a result of your insolvency. As is the case with unjust enrichment defendants, the only interest these other creditors can set up against my claim for restitution of that money—the only basis on which they may contend that according me priority would do them an injustice—is their interest in taking advantage of an asset the law had marked out as mine and to whose disposition I haven't consented. And so, while giving me priority leaves your other creditors with less, it will typically leave them no worse off than they would have been had the initial unauthorized transfer never been made.[62] The only loss my priority causes is the loss of their not having access to my funds.

Of course, these creditors are going to lose out to some degree come what may and so, unlike the typical unjust enrichment defendant, they are also victims of an injustice. The creditor who has a claim against you in tort or for a breach of contract is, as a matter of justice, owed compensation and he will suffer an on-going injustice if, as a result of your insolvency, he does not get the compensation he is due. It may then seem that, by denying me priority and making the money I paid you available to meet their claims, this injustice can be, in part, corrected and, if so, according me priority elevates my interests over your interest in being fully, or at least better, compensated. But the justness of their compensation does not make just the redistribution of funds from me to them. After all, I'm not implicated in the initial injustices on which their claims rest: *I* don't owe them compensation. That denying me priority would indeed effect such a redistribution is obscured only by the fact that, right now, the money is in your hands, not mine. But my very claim is that, though it is indeed in your hands, it remains my money. If that claim succeeds, the only basis on which your creditors might claim access to those funds fails.

[62] See too Emily L Sherwin, 'Constructive Trusts in Bankruptcy' [1989] *University of Illinois Law Review* 297, 332–33; Vanessa Finch and Sarah Worthington, 'The *Pari Passu* Principle and Ranking Restitutionary Rights' in Francis Rose (ed), *Restitution and Insolvency* (Mansfield Press 2000) 10–11, 16. There are exceptions to this. If a would-be creditor adjudges the defendant creditworthy in part on the basis of the funds I paid him, he may be prejudiced if, having given credit on this basis, the defendant goes insolvent and these funds are not available to his general creditors. This is the problem of 'off-balance sheet liabilities' (see eg *Westdeutsche* (n 59) 705 (Lord Browne-Wilkinson)). This concern, analogous to the concern that underlies the change of position defence, shall be examined in the next chapter: 8.V.

All this is premised on you retaining possession of either the asset I transferred to you or its exchange product. If you don't, then, as we've seen, I may yet have a claim against you on the basis of your dealings with the asset while it was in your hands. But my claim now is effectively compensatory: I am no longer asking you to give up to me something which is rightly mine, but to see that I am not disadvantaged by what you did with it. At this point, the case for giving my claim priority over those of your other creditors falls away. Indeed, it falls away even if your assets remain swollen by virtue of your receipt and use of that asset. Say my mistaken payment prompts you to spend funds of your own which bring you a profit. Despite this profit, you go insolvent. You are wealthier than you would have been had you not received the money from me. But the increased funds at your disposal are not the traceable proceeds of that money and, for the reasons given earlier, the mere fact that they are causally attributable to your use of my money does not support giving me any interest in them. Accordingly, upon your insolvency, I can establish no entitlement to those additional funds that supports applying them to the satisfaction of my claim ahead of the claims of your other creditors.

XI Contracts and Creditors

Much the same position as I've sketched out here is endorsed by those who argue that resulting trusts should be the law's default response where assets are transferred by mistake or under coercion. But they have tended to stop short of proposing that this should be the rule for all unauthorized transfers. One suggestion is that a trust should arise only where 'there is no moment in which the enrichment is held free of any claim'.[63] What this limit is designed to exclude are cases of conditional transfers where the condition fails only after receipt. In these cases, the claim should operate only *in personam*, save where the defendant received the asset on the basis that it was to be 'ring-fenced': kept apart from the rest of his assets and available to the defendant only on certain conditions.[64]

[63] Birks (n 4) 181–82.

[64] Birks, ibid 194–98; Chambers (n 14) 144–53.

Why no trust here? The thinking is that, once the asset has passed absolutely to the recipient, the claimant can't later claw it back, even when the condition he attached to its transfer fails. Either the claimant can make out some right *in rem* subsisting (at least) from the date of transfer or he can make out none at all. But this only begs the question, simply reasserting that no *in rem* claim will lie in these cases. In truth, this restriction is arbitrary. Say I pay you £100, anticipating a debt I believe I will shortly owe to you. I am wrong and no such debt arises. On this view, I can demand that you pay me £100 but, though I can identify the very money I paid you, I have no priority in the event of your insolvency and have no claim against anyone you have since passed that money on to. The upshot is that the failure of condition is taken to justify your liability as my immediate payee, but not of any remote recipients of that money. Yet I no more consented to their having this money than I did you. Nor, by the same token, did I consent to that money being made available to your creditors in the event of your insolvency. Even if we consider that it should make a difference to how the law responds to my claim that here, unlike in cases of mistake, we can't know until later whether the condition I've attached to my payment is met, it's hard to see why this difference should be to limit liability to my initial transferee. If the subsequent failure of condition is enough to recover from you, it should be enough to recover from those who claim through you.

The real motivation for excluding cases of failed conditions subsequent is a concern about extending priority to many claims arising out of failed contracts.[65] The standard view takes payments and other asset transfers made in performance of a contract to be conditional both on the defendant performing his part of the contract in return and on the validity of that contract. When these conditions fail—the defendant fails to perform, the contract is terminated—so does the basis upon which the claimant consented to those transfers. This then looks like a straightforward case of unjust enrichment and so the claimant is entitled to restitution. But were these claims also to operate *in rem*, these claimants would be elevated to the status of secured creditors, notwithstanding that they hadn't bargained, and paid, for that protection. Even those happy to see priority in insolvency given

[65] Cf Peter Birks, 'Restitution and Resulting Trusts' in Stephen Goldstein (ed), *Equity and Contemporary Legal Developments* (The Harry and Michael Sacher Institute for Legislative Research and Comparative Law, Hebrew University of Jerusalem 1992) 347–59.

to the standard mistaken payer have thought extending this advantage this far unacceptable.

Sometimes the conclusion that insolvency priority should be denied to this class of claimants is explained on the basis that they, unlike other unjust enrichment claimants, voluntarily accepted the risk of the defendant's insolvency.[66] Having accepted this risk, there is no objection to them bearing their share of the losses that result from it; indeed, it would be unjust if they didn't. But what it means to say these claimants accepted the risk of insolvency is rarely spelt out. If the parties had agreed that, should the defendant go insolvent, the claimant is to have no priority over other creditors, the law should, no doubt, uphold that agreement and deny the claimant any such priority. Here the transfer is in effect made on terms that, in the event of the defendant's insolvency, the asset will be made available to meet the claims of other creditors. But this isn't the usual case. The mere fact that the claimant was aware of the possibility, even the likelihood, of the defendant's insolvency doesn't provide a reason for denying him the protection he would otherwise be due in that event. Knowledge that one's conduct raises or exposes one to a particular risk is not the same as consenting to, or assuming, that risk. That a claimant knows that the defendant may breach the contract doesn't mean we deny him a remedy on the basis that he 'accepted the risk of breach'. The claimant's awareness that the condition he attached to a transfer may fail does not render that transfer and his consent to it any less conditional.[67] So too his knowledge of the possibility of the defendant's insolvency does not mean he consents to the assets—assets transferred on the condition of the contract's performance—being made available to the defendant's creditors in that event.

Underlying the acceptance of risk argument is the sense that creditors shouldn't be given insolvency protection they haven't bargained for. But the fact that a claimant hasn't bargained for a particular right or protection only matters if he is not due it in any event. If he is, the fact that he didn't bargain and pay for it is neither here nor there. You don't need to bargain for what is yours by right.[68] On the contrary,

[66] See eg *Westdeutsche* (n 59) 684 (Lord Goff); Paciocco (n 60) 340–45; Sherwin (n 62) 335–37; Burrows (n 28) 176–79.

[67] 5.VI, 5.VII.

[68] See too Craig Rotherham, 'Tracing and Justice in Bankruptcy' in Francis Rose (ed), *Restitution and Insolvency* (Mansfield Press 2000) 129.

the only question should be whether you have bargained it away. More fully: contract is just one source of legal rights and duties, and contracting parties don't lose their extra-contractual rights by entering into contracts that make no express provision for them. So where a contracting party doesn't bargain for an insolvency priority, it means only that there's no justification *in the contract* for according him that priority. But it doesn't rule out the possibility that priority may be justified on some other basis. If these restitutionary claims following termination really are claims in unjust enrichment, analogous to cases of mistaken payments, then a basis for recovery and for priority is to be found outside the contract in the claimant's interest in the asset now held by the defendant.

But it's not clear that these are, or should be seen as, claims in unjust enrichment. The argument was set out in full in the previous chapter.[69] In short, a claimant cannot claim in unjust enrichment if he was under an obligation to make the transfer he would now like to see reversed. The obligation means that the claimant has no say over making the transfer, so it is neither here nor there whether he consented to it. Where a contract is terminated, this does not cancel the contract *ab initio* but merely releases the parties from their future obligations. The obligations that have already accrued are not set aside and so the payments and transfers made in performance of that contract thus far remain transfers made in fulfilment of a valid legal obligation. So, though the claimant can indeed maintain that he (say) paid the money on the understanding that the contract would be performed and though the defendant's breach and the contract's termination means this condition fails, no claim lies on the basis that he didn't consent to the defendant having the money in these circumstances because the obligatoriness of the payment means his consent isn't needed.

Instead, the claimant's right to restitution of the value of assets transferred under the contract, likewise his right to payment for work he has done, may be better seen as grounded in the contract. It is the contract that grants the right to terminate the contract and so it is the first place to look if we want to know the consequences of termination. Indeed, since it's clear that restitution for assets transferred and work done in performance of the contract are among the standard consequences of termination, when the parties provide for

[69] 6.III, 6.IV.

termination they are, absent some indication to the contrary, providing for these consequences. If this is correct, then there is no reason to think these claims should have the same priority in insolvency as unjust enrichment claims. On the contrary, we should expect them to take no priority unless this was what the contract provided.

8

Defences

1 Denials and Defences

Where some asset of mine ends up in your hands without my proper consent, there is a reason to require you to make restitution to me. I pay you £100 mistakenly believing this is money I owe you. The money was mine to spend as I chose. My choice to give it to you was conditional on my owing you this sum. My mistake as to my indebtedness means that this condition wasn't satisfied. Since I consented to your having only the money you were due, I did not and do not consent to you having this money in these circumstances, and I can call on you to repay me. You can, of course, defeat my claim by showing that this is not in fact what happened: for instance, that I was not in truth mistaken or that, though mistaken, I intended you to have the money in any event. If you're right, my interest in determining the disposition of that money provides no grounds for a claim to restitution. Indeed, this interest then provides a reason to treat my payment as final.

But you may also be able to resist my claim, not by denying my version of events but by showing that there is more to the story. Take an example outside the law of unjust enrichment, though also concerning the protection of private property interests. My ownership of my land gives me presumptive authority over others' access to and use of it and so puts you under a presumptive duty not to enter without my permission. Accordingly, I can make out a claim in trespass simply by showing that you went onto my land without that permission. Again, you can resist my claim by showing that you did in fact have my permission or by establishing that the land wasn't mine so it wasn't my permission you needed. But you can also defeat my claim by admitting this much but showing that you entered to escape a murderous stalker or to save the baby drowning in the puddle on my lawn. (In both cases, let us assume this was the only ready means of averting the threatened evil.) Here you're not denying my interest in the land. Nor need you deny that this interest gives a reason for you to keep off. Rather, you're saying that this interest of mine cannot be protected without doing harm to you or to others, that though there may be a reason for imposing liability there is also a reason against it. The same is true with unjust enrichment. My ownership interest is just one good among many which merit the law's protection and promotion. Where other goods, other values would be threatened by ordering you to make restitution, it may be reasonable to deny my claim or to limit what I recover from you.

To put it another way, these competing goods and values are grounds for according you a defence. It has been said with surprising frequency that defences to claims in unjust enrichment must logically amount to a denial of some element of the cause of action.[1] But the logic is specious and the claim simply wrong. No doubt the term 'defences' can be used in different ways and so may include what are no more than denials of some such element of the cause of action. But defences are of distinct analytical interest only where they raise considerations that are not already factored into the claim.[2] (Though

[1] See eg Peter Birks, *Restitution—The Future* (The Federation Press 1992) 125–26; Richard Nolan, 'Change of Position' in P B H Birks (ed), *Laundering and Tracing* (Clarendon Press 1995) 136; Ross B Grantham and Charles E F Rickett, *Enrichment and Restitution in New Zealand* (Hart Publishing 2000) 334; cf 314. The distinctiveness of defences has been better grasped by criminal lawyers: see eg Kenneth Campbell, 'Offence and Defence' in I H Dennis (ed), *Criminal Law and Justice: Essays from the W G Hart Workshop 1986* (Sweet and Maxwell 1987); John Gardner, 'Justifications and Reasons' in A P Simester and A T H Smith (eds), *Harm and Culpability* (Clarendon Press 1996). Cf Luis Duarte d'Almeida, *Allowing for Exceptions: A Theory of Defences and Defeasibility in Law* (Oxford University Press 2015). See too James Goudkamp and Charles Mitchell, 'Denials and Defences in the Law of Unjust Enrichment' in Charles Mitchell and William Swadling (eds), *The Restatement Third, Restitution and Unjust Enrichment: Critical and Comparative Essays* (Hart Publishing 2013), where this distinction is, it seems, drawn but not grasped (see eg 143: 'it would be possible to do away with defences by assimilating all of the liability rules in unjust enrichment into elements of an action').

[2] The conventional framework for addressing unjust enrichment claims asks: (1) Was the defendant enriched?; (2) Was the enrichment at the claimant's expense?; (3) Was the enrichment unjust?; (4) Are there any defences? If defences are merely denials of some element of the cause of action, the fourth of these questions adds nothing, amounting simply to 'Are you sure?'

the line between reasons for liability and reasons against may be conceptually clear, it won't always clear to draw in practice. On occasion, elements of the cause of action will already factor in some competing interests and goods. This may be true of many fault requirements. My interest in my person and property is a good worth protecting, again at least presumptively, against all unjustified invasions. But strict liability for all such invasions may pose an unreasonable burden on others. Duties of reasonable care may therefore be best seen as balances of the interests of the claimant with the interests of those around him.)

There is no limit on the goods and values that may, at least on occasion, be at stake in the law's resolution of unjust enrichment claims. Accordingly, there is no limit on the reasons that may bear on their proper treatment. Defences to claims in unjust enrichment are, in principle, as many and as diverse as the reasons we have to reject or to restrict these claims. Nonetheless some of these defences have broader application than others, some are more closely or more often linked to the cause of action in unjust enrichment than others. This chapter looks at three: change of position, bona fide purchase, and passing on.

II Change of Position

Liability in cases of unjust enrichment is presumptively strict. The claimant need make no allegation of wrongdoing or fault on the defendant's part. He is simply alleging that he has a legally recognized interest in something in the defendant's hands, something he has not authorized the defendant to have and which should, therefore, be returned. The defendant is being asked to do no more than give up an item to which he had no prior entitlement and to which no entitlement was properly granted to him by the one person entitled to do so. Of course, requiring him to give up that asset or its monetary equivalent leaves the defendant worse off than he would have been if he were under no such liability. But this does him no injustice for, as we have seen, the harm this does him is only the harm of being deprived of something which is, as a matter of justice, not his but the claimant's.[3] So, in the straightforward case, the defendant is left in no

[3] 7.VI.

worse a position than he would have been in had the transfer not been made. He gains, but also loses, nothing.

But this changes where the defendant has begun to arrange his affairs on the understanding that the asset he received is his to keep. Most tailor their expenditure to the resources at their disposal. If you have more money in your pocket or in your bank account, you may buy things you wouldn't have bought if you'd had less. If you are the recipient of a sum of money of which, months or perhaps years later, the payer seeks restitution, you may have made any number of purchasing decisions on the understanding that the money was yours to spend as you like, decisions you wouldn't have made had you not received that money or had you known that you would have to return it to me. Say I pay you £100 by mistake. Neither knowing or suspecting I was mistaken, and hence thinking this money is yours, you treat yourself to something—a meal out, a day at the races—you wouldn't have indulged in if you hadn't thought you truly had these increased funds at your disposal. Now requiring you to repay in full would leave you disadvantaged. You would then be down not just the money I paid you but also the money you spent on the meal or at the races. True, you have the benefit of that meal or of the day out. But this is a benefit towards which you wouldn't have committed your resources without the addition of the money I paid you, a benefit which was not, to you—in these circumstances, given your other expenses and priorities—worth the money you spent on it. Here then it is less clear that it is reasonable for the law to demand that you make full restitution of the money you received from me.

It is to protect defendants in such cases that the courts have developed the defence of change of position. It has been suggested that the defence is specifically tied to the cause of action in unjust enrichment and indeed is better characterized as a defence of disenrichment: the defendant's plea that, though he was at one point unjustly enriched, he is enriched no more.[4] On this basis, change of position looks less like a defence than a denial. If enrichment provides a ground for liability, it is for enrichment retained rather than enrichment once held. That you have a benefit you shouldn't have is a reason to make you give

[4] See eg Andrew Burrows, *The Law of Restitution* (3rd edn, Oxford University Press 2011) 526–27. Cf Peter Birks, *Unjust Enrichment* (2nd edn, Clarendon Press 2005) 208–09; James Edelman, 'Change of Position: A Defence of Unjust Disenrichment' (2012) 92 *Boston University Law Review* 1009.

it up; that you once did isn't. So what should matter is not whether you were unjustly enriched at some earlier time but whether you are unjustly enriched now, at the point at which you are being asked to give up your enrichment. This view is sometimes challenged on the basis that the cause of action is complete at the moment the enrichment is received.[5] But there is no inconsistency between holding that unjust enrichment liability arises as soon as the defendant is unjustly enriched and that this liability then extends only so far as his extant enrichment. Nor does this view rule out putting the burden of proof of what enrichment survives onto the defendant.

But, as we've seen, to see these cases and claims as concerned with the defendant's unjust enrichment is, in truth, a mischaracterization.[6] Their true focus is not what benefit the defendant obtains from the transfer but rather the very thing transferred and their true ground the claimant's interest in that asset and in its disposition. My interest in my assets is not simply an interest in their value and, where some asset of mine ends up in your hands without my authorization, this interest provides a reason for restitution whatever value you or I put on it. If you come into possession of my copy of this book without my consent, my claim for its return doesn't require me to show you were enriched by its receipt and so isn't weakened by you showing that it's worth nothing to you, that you were happier without it. So long, therefore, as my claim is directed to some asset of mine presently in your hands, your change of position, or disenrichment, is no denial of the reason for restitution my interest in that asset provides. Rather it is a true defence, offering a reason why restitution should nonetheless be denied.

What reason? The effect of your change of position is that my interests cannot now be secured, or secured in full, without doing harm to yours. If restitution is ordered, then, to the extent of your change of position, your interests are sacrificed for mine. It is often said that the interest the law is recognizing here is in the security of your receipts.[7] And this is true so far as it goes: the harm you would suffer in these cases comes from your assumption that the money you received from

[5] See eg Charles Mitchell, Paul Mitchell, and Stephen Watterson (eds), *Goff and Jones: The Law of Unjust Enrichment* (8th edn, Sweet and Maxwell 2011) [4-34].

[6] 7.II, 7.III, 7.V.

[7] See eg Birks (n 4) 209; Michael Jewell, 'Change of Position' in Peter Birks and Francis Rose (eds), *Lessons of the Swaps Litigation* (Mansfield Press 2000) 273.

me was yours to keep, that you could go ahead and plan and spend on that basis. No doubt being able to plan in this way, to rely on the assumption that resources that appear to be yours *are* yours is valuable. But the effect of ordering full restitution in these cases is not just to impair your ability to make these plans but to undermine the very plans you have made, and would otherwise go on to make.

In our example, your change of position comes from an application of your own resources triggered by my payment to you. You spend your money on the meal or a day at the races thinking you had the money I'd paid you to fall back on. So we might say that here it is not simply your interest in security of receipt which is at stake in my claim to restitution but your own interest in determining the disposition of *your* assets. If I can recover the money I paid you, the money you paid on the meal or the day out becomes money paid by mistake, money paid on a misunderstanding as to your true wealth. This then provides what some have found a pleasing symmetry: the claimant cannot assert his interest in disposing of his assets without granting the defendant his equivalent interest.[8] But, while this interest of the defendant's is indeed worthy of protection and while the change of position defence serves this function, the reach and rationale of the defence are broader still. Say, in reliance on the money I paid you, you turn down an opportunity to earn some additional cash that you'd otherwise have taken up. Requiring you to make restitution would leave you poorer. But it leaves you poorer without undermining any disposition of your existing funds.

So the change of position defence does protect your interest in the security of your receipts and often too your interest in determining the use and disposition of your assets. But, more than this, it serves to ensure that your plans are not disrupted, that your goals are not frustrated. Accordingly, the harm you are done if you are required to make restitution despite your change of position is not merely the harm of having less wealth than you believed you had or than you would have had had I not paid you, but the damage this does to the life you've chosen and its impact on the choices that lie before you.[9]

[8] See eg Nicholas J McBride and Paul McGrath, 'The Nature of Restitution' (1995) 15 *Oxford Journal of Legal Studies* 33, 40–43; Hanoch Dagan, *The Law and Ethics of Restitution* (Cambridge University Press 2004) 45–46, 66–67; Edelman (n 4) 1021–23.

[9] Cf Dagan, ibid 47–49; Elise Bant, *The Change of Position Defence* (Hart Publishing 2009) 212–16.

Indeed, we might see change of position as just one instance of a broader concern to ensure that protection of the claimant's interests does not undermine the interests of the defendant, a concern relevant to any private law dispute; indeed any private law rule or relationship. It is, for instance, the same concern as motivates some of the unease over strict liability for loss. While the claimant's interests are served by having his losses made good, this comes at the expense of the defendant and his interests. In the absence of fault or consent, this looks like the defendant's interests are being relegated to those of the claimant, that the defendant is being used as a means to the claimant's ends. So we saw in the previous chapter that a defendant who doesn't retain any asset of the claimant's cannot now be liable on the basis of what he has.[10] He may still be liable, however, on the basis of what he did, for his dealings with that asset when it was in his hands. Where these dealings have caused the claimant harm, we can see that he is not left disadvantaged and that his broader interests are secured by requiring the defendant to make compensation. But if the defendant was not at fault for causing these harms, why should the law require him to make good these harms at cost to his own interests? As we saw then, this concern is answered, or simply avoided, where the defendant's dealings with the claimant's asset have left him enriched. To this extent, any requirement that the defendant make good the harms his actions have caused to the claimant will set back the defendant's interests only so far as they have been advanced by his unauthorized receipt and use of that asset. The result is that he is left no better but no worse off than he would have been had that transfer not been made. The upshot is that strict liability for harms caused by unauthorized use of another's asset can be justified where combined with a defence of change of position.[11]

III Harm

The rationale of the change of position defence extends to all claims which threaten to leave the recipient worse off, worse placed to achieve his chosen projects and goals, than had the impugned transfer

[10] 7.V.

[11] See too *Iraqi Airways Corporation v Kuwait Airways Co (Nos 4 and 5)* [2002] UKHL 19, [2002] 2 AC 883, para 79 (Lord Nicholls); Andrew Tettenborn, *Law of Restitution in England and Ireland* (3rd edn, Cavendish Publishing 2002) 278.

not been made. Of course, our plans and goals can be set back in any number of ways, both by others' design and by misfortune. In the main, we have to deal with these setbacks ourselves, without the law's assistance. But the question to which the defence of change of position is directed is not whether the law should step in to assist you when you've suffered some harm, but whether it should itself do harm to you. My interest in the money I paid you cannot now be fully vindicated without harming your interests in turn. So if I seek repayment, you may well ask what warrants the law not just placing my interests before yours, but intervening to ensure this.

Perhaps this challenge can be answered. English law at present recognizes change of position as a defence only to some claims following mistaken and other unauthorized transfers. In particular, the defence is not available in those cases where title does not pass to the defendant when the asset changes hands. Sometimes this is explained on the basis that change of position is a defence unique to claims in unjust enrichment and the defendant's unjust enrichment is foreclosed by the claimant's retention of title.[12] However, the need to see that the defendant's interests are not sacrificed for those of the claimant arises whatever the claimant's cause of action. Another suggestion is that change of position cannot be used to defeat claims to enforce property interests.[13] However, this both begs the question and commits the same old error of confusing what are different modes of protecting a single interest for the protection of different interests. Even in those cases where title does pass, it is the claimant's interest in the asset that grounds the recipient's liability to make restitution. If property interests are, by their nature or import, to be immune to the defence of change of position, the defence should be denied in the standard cases of unjust enrichment too.

A stronger cases for requiring the defendant to make restitution, notwithstanding his change of position and the harm this will cause him, can be made where he bears some responsibility for that harm. Say you know that the money you received was paid by mistake and hence that you weren't intended to have it. Any harm you would then be caused by being ordered to repay me is harm brought about by

[12] See eg Grantham and Rickett (n 1) 361; Burrows (n 4) 547. Cf Bant (n 9) 209–10.

[13] See eg David Fox, 'Legal Title as a Ground of Restitutionary Liability' [2000] *Restitution Law Review* 465, 488; Graham Virgo, *The Principles of the Law of Restitution* (2nd edn, Oxford University Press 2006) 708–10.

your treating as your own that which you had reason to know was not properly yours. Any complaint that my claim to restitution would undermine the plans you have made is itself undermined by the fact that you had all the relevant facts before you and were in a position to plan accordingly. In these circumstances, you are done no injustice by being required to make restitution in full, even where the result is that you are left worse off.

Where there has been a change of position, the transfer can no longer be reversed without loss to one or other of the parties. Though it may be unjust for the law to make you bear the loss where you are blameless, it is a different matter where the loss is one you have, in one way or another, brought on yourself. So the defence should likewise be denied where you are responsible for the impugned transfer, as where you induce the transfer by misrepresentation or coercion. Here too any loss you'd suffer by having to make restitution is loss for which you are, in this way, responsible. We see this idea in the rule that change of position cannot be invoked by wrongdoers.[14] However, the rule as framed is in part too wide, in part not wide enough. Not wide enough as the defendant's responsibility for the loss that one or the other of the parties will now suffer may justify leaving the loss on him rather than the claimant, even where the defendant commits no wrong, breaches no duty. The question of whether the defendant is a wrongdoer is often decisive where the claimant seeks to hold him liable for some loss the claimant has suffered. That the defendant was under a duty not to cause that loss is then a reason, or one part of a reason, for requiring him to bear it. But the question here is not whether the defendant is under a duty to make good a loss suffered by the claimant but whether the loss that he—the defendant—would suffer if restitution were ordered is sufficient reason to refuse that order. So in our case, what we need to ask is not whether there is reason to require you to bear a loss but whether there is reason to deny my claim to restitution. It will sometimes be reasonable to allow me to recover in full, though this will cause a loss to you, in circumstances where I could not demand you to cover my losses.

By the same token, however, the mere fact that you are a wrongdoer should not deny you this defence if the losses that you or I are now in line to suffer are not your responsibility. So English law presently treats all those who make use of another's goods as tortfeasors,

[14] *Lipkin Gorman v Karpnale Ltd* [1991] 2 AC 548 (HL) 580.

regardless of fault, even if they have every reason to think those goods their own. Sometimes this strict liability is taken to signal the priority the law rightly accords to the protection of property interests.[15] So viewed, the fact that allowing a change of position defence to blameless defendants would weaken that protection is a reason for its rejection. (Indeed, if we really were committed to resisting any inroads to the protection the law accords to property interests, we should deny the defence in the standard cases of unjust enrichment too, for these claims are no less assertions of the claimant's interest in the asset received by the defendant.) However, as mentioned earlier, an alternative explanation sometimes given for the strict liability in tort for interference with another's assets is to be found in the need to fill the gap left by the common law having no cause of action that serves as a direct vindication of property interests.[16] On this view, the designation of innocent converters as tortfeasors is no more than a means of ensuring that owners have some redress against those who now have unauthorized possession of their assets. This doesn't tell us anything about the weight to be accorded to these interests and so doesn't indicate that this redress ought to extend as far as recovering from innocent recipients who have changed their position. What matters then is not whether the defendant is classified as a wrongdoer but the reasons for this classification. Only where these reasons also go to the justness of requiring the defendant to make restitution should the defendant's status as a wrongdoer have any bearing on the defences available to him.

To recap: the consequence of a change of position is that the claimant's interests cannot be secured in full without doing harm to the defendant. In this event, the question is whether restitution should nonetheless be ordered and this harm then done to the defendant or, alternatively, whether restitution should be denied, leaving the claimant instead to suffer a loss. One factor bearing on the reasonableness of this determination is the defendant's role in and responsibility for bringing about the present state of affairs. But by parity of reasoning we should attend to the claimant's responsibility too. Just as the defendant's responsibility for the loss that one or other of the parties will suffer is a reason for his bearing that loss, where the claimant

[15] See eg *Fowler v Hollins* (1872) LR 7 QB 616, 639 (Cleasby B).
[16] 7.VIII.

bears this responsibility there is likewise reason for leaving the loss with him.

It has been said that the claimant's fault should not bear on the application of the change of position defence if his fault is no bar to establishing a claim.[17] But this doesn't follow. That my carelessness shouldn't defeat my claim where it would leave you no worse off doesn't mean that it shouldn't do so where it would do you harm. Where there has been no change of position, the claimant's interest can be secured without cost to the defendant. Once there has been, however, we can't secure one party's interests without harming the other's. Someone must be disadvantaged, and fault provides a just basis for determining who this should be.[18]

It is said that attempting an assessment of the degree to which each of the parties was at fault would be simply too complex, and any such determinations arbitrary.[19] But if this is true in some cases, it won't be in all. For one thing, an inquiry into the responsibility each party bears for creating the situation in which they now find themselves need not be undertaken with a view to identifying some ratio of responsibility between the two that can then be used to split any losses between them.[20] Instead, we might simply ask which of the two parties was more at fault, or bears the greater responsibility.[21] If it were the claimant, then the defence of change of position would be open to the defendant even if he were also, in part, to blame. Only where the defendant's fault is greater would the defence be ruled out.

Though the courts have rejected this approach, English law already provides a rough-and-ready approximation of the answers it would give. The claimant will often bear greater responsibility simply by virtue of the fact that it was he who made the initial transfer. This

[17] See eg *Dextra Bank & Trust Co Ltd v Bank of Jamaica* [2001] UKPC 50, [2002] 1 All ER (Comm) 193, para 45; Grantham and Rickett (n 1) 358 and wrongly endorsed in Tim Akkouh and Charlie Webb, 'Mistake, Misprediction and Change of Position' [2002] *Restitution Law Review* 107, 111.

[18] See too *National Bank of New Zealand Ltd v Waitaki International Processing (NI) Ltd* [1997] 2 NZLR 211, 229 (Thomas J); Dagan (n 8) 49–65; Bant (n 9) 178–79.

[19] See eg Birks (n 4) 219; John P Dawson, 'Restitution Without Enrichment' (1981) 61 *Boston University Law Review* 561, 571–73.

[20] Cf *National Bank of New Zealand v Waitaki* (n 18).

[21] This has been labelled a relative fault approach, in contrast to one directed to comparative fault (see J Beatson and W Bishop, 'Mistaken Payments in the Law of Restitution' (1986) 36 *University of Toronto Law Journal* 149, 154–55), though this terminology is not used consistently elsewhere.

supports making the defence generally available, with the denial of the defence to wrongdoers in turn covering many, though certainly not all, cases where the defendant's responsibility is greater. Moreover, in those cases where the claimant played no part in the transfer and so (typically) bears no responsibility at all for it, as where the asset is simply taken from him, change of position is at present denied.

The relevance of the claimant's own responsibility for the losses which would result from ordering restitution is also illustrated by the extension of the defence to anticipatory changes of position. An anticipatory change of position is one that occurs prior to the impugned transfer. So, rather than waiting until I have paid you, you treat yourself to the meal out in anticipation of the money you expect to be receiving from me. I then pay you and later seek restitution. Most formulations of the defence require your pleaded change of position to be caused by the payment I made to you: but for your receipt of this money from me, you would not have acted as you did.[22] This sounds reasonable: if I am seeking restitution of the payment I made, it matters whether the harm you say you'd suffer if you were to make restitution is in fact attributable to that payment. But if this is correct, it would mean anticipatory changes of position could never provide a defence. My payment cannot cause something that has already happened.[23]

Why then allow decisions pre-dating the payment to count in determining whether to grant restitution of that payment? The answer is that it is fair to factor this in when I have created the expectation of payment on which you acted and so am responsible for the harm you'd be caused should I then seek repayment. So if I, mistakenly believing I owe you £100, tell you I'll pay you that money tomorrow and on the back of this you treat yourself to a meal at once, you should have a defence to my claim.[24] Here, were restitution to be ordered, the effect of my intrusion into your life would be to leave

[22] See eg *Philip Collins Ltd v Davis* [2000] 3 All ER 808 (Ch) 827 (Jonathan Parker J); *Scottish Equitable Plc v Derby* [2001] EWCA Civ 369, [2001] 3 All ER 818, para 31 (Robert Walker LJ); Bant (n 9) 4. Cf *Commerzbank AG v Price-Jones* [2003] EWCA Civ 1663, [2004] 1 P & CR DG15, para 41 (Mummery LJ).

[23] Cf Birks (n 4) 212: 'Effect can precede cause when the medium is reliance.' Not true. See Akkouh and Webb (n 17) 110–11.

[24] See too Ajay Ratan, 'The Unity of Pre-Receipt and Post-Receipt Detriment' in Andrew Dyson, James Goudkamp, and Frederick Wilmot-Smith (eds), *Defences in Unjust Enrichment* (Hart Publishing 2016). Cf *Buller v Harrison* (1777) 2 Cowp 565, 566 (Lord Mansfield).

you worse off, no less than had you incurred this expense only after my payment. And so, here too, the harm that I would thereby do to you is, to this extent, sufficient reason to deny my claim for restitution. By contrast, when I played no part in creating the expectation that triggered your expenditure, your anticipatory change of position is effectively coincidental and provides no reason to defeat my claim.

IV Bona Fide Purchase

The change of position defence is not the only means the common law developed to protect recipients of mistakenly transferred or otherwise misapplied assets. Indeed for most of the common law's history the defence was unrecognized and the interests of recipients were protected, if at all, through other doctrinal means. For immediate transferees, such protection as there was came in the form of restrictions to the cause of action, in particular limits to the sorts of mistakes which would support claims to restitution, backed up by the defence of estoppel. But for remoter recipients the common law accorded far greater protection, with the bulk of the work done by the rules on the passing of title and the allied defence of bona fide purchase. Where title passed, no claim would ordinarily lie against those who received the asset from the immediate transferee. One effect of—or, perhaps better to say, one reason for—holding title to pass in the majority of these cases, was then to grant an immunity to remote recipients. (Of course, this rule did not alone guarantee this immunity and it could yet be undone by, say, imposing a trust over the asset, or simply allowing the claimant to sue remote recipients notwithstanding his loss of title. But in the main the courts did not take these steps.) In those rare cases where title did not pass, a later recipient would sometimes be able to raise a defence of bona fide purchase, which would wipe out the claimant's title and similarly grant an immunity to all subsequent recipients.

The change of position defence provides a more direct and potentially more effective means of reconciling the interests of owners and recipients. Accordingly, it is said that its recognition allows the courts to ease some of the limits on the cause of action developed in its absence. There is some indication that this has happened. But, thus far, the development of change of position hasn't been taken to support any equivalent change to the rules of title and the bona fide purchase defence. One reason for this is that these rules are commonly thought to fulfil a different function to the change of position defence. So the rules on the passing of title are typically viewed as being responsive primarily to the title holder's interests and intentions rather than to the interests of recipients, notwithstanding that these rules often provide for title to pass in conditions where this is not what the title holder truly intended. The bona fide purchase defence is in turn seen as concerned with the facilitation of trade or the security of commercial transactions.[25] If purchasers are at risk of unexpected liabilities on account of the assets they buy, they'll be discouraged from entering into such transactions. If we want to see trade encouraged and to see commercial activity facilitated rather than impeded, we need to see that those who buy such assets in good faith are protected.

Let's grant all this. The question is whether meeting these concerns requires anything more than a properly functioning change of position defence. These risks inhibit trade because they carry with them potential losses to the buyer, either because some liability may then attach to him or because he'll not be free to deal as he wishes with the asset he has acquired. But the avoidance of losses like these is the very function of the change of position defence. So long as this defence does its job, innocent purchasers will not be left worse off by virtue of their receipts. If so, the risks that would otherwise arise in these transactions are removed, as are the barriers to trade to which they would lead.[26] Providing effective protection of the interests of those entering the market ensures the effective protection of the market.

If this is right, the principal difference between the change of position and bona fide purchase defences lies not in their rationale or in the concerns to which they are addressed, but in how they in fact address those concerns. Where the bona fide purchase defence can be raised, the protection it provides goes beyond that accorded by change of position. For one thing, change of position operates only *pro tanto*: reducing the defendant's liability by only so much as is necessary to ensure he isn't harmed on account of his receipt of the asset

[25] See eg Kit Barker, 'After Change of Position: Good Faith Exchange in the Law of Restitution' in P B H Birks (ed), *Laundering and Tracing* (Clarendon Press 1995) 195–98; Peter Birks, 'Change of Position and Surviving Enrichment' in William Swadling (ed), *The Limits of Restitutionary Claims: A Comparative Analysis* (British Institute of International and Comparative Law 1997) 56–7; Bant (n 9) 240–41.

[26] Cf Barker, ibid 198.

and the liability which results from it. Bona fide purchase, by contrast, operates in all cases as a complete defence. For the defence to apply, the recipient need only have given something of value in return for the asset. If he did, and so long as he had no notice of the claimant's rights in the asset, the claimant's title is extinguished and the purchaser becomes title-holder in his place. Since there is no inquiry into whether the value the purchaser gave matched the value of the asset he received in return, the defence seems to go beyond what is necessary to ensure that the recipient is not left worse off.

For example, you buy my watch for £50 from a third party who has possession of it without my consent. If you can raise the bona fide purchase defence, my title is extinguished and you come under no liability. This goes even if the market value of the watch is £1,000. Yet if all we want is to ensure is that my claim leaves you no worse off than you would have been had you not acquired the watch, it would seem to be enough that my claim is reduced by the price you paid. Defeating my claim entirely goes beyond what is necessary to protect your interests. It has been suggested that the law has no option but to treat the asset and the price you paid as equivalents.[27] And if they are, or are to be taken as, equivalents, it follows that my claim must be ruled out because you have already lost and gained in equal measure. But it's not at all clear that we must, or ought to, assume equivalence. That contract law conducts no inquiry into the adequacy of the consideration provided by each party does not mean it takes it to be, in all cases, adequate, let alone equivalent. (Indeed the reality of our exchange may be thought to presuppose that we *don't* see our respective performance as equivalents, for why else make the exchange?) In any event, even if the rules of contract formation did employ some irrebuttable presumption of equivalence, it wouldn't follow that we would be foreclosed from looking into the value of each party's performances for other purposes.

Nonetheless, we can understand why courts might in practice be slow to open up the question of what values the parties attached to their respective performances. A rule of thumb that the value the recipient gave in return for his acquisition of the asset stands in rough equivalence to the value he takes from that asset is both plausible and workable. On this basis, bona fide purchase can be viewed as an instance of change

[27] Birks (n 4) 241–42.

of position that, at least presumptively, leaves the recipient with no substantial net gain. And if this is right, it supports a default rule that the recipient's defence should be, in these instances, complete.

But the bona fide purchase defence is without doubt broader than change of position in another way. Change of position is a defence responsive to the circumstances of the given defendant. What matters is how *your* position has changed, not how others who held the asset before you might have changed their positions. The bona fide purchase defence works differently. When it operates, my title is extinguished. Later recipients are immune from any claim, whether or not they themselves are bona fide purchasers, whether or not their positions have changed on account of their receipt. To this extent the bona fide purchase defence provides protection beyond that which change of position accords, extending an immunity to recipients who would not themselves be harmed in the event of their liability.

Can this be justified? It has been said that bona fide purchase is needed as a defence to claims in unjust enrichment to ensure that the rule that title passes (in these cases) to the bona fide purchaser is not undermined.[28] But we should first ask why title *does* pass here, given the claimant's lack of true consent to its disposition; a question raised all the more starkly if the effect of holding title to have passed is then to rule out any claim against not only the purchaser but all subsequent recipients. The effect of the bona fide purchase rule, where it applies, is that later recipients don't need to concern themselves with the asset's full history. Nothing that occurred before the bona fide purchase poses any threat to their claim to the asset. But, we might ask, what threat would they otherwise face? The change of position defence is aimed at ensuring innocent recipients won't be prejudiced

[28] Ibid 242–43. Birks' argument poses a challenge to his own account—indeed, to all orthodox accounts—of unjust enrichment liability. If the bona fide purchaser must be accorded a defence to an *in personam* claim in unjust enrichment so as to ensure that the rule that title passes to that purchaser (and the goods and values which support that rule) is not undermined, why isn't the same true of the immediate recipient in the standard case of the mistaken payment? There too, as we've seen, title passes. But no unjust enrichment lawyer argues that the payer's claim should be denied on the basis that this undermines the rule that title passes. Why? Not because the claim doesn't undermine this rule. Rather, because this rule *ought* to be undermined, because the conclusion that title passes is (at the very least) unreasonable unless the payer is provided with some other means of redress. But that only goes to show that, contrary to the position these accounts take, the rules of unjust enrichment liability are in the service of the same interests as are (ordinarily) supported through the provision of title.

by the claims of prior holders. Accordingly, a recipient needn't be concerned about the possibility of his claim to the asset being challenged since, even if this challenge is successful, change of position ensures he'll be left in no worse a position than had he not made the purchase. In this way, his acquisition and use of the asset is, so far as any potential liability is concerned, risk-free. So it seems that change of position provides all the protection recipients need. Any additional protection is then not only unnecessary to see their interests secured, but comes at the cost of an unwarranted reduction in the protection accorded to claimants' interests.

But this is true only if change of position does its job. Unless the defence, when applied in practice, does catch all those recipients who would be left worse off were the claimant to recover in full, it will fail to provide adequate protection to recipients' interests. Do we have any reason to doubt that it does? Perhaps. Change of position lies, in most cases, in decisions the defendant has made which he would not have made had he not believed he had the relevant asset or funds at his free disposal. But establishing the counterfactual won't always be straightforward. Would you have treated yourself to this meal out if you hadn't received the £100 from me? You say no. But if we look at your bank statements, we can see that you go out for meals such as this every so often in any case, so it's not plain that this meal was exceptional. We have only your word for it.

More to the point, though almost every expenditure is chosen on the back of an understanding of the funds available to us and the competing possible uses of those funds, rarely will the decision to incur a given expenditure follow from a conscious working out of quite how great our funds would have to be to make that expenditure worthwhile. In other words: say I go into a book shop and see a book I like. The book has its price and I simply have to decide whether to pay it, whether this would be a worthwhile use of my money. I conclude it is. That decision is, no doubt, based on some sense of my own wealth and how else my money could be spent. But where I decide to spend my money in this way I normally won't also work out how much poorer I would have had to be to have decided not to, just as I won't work out how much higher the price would have had to be before I chose not to make the purchase. If this is true, particular purchases will rarely be consciously tied to particular receipts. So the causal links on which the change of position defence is dependent won't even be clear to the defendant, let alone a court.

So, while it is right to leave the burden of establishing a change of position on the defendant recipient, since he'll be better placed than the claimant to bring evidence of this, such evidence will often be scant. Even if courts acknowledge these difficulties and so do not demand evidence tying particular receipts to particular items of expenditure, these features of the change of position defence mean that the confidence that recipients can have in the defence in fact securing their interests must be limited. And if this is true, then the availability of change of position as a defence to these claims will not assuage all the concerns of potential purchasers. Against this backdrop, a bona fide purchase defence, granting an immunity not only to those purchasers but to those who go on to receive the asset from them, makes some sense.

V Specific Recovery and Insolvency

The courts have recognized the change of position defence, at least explicitly, only in relation to monetary (*in personam*) restitutionary awards. Here the defence operates through a reduction of the sum payable by such amount as is needed to ensure the defendant is not left worse off as a result of the initial transfer. But change of position should be no less a defence to claims in unjust enrichment where the claimant seeks, or the court orders, restitution *in specie*. If specific restitution is to be ordered as against an innocent defendant who has changed his position, it should be on terms that the claimant compensate the defendant for the harm this would do him.[29]

A similar technique can be adopted in the event of the defendant's insolvency, if there is a risk of analogous harm to one or more of the defendant's general creditors. For reasons given in the previous chapter, so long as the defendant still holds some asset of the claimant's, unjust enrichment claims can justifiably be granted priority in a defendant's insolvency. Doing so leaves the defendant's other creditors with lesser funds from which their claims can be met and so leaves them worse off than they would have been if my claim were not to take priority over theirs. But ordinarily it won't leave them in any worse a position than had the impugned transfer not been made. Sometimes, however, things will be different.

[29] See too ibid 210.

I pay you a sum of money by mistake. You become insolvent before I bring my claim. One of your other creditors alleges that he advanced you credit only having first checked that you were creditworthy and his judgment as to your creditworthiness was grounded, in part, on his belief that the money you received from me was indeed yours. If my claim takes priority and I recover in full, that creditor will be harmed: he will be denied access to those funds to meet his claim, yet he would not now be a creditor had I not made the payment and led him to believe those funds would be available to creditors. The concern here is analogous to that underlying the change of position defence. Indeed, since your creditors stand as potential recipients of that money, your creditor's complaint here is in substance one of anticipatory change of position: thinking he would receive a portion of those funds in the event of your insolvency, he gave credit to you.

Some have taken this risk to creditors as a reason for denying unjust enrichment claims any such priority.[30] Even if there were no way to protect these creditors, it's doubtful that the mere possibility of such harms is sufficient to deny priority in all cases.[31] But again we can see that the interests of your creditors are protected by ordering restitution on terms: allowing my claim to take priority on the condition that I compensate those creditors who had relied on your apparent entitlement to the funds I paid. This means my paying them whatever portion of those funds they would have received had that money been available for distribution amongst your general creditors.

But can't your creditor claim that he would not be your creditor and so would have suffered no losses *at all*, had it not been for my mistaken payment? If so, it looks like merely giving him the portion of those funds he'd have received had they been distributed amongst your general creditors doesn't go far enough, for the losses he'll still suffer on account of your insolvency are losses he'd have avoided but for my payment. True, but these additional losses are not caused by my claim taking priority, for he'd have suffered them even were my claim to rank alongside his. Unless the creditor's reliance on my mistaken payment to you is to make me his insurer in the event of your

[30] Cf *Westdeutsche Landesbank Girozentrale v Islington London Borough Council* [1996] AC 669 (HL) 705 (Lord Browne-Wilkinson).

[31] See too Emily L Sherwin, 'Constructive Trusts in Bankruptcy' [1989] *University of Illinois Law Review* 297, 323–24, 360, where it is suggested that it is rare for creditors to base their decision to give credit on the debtor's entitlement to particular assets in his possession, and are instead more likely to rely on the debtor's general ability to generate income.

insolvency, the most we should do is to see that my claim is not preferred to his. We do this by ensuring that the priority my claim is accorded does not come at his expense, by allowing him to take out that portion of my funds which would otherwise have come his way.

VI Loss and Gain

An order that the defendant must make restitution of his unjust enrichment operates as a corrective to the injustice of that enrichment. There is no difficulty then in describing claims in unjust enrichment as claims of corrective justice. Designating these claims as claims of corrective justice is sometimes thought to make a difference to how they are to be addressed and answered.[32] One example comes where the gains the defendant makes from the unauthorized transfer exceed the claimant's losses. On one account of corrective justice—Aristotle's—the injustices which corrective justice corrects can be figured as inequalities whereby one party unjustly gains what another has lost.[33] Corrective justice is done when equality is restored by returning what was gained to he who lost it. It takes no leap to see how this can capture cases of unjust enrichment. If corrective justice is called into operation only where there exists some such correspondence of loss and gain, some have extrapolated that, where an unjust enrichment defendant's gain exceeds the claimant's losses, recovery should be capped at the measure of those losses.[34]

Even on its face, this looks mistaken. Let's grant that corrective justice is done only where one person's loss is another's gain and so both can be simultaneously reversed. All that follows is that a restitutionary award does corrective justice only where the claimant's loss matches the defendant's gain. It doesn't follow that it is unjust or unreasonable to allow recovery in other circumstances or in other measures. There's more to justice than corrective justice, all the more when correction is framed so narrowly.

[32] See too 3.II.

[33] Aristotle, *Nicomachean Ethics*, V, 1131b25–1132b20.

[34] See Lionel Smith, 'Restitution: The Heart of Corrective Justice' (2001) 79 *Texas Law Review* 2115, 2146–48; Mitchell McInnes, '"At the Claimant's Expense": Quantifying Restitutionary Relief' [1998] *Cambridge Law Journal* 472, 474–75; Virgo (n 13) 112–15.

But why frame it so narrowly? Here these accounts depart from Aristotle's. For the examples he gave of injustices to which corrective justice responds include many—killing, assault, adultery—where there is no such correspondence of loss and gain, no possibility of any such mutual material restoration. So Aristotle can only have intended the terms 'loss' and 'gain' to carry some meaning other than material, factual loss and gain. What meaning? Weinrib's suggestion is that loss and gain here should be understood as 'normative' loss and gain.[35] Sometimes normative gain and loss appears simply to represent the doing and suffering of an injury.[36] So, the assailant does an injury to (violates the rights or entitlements of) his victim, with the very doing of that injury the 'gain' to which corrective justice responds. Loss and gain necessarily correlate, whatever the material, factual consequences of the assault, since it is the same injury done and suffered. But if this is right, it looks like we have to reject the suggestion that corrective justice is the reversal of this loss and gain, for while the gains and losses which result from injuries may often be corrected, these doings cannot themselves be undone.

Elsewhere, Weinrib offers a different understanding of normative gains and losses: 'a person enjoys a normative gain when there is justification for the law's diminishing his or her holdings...a person endures a normative loss when there is justification for the law's augmenting his or her holdings'.[37] So, the assailant comes under a duty to compensate his victim; until he makes this compensation, he has more and his victim less than they are due. Now we have no difficulty seeing how these gains and losses can be reversed: the payment of compensation simultaneously removes the defendant's gain and makes good the claimant's loss. However, so understood, loss and gain no longer identify the grounds of the injustice which calls for correction but rather the correction which justice requires. The perpetrator of the assault owes compensation to his victim and so we can say that, until he pays that compensation, he has more than he is due. But it is not because of the assailant's (normative) gain that he must compensate his victim. That gain is no more than a restatement or reflection of his duty to make compensation. Accordingly, if we want to know why he is under a duty to compensate his victim,

[35] Ernest J Weinrib, *The Idea of Private Law* (Harvard University Press 1995) 114–19.
[36] Ibid 133. See too Aristotle (n 33) 1132a5–15.
[37] Weinrib (n 35) 116.

the answer is not to be found in this gain (which merely repeats the existence of that duty), but rather in the wrongfulness of his assault (a wrong which cannot in turn be reduced to a failure to compensate for the injury caused).

So neither of Weinrib's re-readings of Aristotle succeeds in making good the claim that corrective justice is the restoration of what one party has gained and another lost. Perhaps this claim can't be made good. It is in any case doubtful whether these efforts to decode Aristotle's account promise any real pay off. We don't need to find some way in which the assailant may be said to have gained from his assault to make sense of his obligation to compensate his victim. There is no question that assailants and other wrongdoers have reason to pay compensation, whether or not their wrongs brought them any material reward. If called on to explain why this is, our focus would be on the nature of the wrong, the harms the claimant suffered, and the wrongdoer's responsibility for them. Here, and I suspect elsewhere, our understanding of corrective justice and of its practical demands appears not to be hampered by uncertainty over this aspect of Aristotle's account.

We can leave these doubts to one side. For present purposes, what matters is that Aristotle's account doesn't support the conclusions some unjust enrichment lawyers have drawn from it. No doubt we can class claims in unjust enrichment as claims of corrective justice. This tells us something: that these awards aim to put right some prior injustice. But beyond this, it sheds no real light on why these claims arise or how they should be resolved. Even if, as Aristotle claimed, corrective justice responds to the injustice of one gaining what another has lost, these losses and gains need not, on Aristotle's own account, correspond to material, factual losses and gains. And so, accepting that claims in unjust enrichment are claims of corrective justice does not support, even on Aristotle's account, the conclusion that recovery should not go beyond the measure of the claimant's factual losses.

Indeed, as we saw in the previous chapter, claims following unauthorized transfers are better conceived as concerned, in the first instance, with neither gains nor losses. My claim that what you now hold is, or should be regarded as, properly mine is one which requires no inquiry into the values we attach to the item I have lost and you have gained. Often these values will differ. What you stand to gain if the transfer goes unreversed will be sometimes more, sometimes less than I would lose. In all cases the presumptive primary response should be to return what is mine to me. Sometimes this will leave me to bear a loss. This will often be the result of a successful plea of change of position, so too where being dispossessed of my asset caused me consequential losses for which you cannot reasonably be held responsible. At other times, however, my claim may leave me in a better position than I would have been in had the relevant transfer not been made. I pay you £100 by mistake. The next day my wallet is stolen. Assume that if I hadn't paid you, that money would have been in my wallet. I am entitled to restitution from you even though this would then leave me £100 better off than I would have been had I not made the payment. (Of course, I have a claim against the thief, for what it's worth. Perhaps this might get me my £100 back. But the same goes were I carelessly to drop my wallet in the Thames, with no chance of recompense.) Again, my claim is not that the payment has left me—now—worse off but that that money you received and which you still hold was, and should remain, mine. Your liability is not avoided or circumscribed by showing that you would make or have made better use of my funds than I would have done.

The same goes if you invest the very money I paid you, generating a profit of an additional £100. Let's also assume you would not have made any such investment had you not received this money from me. (Were this not true, your use of this money rather than your own to invest would be a change of position.) As we saw in the previous chapter, it may be reasonable to take my ownership of my money as supporting a parallel interest in what is bought with it.[38] If so, I should now be entitled to the £200 of profit you now hold, and it is again immaterial that I would not have secured any such gain had the money remained in my hands.

For the same reasons, it does not matter here that any loss I did suffer from being deprived of my asset for this period has been made good by the time I bring my claim. I pay you by mistake. Now out of pocket, I take on extra work—work I wouldn't otherwise have taken on—to put me back in funds. Or my friend, Dan, hearing of my misfortune, makes a gift of some money to me. I am now no worse off than I would have been had I not made the payment to you. Nonetheless, on the basis that the money I paid you remains in your hands, I can recover what was and should still be mine. (If I do recover

[38] 7.IV.

from you, Dan, depending on his intentions when making his payment, may have a claim to recover the money he paid me.)

So there is good reason to reject a defence of passing on or dis-impoverishment to claims of this sort. But the position is not quite so clear-cut where there is no longer any asset in your hands that I can maintain is, in truth, mine. At this point, any claim I have against you must rest on some other basis. If you spend the £100 I paid you paying a utility bill, I should nonetheless be entitled to demand that you pay me £100 out of your other funds. It is now standard to see your liability as grounded in your unjust enrichment, in the gain you made and retain from my payment to you. So, here, you remain enriched by your receipt and use of the money I paid you since, by using that money to pay your bill, you avoided having to find such money elsewhere, preserving your existing holdings. However, as I argued in the previous chapter, it is doubtful that the fact that you acquire or retain wealth as a result of your unauthorized use of some asset of mine by itself gives me any interest in or claim to that wealth. On this basis, it would be a mistake to see your enrichment as the gist or focus of my claim. Instead, my claim is, I think, better conceived as directed to the loss I have suffered as a result of your unauthorized dealings with my assets, with your enrichment relevant to the extent it helps show why it would not be unfair to require you to make good that loss.

If so, for these claims, the standard argument against a defence of passing on—that claims following unauthorized transfers are concerned not with making good losses but with removing gains—falls away. So say again that you spend the money I mistakenly pay you to pay your utility bill. Now, I can't demand that you return my money to me, since you no longer have it to return. Nor can I demand that you give up its proceeds, since there are none. All I can ask is that you secure my broader interests by making good the loss you've caused me by your use of my money. The question now then is whether you can defeat my claim by showing that there is in fact no loss to compensate since, though that money is gone, I have now received other funds which I would not have received but for my initial mistaken payment.

Here's why we might still think not. My claim against you is directed not to the loss my payment caused me but to the loss *you* caused me by your use of the money I paid you. Whether I am now worse off than I would have been had I not made the payment does not, therefore, matter so long as I am worse off than I would have been had you not used that money as you did. So if it was my payment away of the money, rather than your subsequent expenditure of that money, which motivated me to take on the extra work or which prompted Dan to make the gift to me, the money I make from that extra work or which Dan gives to me is money I'd have either way. That is to say: but for your spending the money I paid you, I'd be able to recover that money from you *on top of* the money I made from the extra work or which was given me by Dan. The only cases where passing on might provide you with a defence are where my loss is made good on account of, or is otherwise causally attributable to, what you have done with my money and hence where, without your use of my money, I would now be no better off. In these (likely rare) circumstances, we might expect the question of whether I should nonetheless be able to recover from you to turn on the same considerations which determine the effect of collateral benefits on compensatory claims generally.

VII Retrospect

The last two chapters provide what is no more than a selective sketch of how a legal system which had a clear grasp of the reasons which bear on the resolution of claims in unjust enrichment would approach them. Any number of questions that a comprehensive scheme for dealing with such claims must answer are left unanswered. Sometimes answering these questions would require no more than a working through of arguments I have set out. Elsewhere, however, coming to a fully reasonable answer would require consideration of arguments I have neither made nor foreshadowed. Even once these various arguments are given their proper place and weight, there will often be a range of responses a legal system may reasonably adopt and between which it must simply choose.

The account I offer here is not put forward as an interpretation or rationalization of English law, or of the law of any other jurisdiction, as it is today or was at any other time. Nonetheless, many of the positions I take here mirror positions taken by the English common law. Indeed, one conclusion which we might draw here is that the failure to develop any theory of unjust enrichment claims or to inquire into their grounds has not precluded judges from developing a body of laws which is, on the whole, reasonable, sometimes more reasonable than the revisions of those laws modern unjust enrichment scholars have proposed. Where the common law does depart from the positions argued for in these two chapters, it is, so I suggest, less than fully reasonable. But it doesn't follow that judges act unreasonably when applying these less-than-fully-reasonable rules. There is often good reason for judges to conform their own decisions to the decisions reached and directives issued by other legal officials, even where those prior decisions and directives were themselves unreasonable.[39] Moreover, where it is, all things considered, reasonable to depart from previous authority, there may be good reason to leave this decision to legislators or to higher courts. It may be reasonable for a trial judge to apply a rule that an appellate court will reasonably strike down.

So this account provides no one-size-fits-all model for across-the-board adoption by judges and law-makers. None exists. Nevertheless the account and the arguments of this book generally are *for* judges and law-makers, and for all those concerned with guiding or assessing their decisions. For judges deciding unjust enrichment claims and for legislators framing rules for their resolution, the basic question they must answer is when there is good reason to require a defendant to make restitution. The value of conformity to past rules and rulings of legal officials provides its own reasons for and against restitution. But the question of whether there is good reason to order restitution is never simply a matter of inquiry into such past practices, and there are reasons for ordering restitution which exist and operate independently of those practices and are not displaced by them. These are the reasons this book has examined.

I've made much of the failings of the accounts unjust enrichment lawyers have put forward, but in their core claim they were right. There is a body of like cases, exemplified by cases of mistaken payments, which support liability to make restitution in the absence of a contract and any wrongdoing on the part of the recipient. They were right too about why this mattered: since these cases are like cases, they should receive (to this extent) like treatment. But by insisting that unjust enrichment only looked down to the cases, they shut off the one route by which these claims could be made good. This book shares the principal aims of these accounts: to mark out this class of like cases and the treatment they merit. Where those accounts went wrong was in thinking that these were questions that could be

[39] I.VI.

addressed without reference to or inquiry into the reasons for restitution unjust enrichment gives. The opposite is true. Unjust enrichment's distinctiveness as a ground of private law liability lies in the distinctive reasons it provides. Identifying these reasons and determining their proper reach and operation is not simply the task of unjust enrichment theory. It is the defining role of unjust enrichment law.

Bibliography

Akkouh T and Webb C, 'Mistake, Misprediction and Change of Position' [2002] *Restitution Law Review* 107.

Akkouh T and Worthington S, '*Re Diplock* (1948)' in C Mitchell and P Mitchell (eds), *Landmark Cases in the Law of Restitution* (Oxford: Hart Publishing 2006).

American Law Institute, *Restatement (Third) of Restitution and Unjust Enrichment* (St Paul, MN: American Law Institute 2011).

Anscombe G E M, *Intention* (2nd edn, Oxford: Basil Blackwell 1963).

____ 'Under a Description' (1979) 13 *Nous* 219.

Aquinas, *Summa Theologiae*.

Aristotle, *Nicomachean Ethics*.

____ *Politics*.

Baker J H, *An Introduction to English Legal History* (4th edn, London: Butterworths 2002).

Baloch T, *Unjust Enrichment and Contract* (Oxford: Hart Publishing 2009).

Bant E, *The Change of Position Defence* (Oxford: Hart Publishing 2009).

Barker K, 'After Change of Position: Good Faith Exchange in the Law of Restitution' in P Birks (ed), *Laundering and Tracing* (Oxford: Clarendon Press 1995).

____ 'Responsibility for Gain: Unjust Factors or Absence of Legal Ground? Starting Points in Unjust Enrichment Law' in C Rickett and R Grantham (eds), *Structure and Justification in Private Law* (Oxford: Hart Publishing 2008).

____ 'The Nature of Responsibility for Gain: Gain, Harm and Keeping the Lid on Pandora's Box' in R Chambers, C Mitchell, and J Penner (eds), *Philosophical Foundations of the Law of Unjust Enrichment* (Oxford: Oxford University Press 2009).

Beatson J, *The Use and Abuse of Unjust Enrichment: Essays on the Law of Restitution* (Oxford: Clarendon Press 1991).

____ 'Restitution and Contract: Non-Cumul?' (2000) 1 *Theoretical Inquiries in Law* 83.

____ and Bishop W, 'Mistaken Payments in the Law of Restitution' (1986) 36 *University of Toronto Law Journal* 149.

Birks P, *An Introduction to the Law of Restitution* (Oxford: Clarendon Press 1985).

____ 'Unjust Enrichment—A Reply to Mr Hedley' (1985) 5 *Legal Studies* 67.

____ *An Introduction to the Law of Restitution* (rev edn, Oxford: Clarendon Press 1989).

____ 'Restitution and Resulting Trusts' in S Goldstein (ed), *Equity and Contemporary Legal Developments* (Jerusalem: The Harry and Michael Sacher Institute for Legislative Research and Comparative Law, Hebrew University of Jerusalem 1992).

____ *Restitution: The Future* (Annandale, NSW: The Federation Press 1992).
____ 'No Consideration: Restitution after Void Contracts' (1993) 23 *University of Western Australia Law Review* 195.
____ 'Equity in the Modern Law: An Exercise in Taxonomy' (1996) 26 *University of Western Australia Law Review* 1.
____ 'Change of Position and Surviving Enrichment' in W Swadling (ed), *The Limits of Restitutionary Claims: A Comparative Analysis* (London: British Institute of International and Comparative Law 1997).
____ 'Definition and Division: A Meditation on *Institutes* 3.13' in P Birks (ed), *The Classification of Obligations* (Oxford: Clarendon Press 1997).
____ 'Property and Unjust Enrichment: Categorical Truths' [1997] *New Zealand Law Review* 623.
____ 'The Concept of a Civil Wrong' in D Owen (ed), *Philosophical Foundations of Tort Law* (Oxford: Clarendon Press 1997).
____ 'Misnomer' in W Cornish, R Nolan, J O'Sullivan, and G Virgo (eds), *Restitution—Past, Present and Future: Essays in Honour of Gareth Jones* (Oxford: Hart Publishing 1998).
____ 'The Law of Unjust Enrichment: A Millennial Resolution' [1999] *Singapore Journal of Legal Studies* 318.
____ 'Property, Unjust Enrichment, and Tracing' (2001) 54 *Current Legal Problems* 231.
____ 'Unjust Enrichment and Wrongful Enrichment' (2001) 79 *Texas Law Review* 1767.
____ *Unjust Enrichment* (2nd edn, Oxford: Clarendon Press 2005).
____ and Chambers R, *The Restitution Research Resource* (Oxford: Mansfield Press 1997).
Botterell A, 'Property, Corrective Justice, and the Nature of the Cause of Action in Unjust Enrichment' (2007) 20 *Canadian Journal of Law and Jurisprudence* 275.
Burrows A, *The Law of Restitution* (London: Butterworths 1993).
____ *Understanding the Law of Obligations* (Oxford: Hart Publishing 1998).
____ 'Proprietary Restitution: Unmasking Unjust Enrichment' (2001) 117 *Law Quarterly Review* 412.
____ *The Law of Restitution* (3rd edn, Oxford: Oxford University Press 2011).
____ *A Restatement of the English Law of Restitution* (Oxford: Oxford University Press 2012).
Campbell K, 'Offence and Defence' in I H Dennis (ed), *Criminal Law and Justice: Essays from the W G Hart Workshop 1986* (London: Sweet and Maxwell 1987).
Cane P, *Atiyah's Accidents, Compensation and the Law* (8th edn, Cambridge: Cambridge University Press 2013).
Cartwright J P W, 'Conditional Intention' (1990) 60 *Philosophical Studies* 233.
Chambers R, *Resulting Trusts* (Oxford: Clarendon Press 1997).
____ 'Two Kinds of Enrichment' in R Chambers, C Mitchell, and J Penner (eds), *Philosophical Foundations of the Law of Unjust Enrichment* (Oxford: Oxford University Press 2009).

____ 'Trust and Theft' in E Bant and M Harding (eds), *Exploring Private Law* (Cambridge: Cambridge University Press 2010).

Coleman J, *The Practice of Principle: In Defence of a Pragmatist Approach to Legal Theory* (Oxford: Oxford University Press 2003).

Dagan H, *The Law and Ethics of Restitution* (Cambridge: Cambridge University Press 2004).

____ *Property: Values and Institutions* (Oxford: Oxford University Press 2011).

Davidson D, 'Actions, Reasons, and Causes' (1963) 60 *Journal of Philosophy* 685.

____ *Essays on Actions and Events* (2nd edn, Oxford: Clarendon Press 2001).

Dawson J, *Restitution without Enrichment* (1981) 61 *Boston University Law Review* 563.

Dickson J, *Evaluation and Legal Theory* (Oxford: Hart Publishing 2001).

Dietrich J, *Restitution: A New Perspective* (Annandale, NSW: The Federation Press 1998).

____ '*Quantum Meruit* for Services Rendered in a Three-Party Context: (Implied) Contract, Restitution, or Unjust Enrichment?' [2009] *Restitution Law Review* 98.

Duarte d'Almeida L, *Allowing for Exceptions: A Theory of Defences and Defeasibility in Law* (Oxford: Oxford University Press 2015).

Dworkin R, *Law's Empire* (Cambridge, MA: Belknap Press 1986).

____ *Justice in Robes* (Cambridge, MA: Belknap Press 2006).

Edelman J, *Gain-Based Damages: Contract, Tort, Equity and Intellectual Property* (Oxford: Hart Publishing 2002).

____ 'Change of Position: A Defence of Unjust Disenrichment' (2012) 92 *Boston University Law Review* 1009.

____ and Bant E, *Unjust Enrichment in Australia* (Oxford: Oxford University Press 2006).

Edwards H, 'The Growing Disjunction between Legal Education and the Legal Profession' (1992) 91 *Michigan Law Review* 14.

Evans S, 'Rethinking Tracing and the Law of Restitution' (1999) 115 *Law Quarterly Review* 469.

Finch V and Worthington S, 'The *Pari Passu* Principle and Ranking Restitutionary Rights' in F Rose (ed), *Restitution and Insolvency* (Oxford: Mansfield Press 2000).

Finnis J, 'Law as Co-ordination' (1989) 2 *Ratio Juris* 97.

____ 'Intention and Side-effects' in R Frey and C Morris (eds), *Liability and Responsibility: Essays in Law and Morals* (Cambridge: Cambridge University Press 1991).

____ 'Natural Law and Legal Reasoning' in R George (ed), *Natural Law Theory: Contemporary Essays* (Oxford: Clarendon Press 1992).

____ 'On Conditional Intentions and Preparatory Intentions' in L Gormally (ed), *Moral Truth and Moral Tradition: Essays in Honour of Peter Geach and Elizabeth Anscombe* (Dublin: Four Courts Press 1994).

____ 'Intention in Tort Law' in D Owen (ed) *Philosophical Foundations of Tort Law* (Oxford: Clarendon Press 1995).

____ 'Natural Law: The Classical Tradition' in J Coleman and S Shapiro (eds), *The Oxford Handbook of Jurisprudence and Philosophy of Law* (Oxford: Oxford University Press 2002).

____ 'Law and What I Truly Should Decide' (2003) 48 *American Journal of Jurisprudence* 107.

____ 'On Hart's Ways: Law as Reason and as Fact' (2007) 52 *American Journal of Jurisprudence* 25.

____ *Natural Law and Natural Rights* (2nd edn, Oxford: Oxford University Press 2011).

____ 'Reflections and Responses' in J Keown and R George (eds), *Reason, Morality, and Law: The Philosophy of John Finnis* (Oxford: Oxford University Press 2013).

Fitzgerald B, 'Ownership as the Proximity or Privity Principle in Unjust Enrichment Law' (1995) 18 *University of Queensland Law Journal* 166.

Fox D, 'The Transfer of Legal Title to Money' [1996] *Restitution Law Review* 60.

____ 'Legal Title as a Ground of Restitutionary Liability' [2000] *Restitution Law Review* 465.

____ *Property Rights in Money* (Oxford: Oxford University Press 2008).

Fried C, *Contract as Promise: A Theory of Contractual Obligation* (Cambridge, MA: Harvard University Press 1981).

Friedmann D, 'Restitution of Benefits Obtained through the Appropriation of Property or the Commission of a Wrong' (1980) 80 *Columbia Law Review* 504.

____ 'Valid, Voidable, Qualified, and Non-existing Obligations: An Alternative Perspective on the Law of Restitution' in A Burrows (ed), *Essays on the Law of Restitution* (Oxford: Clarendon Press 1991).

____ 'The Protection of Entitlements via the Law of Restitution—Expectancies and Privacy' (2005) 121 *Law Quarterly Review* 400.

Fuller L L and Perdue Jr W, 'The Reliance Interest in Contract Damages: 1' (1936) 42 *Yale Law Journal* 52.

Gardner J, Justifications and Reasons' in A P Simester and A T H Smith (eds), *Harm and Culpability* (Oxford: Clarendon Press 1996).

____ 'Obligations and Outcomes in the Law of Torts' in P Cane and J Gardner (eds), *Relating to Responsibility: Essays in Honour of Tony Honoré on the Occasion of his 80th Birthday* (Oxford: Hart Publishing 2001).

____ 'Ethics and Law' in J Skorupski (ed), *The Routledge Companion to Ethics* (Abingdon: Routledge 2010).

____ 'What is Tort Law for? Part 1. The Place of Corrective Justice' (2011) 30 *Law and Philosophy* 1.

____ and Macklem, T, 'Reasons' in J Coleman and S Shapiro (eds), *The Oxford Handbook of Jurisprudence and Philosophy of Law* (Oxford: Oxford University Press 2002).

Gardner S, *An Introduction to the Law of Trusts* (3rd edn, Oxford: Clarendon Press 2011).

Gilmore G, *The Death of Contract* (Columbus, OH: Ohio State University Press 1974).
Goff R and Jones G, *The Law of Restitution* (London: Sweet and Maxwell 1966).
Goodhart W and Jones G, 'The Infiltration of Equitable Doctrine into English Commercial Law' (1980) 43 *Modern Law Review* 489.
Gordley J, *Foundations of Private Law: Property, Tort, Contract, Unjust Enrichment* (Oxford: Oxford University Press 2006).
Goudkamp J and Mitchell C, 'Denials and Defences in the Law of Unjust Enrichment' in C Mitchell and W Swadling (eds), *The Restatement Third, Restitution and Unjust Enrichment: Critical and Comparative Essays* (Oxford: Hart Publishing 2013).
Grantham R and Rickett C, 'Property and Unjust Enrichment: Categorical Truths or Unnecessary Complexity?' [1997] *New Zealand Law Review* 668.
____ *Enrichment and Restitution in New Zealand* (Oxford: Hart Publishing 2000).
____ 'Tracing and Property Rights: The Categorical Truth' (2000) 63 *Modern Law Review* 905.
____ 'On the Subsidiarity of Unjust Enrichment' (2001) 117 *Law Quarterly Review* 273.
____ 'Property Rights as a Legally Significant Event' [2003] *Cambridge Law Journal* 717.
Harris J W, *Property and Justice* (Oxford: Oxford University Press 1996).
Hart H L A, 'Positivism and the Separation of Law and Morals' (1958) 71 *Harvard Law Review* 593.
____ *The Concept of Law* (3rd edn, Oxford: Oxford University Press 2012).
Hedley S, Unjust Enrichment as the Basis of Restitution—An Overworked Concept' (1985) 5 *Legal Studies* 56.
____ 'Unjust Enrichment: A Middle Course?' (2002) 2 *Oxford University Commonwealth Law Journal* 181.
____ 'Implied Contract and Restitution' [2004] *Cambridge Law Journal* 435.
Holdsworth W S, 'Unjustifiable Enrichment' (1939) 55 *Law Quarterly Review* 37.
Holmes Jr O W, *The Common Law* (Boston, MA: Little, Brown, and Company 1881).
Honoré A M, 'Ownership' in A G Guest (ed), *Oxford Essays in Jurisprudence: A Collaborative Work* (Oxford: Oxford University Press 1961).
Ibbetson D, *A Historical Introduction to the Law of Obligations* (Oxford: Oxford University Press 2001).
Jackman I M, *The Varieties of Restitution* (Annandale, NSW: The Federation Press 1998).
Jaffey P, 'Restitutionary Damages and Disgorgement' [1995] *Restitution Law Review* 30.
____ *The Nature and Scope of Restitution* (Oxford: Hart Publishing 2000).
____ 'Two Theories of Unjust Enrichment' in J Neyers, M McInnes, and S Pitel (eds), *Understanding Unjust Enrichment* (Oxford: Hart Publishing 2004).
____ *Private Law and Property Claims* (Oxford: Hart Publishing 2007).

____ 'Unjust Enrichment and Contract' (2014) 77 *Modern Law Review* 983.

Jewell M, 'Change of Position' in P Birks and F Rose (eds), *Lessons of the Swaps Litigation* (Oxford: Mansfield Press 2000).

Jones G (ed), *Goff and Jones: The Law of Restitution* (7th edn, London: Sweet and Maxwell 2007).

Klimchuk D, 'The Normative Foundations of Unjust Enrichment' in R Chambers, C Mitchell, and J Penner (eds), *Philosophical Foundations of the Law of Unjust Enrichment* (Oxford: Oxford University Press 2009).

Kull A, 'Rationalizing Restitution' (1995) 83 *California Law Review* 1191.

____ 'Restitution in Bankruptcy: Reclamation and Constructive Trust' (1998) 72 *American Bankruptcy Law Journal* 265.

Lamond G, 'Do Precedents Create Rules?' (2005) 11 *Legal Theory* 1.

Lobban M, 'Mapping the Common Law: Some Lessons from History' [2014] *New Zealand Law Review* 21.

Lodder A V M, *Enrichment in the Law of Unjust Enrichment and Restitution* (Oxford: Hart Publishing 2012).

Marmor A, 'Should Like Cases be Treated Alike?' (2005) 11 *Legal Theory* 27.

McBride N and McGrath P, 'The Nature of Restitution' (1995) 15 *Oxford Journal of Legal Studies* 33.

McFarlane B, 'Identifying Property Rights: A Reply to Mr Watt' [2003] *Conveyancer and Property Lawyer* 473.

____ 'Unjust Enrichment, Rights and Value' in A Robertson and Tang H W (eds), *The Goals of Private Law* (Oxford: Hart Publishing 2009).

____ 'Reply: Property Law and its Structure' (2011) 2 *Jurisprudence* 217.

____ 'Rights and Value; Means and Ends' in C Mitchell and W Swadling (eds), *The Restatement Third, Restitution and Unjust Enrichment: Critical and Comparative Essays* (Oxford: Hart Publishing 2013).

McInnes M, '"At the Claimant's Expense": Quantifying Restitutionary Relief' [1998] *Cambridge Law Journal* 472.

—— 'Gain, Loss and the User Principle' [2006] *Restitution Law Review* 76.

McKendrick E, 'Mistake of Law—Time for a Change?' in W Swadling (ed), *The Limits of Restitutionary Claims: A Comparative Analysis* (London: United Kingdom National Committee of Comparative Law 1997).

Meier S and Zimmermann R, 'Judicial Development of the Law, Error Iuris, and the Law of Unjustified Enrichment—A View from Germany' (1999) 115 *Law Quarterly Review* 556.

Millett P J, 'Review of A Burrows, *The Law of Restitution*' (1995) 111 *Law Quarterly Review* 517.

____ 'Restitution and Constructive Trusts' (1998) 114 *Law Quarterly Review* 399.

Mitchell C, Mitchell P, and Watterson S (eds), *Goff and Jones: The Law of Unjust Enrichment* (8th edn, London: Sweet and Maxwell 2011).

Murphy M, *Natural Law in Jurisprudence and Politics* (Cambridge: Cambridge University Press 2009).

Nadler J, 'What Right Does Unjust Enrichment Law Protect?' (2008) 28 *Oxford Journal of Legal Studies* 245.

Nolan R, 'Change of Position' in P Birks (ed), *Laundering and Tracing* (Oxford: Clarendon Press 1995).

Paciocco D, 'The Remedial Constructive Trust: A Principled Basis for Priorities over Creditors' (1989) 68 *Canadian Bar Review* 315.

Peel E, *Treitel: The Law of Contract* (13th edn, London: Sweet and Maxwell 2011).

Perillo J, 'Restitution in a Contractual Context' (1973) 73 *Columbia Law Review* 1208.

Pollock F, 'Divisions of Law' (1894) 8 *Harvard Law Review* 187.

____ *Jurisprudence and Legal Essays* (London: MacMillan & Co Ltd 1961).

Priel D, 'In Defence of Quasi-Contract' (2012) 75 *Modern Law Review* 54.

____ 'The Justice in Unjust Enrichment' (2014) 51 *Osgoode Hall Law Journal* 813.

Ratan A, 'The Unity of Pre-Receipt and Post-Receipt Detriment' in A Dyson, J Goudkamp, and F Wilmot-Smith (eds), *Defences in Unjust Enrichment* (Oxford: Hart Publishing 2016).

Rawls J, 'Two Concepts of Rules' (1955) 64 *Philosophical Review* 3.

Raz J, *The Morality of Freedom* (Oxford: Oxford University Press 1995).

____ 'Incorporation by Law' (2004) 10 *Legal Theory* 1.

____ *The Authority of Law: Essays on Law and Morality* (2nd edn, Oxford: Oxford University Press 2009).

____ *From Normativity to Responsibility* (Oxford: Oxford University Press 2011).

Reich C, 'The New Property' (1964) 73 *Yale Law Journal* 733.

Rotherham C, 'Tracing and Justice in Bankruptcy' in F Rose (ed), *Restitution and Insolvency* (Oxford: Mansfield Press 2000).

Saprai P, 'Restitution without Corrective Justice' [2006] *Restitution Law Review* 41.

Seah W, 'Mispredictions, Mistakes and the Law of Unjust Enrichment' [2007] *Restitution Law Review* 93.

Seavey W and Scott A, 'Restitution' (1938) 54 *Law Quarterly Review* 29.

Sharpe R and Waddams S, 'Damages for Lost Opportunity to Bargain' (1982) 2 *Oxford Journal of Legal Studies* 290.

Sheehan D, 'What is a Mistake?' (2000) 20 *Legal Studies* 538.

Sherwin E, 'Constructive Trusts in Bankruptcy' [1989] *University of Illinois Law Review* 297.

Simmonds N E, *The Decline of Juridical Reason: Doctrine and Theory in the Legal Order* (Manchester: Manchester University Press 1984).

Smith L, *The Law of Tracing* (Oxford: Clarendon Press 1997).

____ 'Unjust Enrichment, Property and the Structure of Trusts' (2000) 116 *Law Quarterly Review* 416.

____ 'Restitution: The Heart of Corrective Justice' (2001) 79 *Texas Law Review* 2115.

____ 'Property, Subsidiarity and Unjust Enrichment' in D Johnston and R Zimmermann (eds) *Unjustified Enrichment: Key Issues in Comparative Perspective* (Cambridge: Cambridge University Press 2002).

____ 'Demystifying Juristic Reasons' (2007) 45 *Canadian Business Law Journal* 281.

Smith S, 'Unjust Enrichment: Nearer to Tort than Contract' in R Chambers, C Mitchell, and J Penner (eds), *Philosophical Foundations of the Law of Unjust Enrichment* (Oxford: Oxford University Press 2009).

____ 'A Duty to Make Restitution' (2013) 26 *Canadian Journal of Law and Jurisprudence* 157.

Stevens D, 'Restitution, Property, and the Cause of Action in Unjust Enrichment: Getting by with Fewer Things' (1989) 39 *University of Toronto Law Journal* 258 and 325.

Stevens R, *Torts and Rights* (Oxford: Oxford University Press 2007).

____ 'Is There a Law of Unjust Enrichment?' in S Degeling and J Edelman (eds), *Unjust Enrichment in Commercial Law* (Sydney, NSW: Thomson Reuters 2008).

____ 'When and Why Does Unjustified Enrichment Justify the Recognition of Proprietary Rights?' (2012) 92 *Boston University Law Review* 919.

Stoljar S J, 'The Great Case of *Cutter v Powell*' (1956) 34 *Canadian Bar Review* 288.

____ *The Law of Quasi-Contract* (2nd edn, Sydney, NSW: Law Book Company 1989).

Swadling W, 'A Claim in Restitution' [1996] *Lloyd's Maritime and Commercial Law Quarterly* 63.

____ 'Explaining Resulting Trusts' (2008) 124 *Law Quarterly Review* 72.

____ 'Ignorance and Unjust Enrichment: The Problem of Title' (2008) 28 *Oxford Journal of Legal Studies* 627.

____ 'Policy Arguments for Proprietary Restitution' (2008) 28 *Legal Studies* 506.

Tadros V, *Criminal Responsibility* (Oxford: Oxford University Press 2005).

Tettenborn A, 'Lawful Receipt—A Justifying Factor?' [1997] *Restitution Law Review* 1.

____ 'Conversion, Tort and Restitution' in N Palmer and E McKendrick (eds), *Interests in Goods* (2nd edn, London: LLP 1998).

____ *Law of Restitution in England and Ireland* (3rd edn, London: Cavendish Publishing 2002).

____ 'Restitution of Property You Do Not Own Anyway' in A Hudson (ed) *New Perspectives on Property Law, Obligations and Restitution* (London: Cavendish Publishing 2003).

Virgo G, 'Vindicating Vindication: *Foskett v McKeown* Reviewed' in A Hudson (ed), *New Perspectives on Property Law, Obligations and Restitution* (London: Cavendish Publishing 2004).

____ *The Principles of the Law of Restitution* (2nd edn, Oxford: Oxford University Press 2006).

Von Caemmerer E, 'Grundprobleme des Bereicherungsrechts' in H Leser (ed), *Gesammelte Schriften: Bd I, Rechtsvergleichung und Schuldsrecht* (Tübingen: J C B Mohr (Paul Siebeck) 1968).

Watterson S, '"Direct Transfers" in the Law of Unjust Enrichment' (2011) 64 *Current Legal Problems* 435.

Watts P, 'Restitution—A Property Principle and a Services Principle' [1995] *Restitution Law Review* 49.

____ '"Property and 'Unjust Enrichment'": Cognate Conservators' [1998] *New Zealand Law Review* 151.

Webb C, 'Justifying Damages' in J Neyers, R Bronaugh, and S Pitel (eds), *Exploring Contract Law* (Oxford: Hart Publishing 2009).

____ 'Property, Unjust Enrichment, and Defective Transfers' in R Chambers, C Mitchell, and J Penner (eds), *Philosophical Foundations of the Law of Unjust Enrichment* (Oxford: Oxford University Press 2009).

____ 'What is Unjust Enrichment?' (2009) 29 *Oxford Journal of Legal Studies* 215.

Weinrib E, *The Idea of Private Law* (Cambridge, MA: Harvard University Press 1995).

____ 'Restitutionary Damages as Corrective Justice' (2000) 1 *Theoretical Inquiries in Law* 1.

____ 'Two Conceptions of Remedies' in C Rickett (ed), *Justifying Private Law Remedies* (Oxford: Hart Publishing 2008).

____ 'Correctively Unjust Enrichment' in R Chambers, C Mitchell, and J Penner (eds), *Philosophical Foundations of the Law of Unjust Enrichment* (Oxford: Oxford University Press 2009).

____ *Corrective Justice* (Oxford: Oxford University Press 2012).

Worthington S, *Equity* (2nd edn, Oxford: Clarendon Press 2006).

Zimmermann R, *The Law of Obligations: Roman Foundations of the Civilian Tradition* (Cape Town: Juta & Co 1990).

Index

The manufacturer's authorised representative in the EU for product safety is Oxford University Press España S.A. of El Parque Empresarial San Fernando de Henares, Avenida de Castilla, 2 - 28830 Madrid (www.oup.es/en or product.safety@oup.com). OUP España S.A. also acts as importer into Spain of products made by the manufacturer.
Printed and bound by CPI Group (UK) Ltd, Croydon, CR0 4YY
14/09/2026
02216307-0008